Praise for *Trino: The Definitive Guide*

This book provides a great introduction to Trino and teaches you everything
you need to know to start your successful usage of Trino.

*—Dain Sundstrom and David Phillips, Creators of the Trino
Project and Founders of the Trino Software Foundation*

Trino plays a key role in enabling analysis at Pinterest. This book covers the Trino
essentials, from use cases through how to run Trino at massive scale.

*—Ashish Kumar Singh, Tech Lead,
Bigdata Query Processing Platform, Pinterest*

Trino has been incredibly useful for quick ad hoc queries; that's why it was one of the first
two engines we added Iceberg support to. I'm excited to see Trino taking on more and
more warehouse workloads as the Iceberg connector, now over four years old, has grown
to support materialized views, expressive DML commands, and metadata exploration.

*—Ryan Blue, Cocreator of Apache Iceberg,
Cofounder and CEO of Tabular*

Trino has set the bar in both community building and technical excellence for lightning-
fast analytical processing on stored data in modern cloud architectures. This book is
a must-read for companies looking to modernize their analytics stack.

*—Jay Kreps, Cocreator of Apache Kafka,
Cofounder and CEO of Confluent*

Trino has saved us all— both in academia and industry—countless hours of work, allowing us all to avoid having to write code to manage distributed query processing. We're so grateful to have a high-quality open source distributed SQL engine to start from, enabling us to focus on innovating in new areas instead of reinventing the wheel for each new distributed data system project.

—Daniel Abadi, Professor of Computer Science,
University of Maryland, College Park

SECOND EDITION

Trino: The Definitive Guide

SQL at Any Scale, on Any Storage,
in Any Environment

Matt Fuller, Manfred Moser, and Martin Traverso

Beijing · Boston · Farnham · Sebastopol · Tokyo

Trino: The Definitive Guide

by Matt Fuller, Manfred Moser, and Martin Traverso

Published by O'Reilly Media, Inc., 1005 Gravenstein Highway North, Sebastopol, CA 95472.

O'Reilly books may be purchased for educational, business, or sales promotional use. Online editions are also available for most titles (*http://oreilly.com*). For more information, contact our corporate/institutional sales department: 800-998-9938 or *corporate@oreilly.com*.

Acquisition Editor: Andy Kwan	**Indexer:** Potomac Indexing, LLC
Development Editor: Michele Cronin	**Interior Designer:** David Futato
Production Editor: Kristen Brown	**Cover Designer:** Randy Comer
Copyeditor: Piper Editorial Consulting, LLC	**Illustrator:** Kate Dullea
Proofreader: Sharon Wilkey	

April 2020:	First Edition, Presto
April 2021:	First Edition, Trino
October 2022:	Second Edition

Revision History for the Second Edition

2022-10-03:   First release

See *http://oreilly.com/catalog/errata.csp?isbn=9781098137236* for release details.

978-1-098-13723-6

[LSI]

Table of Contents

Part II. Diving Deeper into Trino

Part III.   Trino in Real-World Uses

Foreword

Has it really been over a decade already? Interesting how it feels like yesterday, and like a long time ago, at the same time. We started the Presto project at Facebook in 2012, and various components and ideas date back even longer. We certainly planned to create something useful. We always wanted to have a successful open source project and community. In 2013 we released a first version of Presto under the Apache License, and the adventure began.

Since then we all moved on from Facebook, the Presto name, and generally well beyond what we dreamed of. We are proud of the project community's accomplishments, and we are very humbled by all the positive feedback and help we have received.

Trino has grown tremendously and provided a lot of value to its large community of users. You can find fellow Trino community members across the globe and developers in Brazil, Canada, China, Germany, India, Israel, Japan, Poland, Singapore, the United States, the United Kingdom, and other countries.

Launching the Trino Software Foundation in early 2019 and moving the project to independence was another major milestone. The not-for-profit organization is dedicated to the advancement of the Trino open source distributed SQL engine. The foundation is committed to ensuring that the project remains open, collaborative, and independent for decades to come.

Renaming the project and the foundation to Trino with the end of 2020 was another milestone for the community. We got a new name, a new look, new interest from around the world, and even a great little mascot, our beloved bunny—Commander Bun Bun. Now, over three years after the launch of the foundation, we can look back at an accelerated rate of impressive contributions from the large and constantly growing community.

We are pleased that Matt, Manfred, and Martin created this updated second edition of the book about Trino with the help of O'Reilly. It provides a great introduction to Trino and teaches you everything you need to know to start using it successfully.

Enjoy the journey into the depths of Trino and the related world of business intelligence, reporting, dashboard creation, data warehousing, data mining, machine learning, and beyond.

Of course, make sure to dive into the additional resources and help we offer on the Trino website at *https://trino.io*, the community chat, the source repository, the Trino Community Broadcast, and other resources.

Welcome to the Trino community!

— Dain Sundstrom and David Phillips
Creators of the Trino Project and
Founders of the Trino Software Foundation

Preface

Trino: The Definitive Guide is the first and foremost book about the Trino distributed query engine. The book is aimed at beginners and existing users of Trino alike. Ideally, you have some understanding of databases and SQL, but if not, you can divert from reading and look things up while working your way through this book. No matter your level of expertise, we are sure that you'll learn something new from this book.

This second edition modernizes the content to keep up with the rapid innovation of Trino. We cover new aspects such as the Helm chart to deploy a Trino cluster to Kubernetes, the new Iceberg and Delta Lake connectors for modern lakehouse architectures, fault-tolerant execution for query processing, expanded SQL language features, and the latest Trino release, now running on Java 17.

The first part of the book introduces you to Trino and then helps you get up and running quickly so you can start learning how to use it. This includes installation and first use of the command-line interface as well as client- and web-based applications, such as SQL database management or dashboard and reporting tools, using the JDBC driver.

The second part of the book advances your knowledge and includes details about the Trino architecture, cluster deployment, many connectors to data sources, and a lot of information about the main power of Trino—querying any data source with SQL.

The third part of the book rounds out the content with further aspects you need to know when running and using a production Trino deployment. This includes Web UI usage, security configuration, and some discussion of real-world uses of Trino in other organizations.

Conventions Used in This Book

The following typographical conventions are used in this book:

Italic
> Indicates new terms, URLs, email addresses, filenames, and file extensions.

`Constant width`
> Used for program listings, as well as within paragraphs to refer to program elements such as variable or function names, databases, data types, environment variables, statements, and keywords.

`Constant width bold`
> Shows commands or other text that should be typed literally by the user.

`Constant width italic`
> Shows text that should be replaced with user-supplied values or by values determined by context.

 This element signifies a tip or suggestion.

 This element signifies a general note.

 This element indicates a warning or caution.

Code Examples, Permissions, and Attribution

Supplemental material for the book is documented in greater detail in "Book Repository" on page 15.

If you have a technical question or a problem using the code examples, please contact us on the community chat—see "Community Chat" on page 14—or you may file issues on the book repository.

This book is here to help you get your job done. In general, if example code is offered with this book, you may use it in your programs and documentation. You do not need to contact us for permission unless you're reproducing a significant portion of the code. For example, writing a program that uses several chunks of code from this book does not require permission. Selling or distributing examples from O'Reilly books does require permission. Answering a question by citing this book and quoting example code does not require permission. Incorporating a significant amount of example code from this book into your product's documentation does require permission.

We appreciate, but generally do not require, attribution. An attribution usually includes the title, author, publisher, and ISBN. For example: "*Trino: The Definitive Guide*, 2nd Edition, by Matt Fuller, Manfred Moser, and Martin Traverso (O'Reilly). Copyright 2023 Matt Fuller, Martin Traverso, and simpligility technologies, Inc., 978-1-098-13723-6."

If you feel your use of code examples falls outside fair use or the permission given above, feel free to contact us at *permissions@oreilly.com*.

O'Reilly Online Learning

 For more than 40 years, O'Reilly Media (*http://oreilly.com*) has provided technology and business training, knowledge, and insight to help companies succeed.

Our unique network of experts and innovators share their knowledge and expertise through books, articles, and our online learning platform. O'Reilly's online learning platform gives you on-demand access to live training courses, in-depth learning paths, interactive coding environments, and a vast collection of text and video from O'Reilly and 200+ other publishers. For more information, visit *https://oreilly.com*.

How to Contact Us

Please address comments and questions concerning this book to the publisher:

O'Reilly Media, Inc.
1005 Gravenstein Highway North
Sebastopol, CA 95472
800-998-9938 (in the United States or Canada)
707-829-0515 (international or local)
707-829-0104 (fax)

We have a web page for this book, where we list errata, examples, and any additional information. You can access this page at *https://oreil.ly/trinoTDG_2e*.

Email *bookquestions@oreilly.com* to comment or ask technical questions about this book.

For news and information about our books and courses, visit *https://oreilly.com*.

Find us on LinkedIn: *https://linkedin.com/company/oreilly-media*.

Follow us on Twitter: *https://twitter.com/oreillymedia*.

Watch us on YouTube: *https://www.youtube.com/oreillymedia*.

Acknowledgments

We would like to thank everyone in the larger Trino community—starting with the founders of the project, the dedicated team of maintainers, and all the contributors since inception of the project. Our gratitude reaches much further, and we appreciate everybody using Trino, spreading the word, helping other users, contributing to related projects and integrations, and simply showing up with questions on our chat. We are excited to be part of the community and look forward to many shared successes in the future.

A critical part of the Trino community is Starburst. We want to thank everyone at Starburst for their help. We really appreciate the work, resources, stability, and support Starburst provides to the project, its customers using Trino, and the authors, who are part of the Starburst team.

Specifically related to the book, we would like to thank everyone who helped us with ideas, input, and reviews. In addition, the authors want to express their personal gratitude:

- Matt would like to thank his wife, Meghan, and his three children, Emily, Hannah, and Liam, for their patience and encouragement while Matt worked on the book. The kids' excitement about their dad becoming an "author" helped Matt through many long weekends and late nights.

- Manfred would like to thank his wife, Yen, and his three sons, Lukas, Nikolas, and Tobias, not only for putting up with the tech mumbo-jumbo but also for genuinely sharing an interest and passion for technology, writing, learning, and teaching.

- Martin would like to thank his wife, Melina, and his four children, Marcos, Victoria, Joaquin, and Martina, for their support and enthusiasm over the past 10 years of working on Trino.

Getting Started with Trino

Trino is a SQL query engine enabling SQL access to any data source. You can use Trino to query very large data sets by horizontally scaling the query processing.

In this first part, you learn about Trino and its use cases. Then you move on to get a simple Trino installation up and running. And finally, you learn about the tools you can use to connect to Trino and query the data. You get to concentrate on a minimal setup so you can start using Trino as quickly as possible.

Introducing Trino

So you heard of Trino and found this book. Or maybe you are just browsing this first section and wondering whether you should dive in. In this introductory chapter, we discuss the problems you may be encountering with the massive growth of data creation and the value locked away within that data. Trino is a key enabler for working with all the data and providing access to it with proven successful tools around Structured Query Language (SQL).

The design and features of Trino enable you to get better insights, beyond those accessible to you now. You can gain these insights faster, as well as get information that you could not get in the past because it cost too much or took too long to obtain. And for all that, you end up using fewer resources and therefore spending less of your budget, which you can then use to learn even more!

We also point you to more resources beyond this book but, of course, we hope you join us here first.

The Problems with Big Data

Everyone is capturing more and more data from device metrics, user behavior tracking, business transactions, location data, software and system testing procedures and workflows, and much more. The insights gained from understanding that data and working with it can make or break the success of any initiative, or even a company.

At the same time, the diversity of storage mechanisms available for data has exploded: relational databases, NoSQL databases, document databases, key-value stores, object storage systems, and so on. Many of them are necessary in today's organizations, and it is no longer possible to use just one of them. As you can see in Figure 1-1, dealing with this can be a daunting task that feels overwhelming.

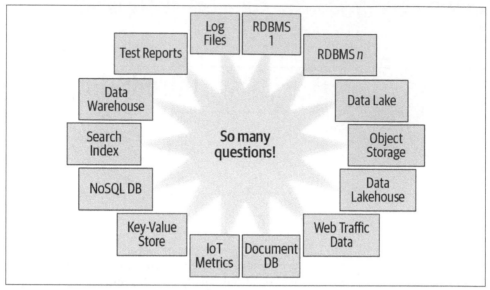

Figure 1-1. Big data can be overwhelming

In addition, all these different systems do not allow you to query and inspect the data with standard tools. Different query languages and analysis tools for niche systems are everywhere. Meanwhile, your business analysts are used to the industry standard, SQL. A myriad of powerful tools rely on SQL for analytics, dashboard creation, rich reporting, and other business intelligence work.

The data is distributed across various silos, and some of them cannot even be queried at the necessary performance for your analytics needs. Other systems, unlike modern cloud applications, store data in monolithic systems that cannot scale horizontally. Without these capabilities, you are narrowing the number of potential use cases and users, and therefore the usefulness of the data.

The traditional approach of creating and maintaining large, dedicated data ware‐houses has proven to be very expensive in organizations across the globe. Most often, this approach is also found to be too slow and cumbersome for many users and usage patterns. The often considered solution of creating a data lake ended up creating a dumping ground for data that no one ever looked at again, or went to great pains to attempt to analyze the data. Even the new approach of a data lakehouse that promises to combine the advantages of warehouses and lakes will not be the sole solution. Data will remain distributed, stored all over the place, and will crop up in more and more systems.

You can see the tremendous opportunity for a system to unlock all this value.

Trino to the Rescue

Trino is capable of solving all these problems and of unlocking new opportunities with federated queries to disparate systems, parallel queries, horizontal cluster scaling, and much more. You can see the Trino project logo in Figure 1-2.

Figure 1-2. Trino logo with the mascot Commander Bun Bun

Trino is an open source, distributed SQL query engine. It was designed and written from the ground up to efficiently query data against disparate data sources of all sizes, ranging from gigabytes to petabytes. Trino breaks the false choice between having fast analytics using an expensive commercial solution or using a slow "free" solution that requires excessive hardware.

Designed for Performance and Scale

Trino is a tool designed to efficiently query vast amounts of data by using distributed execution. If you have terabytes or even petabytes of data to query, you are likely using tools such as Apache Hive that interact with Hadoop and its Hadoop Distributed File System (HDFS), or equivalent systems such as Amazon Simple Storage Service (S3) and others provided by the cloud providers or used in self-hosted, compatible deployments. Trino is designed as an alternative to these tools to more efficiently query that data.

Analysts who expect SQL response times from milliseconds for real-time analysis to seconds and minutes should use Trino. Trino supports SQL, commonly used in data warehousing and analytics for analyzing data, aggregating large amounts of data, and producing reports. These workloads are often classified as *online analytical processing* (OLAP).

Even though Trino understands and can efficiently execute SQL, Trino is *not* a database, as it does not include its own data storage system. It is not meant to be a general-purpose relational database that serves to replace Microsoft SQL Server, Oracle Database, MySQL, or PostgreSQL. Further, Trino is not designed to handle *online transaction processing* (OLTP). This is also true of other databases designed and optimized for data warehousing or analytics, such as Teradata, Netezza, Vertica, and Amazon Redshift.

Trino leverages both well-known and novel techniques for distributed query processing. These techniques include in-memory parallel processing, pipelined execution across nodes in the cluster, a multithreaded execution model to keep all the CPU cores busy, efficient flat-memory data structures to minimize Java garbage collection, and Java bytecode generation. A detailed description of these complex Trino internals is beyond the scope of this book. For Trino users, these techniques translate into faster insights into your data at a fraction of the cost of other solutions.

SQL-on-Anything

Trino was initially designed to query data from HDFS. And it can do that very efficiently, as you will learn later. But that is not where it ends. On the contrary, Trino is a query engine that can query data from object storage, relational database management systems (RDBMSs), NoSQL databases, and other systems, as shown in Figure 1-3.

Trino queries data where it lives and does not require a migration of data to a single location. So Trino allows you to query data in HDFS and other distributed object storage systems. It allows you to query RDBMSs and other data sources. By querying data wherever it lives, Trino can therefore replace the traditional, expensive, and heavy extract, transform, and load (ETL) processes. Or at a minimum, it can help you by providing a query engine to run high-performance ETL processes with modern tools such as dbt across all data sources where necessary, and reduce or even avoid the need for ETL processes. So Trino is clearly not just another SQL-on-Hadoop solution.

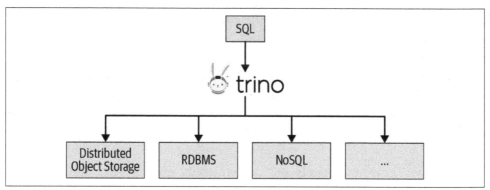

Figure 1-3. SQL support for a variety of data sources with Trino

Object storage systems include Amazon S3, Microsoft Azure Blob Storage, Google Cloud Storage, and S3-compatible storage such as MinIO and Ceph. These systems can use the traditional Hive table format, as well as the newer replacements Delta Lake and Iceberg. Trino can query traditional RDBMSs such as Microsoft SQL Server, PostgreSQL, MySQL, Oracle, Teradata, and Amazon Redshift. Trino can also query NoSQL systems such as Apache Cassandra, Apache Kafka, MongoDB, or Elasticsearch. Trino can query virtually anything and is truly an SQL-on-Anything system.

For users, this means that suddenly they no longer have to rely on specific query languages or tools to interact with the data in those specific systems. They can simply leverage Trino and their existing SQL skills and their well-understood analytics, dashboarding, and reporting tools. These tools, built on top of using SQL, allow analysis of those additional data sets, which are otherwise locked in separate systems. Users can even use Trino to query across different systems with the same SQL they already know.

Separation of Data Storage and Query Compute Resources

Trino is not a database with storage; rather, it simply queries data where it lives. When using Trino, storage and compute are decoupled and can be scaled independently. Trino represents the compute layer, whereas the underlying data sources represent the storage layer.

This allows Trino to scale up and down its compute resources for query processing, based on analytics demand to access this data. There is no need to move your data, provision compute and storage to the exact needs of the current queries, or change that regularly, based on your changing query needs.

Trino can scale the query power by scaling the compute cluster dynamically, and the data can be queried right where it lives in the data source. This characteristic allows you to greatly optimize your hardware resource needs and therefore reduce cost.

Trino Use Cases

The flexibility and powerful features of Trino allow you to decide for yourself how exactly you are using Trino and what benefits you value and want to take advantage of. You can start with only one small use for a particular problem. Most Trino users start like that.

Once you and other Trino users in your organization have gotten used to the benefits and features, you'll discover new situations. Word spreads, and soon you see a myriad of needs being satisfied by Trino accessing a variety of data sources.

In this section, we discuss several of these use cases. Keep in mind that you can expand your use to cover them all. On the other hand, it is also perfectly fine to solve one particular problem with Trino. Just be prepared to like Trino and increase its use after all.

One SQL Analytics Access Point

RDBMSs and the use of SQL have been around a long time and have proven to be very useful. No organization runs without them. In fact, most companies run multiple systems. Large commercial databases like Oracle Database or IBM DB2 are probably backing your enterprise software. Open source systems like MariaDB or PostgreSQL may be used for other solutions and a couple of in-house applications.

As a consumer and analyst, you likely run into numerous problems:

- Sometimes you do not know where data is even available for you to use, and only tribal knowledge in the company, or years of experience with internal setups, can help you find the right data.

- Querying the various source databases requires you to use different connections, as well as different queries running different SQL dialects. They are similar enough to look the same, but they behave just differently enough to cause confusion and the need to learn the details.

- You cannot combine the data from different systems in a query without using the data warehouse.

Trino allows you to get around these problems. You can expose all these databases in one location: Trino.

You can use one SQL standard to query all systems—standardized SQL, functions, and operators supported by Trino.

All your dashboarding and analytics tools, and other systems for your business intelligence needs, can point to one system, Trino, and have access to all data in your organization.

Access Point to Data Warehouse and Source Systems

When organizations find the need to better understand and analyze data in their numerous RDBMSs, the creation and maintenance of data warehouse systems comes into play. Select data from various systems is then going through complex ETL processes and, often via long-running batch jobs, ends up in a tightly controlled, massive data warehouse.

While this helps you a lot in many cases, as a data analyst, you now encounter new problems:

- Now you have another entry point, in addition to all the databases themselves, for your tools and queries.
- The data you specifically need today is not in the data warehouse. Getting the data added is a painful, expensive process full of hurdles.

Trino allows you to add any data warehouse database as a data source, just like any other relational database.

If you want to dive deeper into a data warehouse query, you can do it right there in the same system. You can access the data warehouse *and* the source database system in the same place and even write queries that combine them. Trino allows you to query any database in the same system, data warehouse, source database, and any other database.

Provide SQL-Based Access to Anything

The days of using only RDBMSs are long gone. Data is now stored in many disparate systems optimized for relevant use cases. Object-based storage, key-value stores, document databases, graph databases, event-streaming systems, and other so-called NoSQL systems all provide unique features and advantages.

At least some of these systems are in use in your organization, holding data that's crucial for understanding and improving your business.

Of course, all of these systems also require you to use different tools and technologies to query and work with the data.

At a minimum, this is a complex task with a huge learning curve. More likely, however, you end up only scratching the surface of your data and not really gaining a complete understanding. You lack a good way to query the data. Tools to visualize and analyze in more detail are hard to find or simply don't exist.

Trino, on the other hand, allows you to connect to all these systems as a data source. It exposes the data to query with standard American National Standards Institute (ANSI) SQL and all the tooling using SQL, as shown in Figure 1-4.

Figure 1-4. One SQL access point for many use cases to all data sources

So with Trino, understanding the data in all these vastly different systems becomes much simpler, or even possible, for the first time.

Federated Queries

Exposing all the data silos in Trino is a large step toward understanding your data. You can use SQL and standard tools to query them all. However, often the questions you want answered require you to reach into the data silos, pull aspects out of them, and then combine them in one location.

Trino allows you to do that by using federated queries. A *federated query* is an SQL query that references and uses databases and schemas from entirely different systems in the same statement. All the data sources in Trino are available for you to query at the same time, with the same SQL in the same query.

You can define the relationships between the user-tracking information from your object storage with the customer data in your RDBMS. If your key-value store contains more related information, you can hook it into your query as well.

Using federated queries with Trino allows you to gain insights that you could not learn about otherwise.

Semantic Layer for a Virtual Data Warehouse

Data warehouse systems have created not only huge benefits for users but also a burden on organizations:

- Running and maintaining the data warehouse is a large, expensive project.
- Dedicated teams run and manage the data warehouse and the associated ETL processes.
- Getting the data into the warehouse requires users to break through red tape and typically takes too much time.

Trino, on the other hand, can be used as a virtual data warehouse. It can be used to define your semantic layer by utilizing one tool and standard ANSI SQL. Once all the databases are configured as data sources in Trino, you can query them. Trino provides the necessary compute power to query the storage in the databases. Using SQL and the supported functions and operators, Trino can provide you the desired data straight from the source. There is no need to copy, move, or transform the data before you can use it for your analysis.

Thanks to the standard SQL support against all connected data sources, you can create the desired semantic layer for querying from tools and end users in a simpler fashion. And that layer can encompass all underlying data sources without the need to migrate any data. Trino can query the data at the source and storage level.

Using Trino as this "on-the-fly data warehouse" provides organizations the potential to enhance their existing data warehouse with additional capabilities or even to avoid building and maintaining a warehouse altogether.

Data Lake Query Engine

The term *data lake* is often used for a large HDFS or similar distributed object storage system into which all sorts of data is dumped without much thought about accessing it. Trino unlocks this to become a useful data warehouse. In fact, Trino emerged from Facebook as a way to tackle faster and more powerful querying of a very large Hadoop data warehouse than what Hive and other tools could provide. This led to the Trino Hive connector, discussed in "Hive Connector for Distributed Storage Data Sources" on page 102.

Modern data lakes now often use other object storage systems beyond HDFS from cloud providers or other open source projects. Trino is able to use the Hive connector against any of them and hence enable SQL-based analytics on your data lake, wherever it is located and however it stores the data.

The creation of new table formats such as Delta Lake and Iceberg allowed data lakes to tremendously improve the usability of the data lake, so much so that the new term *data lakehouse* was created. With the Delta Lake and Iceberg connectors, Trino is a first-class choice to query these new lakehouses.

SQL Conversions and ETL

With support for RDBMSs and other data storage systems alike, Trino can be used to move data. SQL, and the rich set of SQL functions available, allow you to query data, transform it, and then write it to the same data source or any other data source.

In practice, this means that you can copy data out of your object storage system or key-value store and into a RDBMS and use it for your analytics going forward. Of course, you also can transform and aggregate the data to gain new understanding.

On the other hand, it is also common to take data from an operational RDBMS, or maybe an event-streaming system like Kafka, and move it into a data lake to ease the burden on the RDBMS in terms of querying by many analysts. ETL processes, now often also called *data preparation*, can be an important part of this process to improve the data and create a data model better suited for querying and analysis.

In this scenario, Trino is a critical part of an overall data management solution, and the support for fault-tolerant execution of queries with modern data lakehouses makes Trino an excellent choice for such use cases.

Better Insights Due to Faster Response Times

Asking complex questions and using massive data sets always runs into limitations. It might end up being too expensive to copy the data and load it into your data warehouse and analyze it there. The computations require too much compute power to be able to run them at all, or it takes numerous days to get an answer.

Trino avoids data copying by design. Parallel processing and heavy optimizations regularly lead to performance improvements for your analysis with Trino.

If a query that used to take three days can now run in 15 minutes, it might be worth running it after all. And the knowledge gained from the results gives you an advantage and the capacity to run yet more queries.

These faster processing times of Trino enable better analytics and results.

Big Data, Machine Learning, and Artificial Intelligence

The fact that Trino exposes more and more data to standard tooling around SQL, and scales querying to massive data sets, makes it a prime tool for big data processing. Now this often includes statistical analysis and grows in complexity toward machine learning and artificial intelligence systems. With the support for R and other tools, Trino definitely has a role to play in these use cases.

Other Use Cases

In the prior sections, we provided a high-level overview of Trino use cases. New use cases and combinations are emerging regularly.

In Chapter 13, you can learn details about the use of Trino by some well-known companies and organizations. We present that information toward the end of the book so you can first gain the knowledge required to understand the data at hand by reading the following chapters.

Trino Resources

Beyond this book, many more resources are available that allow you to expand your knowledge about Trino. In this section, we enumerate the important starting points. Most of them contain a lot of information and include pointers to further resources.

Website

The *Trino Software Foundation* governs the community of the open source Trino project and maintains the project website. You can see the home page in Figure 1-5. The website contains documentation, contact details, community blog posts with the latest news and events, Trino Community Broadcast episodes in audio and video format, and other information at *https://trino.io*.

Figure 1-5. Home page of Trino website at trino.io

Documentation

The detailed documentation for Trino is maintained as part of the codebase and is available on the website. It includes high-level overviews as well as detailed reference information about the SQL support, functions and operators, connectors, configuration, and much more. You also find release notes with details of latest changes there. Get started at *https://trino.io/docs*.

Community Chat

The community of beginner, advanced, and expert users, as well as the contributors and maintainers of Trino, is very supportive and actively collaborates every day on the community chat available at *https://trinodb.slack.com*.

Join the *announcements* channel, and then check out the numerous channels focusing on various topics such as help for beginners, bug triage, releases, development, and more specific channels to discuss Kubernetes or specific connectors.

 You can find Matt, Manfred, and Martin on the community chat nearly every day, and we would love to hear from you there.

Source Code, License, and Version

Trino is an open source project distributed under the Apache License, v2 with the source code managed and available in the Git repository at *https://github.com/tri nodb/trino*.

The `trinodb` organization at *https://github.com/trinodb* contains numerous other repositories related to the project, such as the source code of the website, clients, other components, or the contributor license management repository.

Trino is an active open source project with frequent releases. By using the most recent version, you are able to take advantage of the latest features, bug fixes, and performance improvements. This book refers to, and uses, the latest Trino version 392 at the time of writing. If you choose a different and more recent version of Trino, it should work the same as described in this book. While it's unlikely you'll run into issues, it is important to refer to the release notes and documentation for any changes.

Contributing

As we've mentioned, Trino is a community-driven, open source project, and your contributions are welcome and encouraged. The project is very active on the community chat, and committers and other developers are available to help there.

Here are a few tasks to get started with contributing:

- Check out the Developer Guide section of the documentation.
- Learn to build the project from source with instructions in the *README* file.
- Read the research papers linked on the Community page of the website.
- Read the Code of Conduct from the same page.
- Find an issue with the label *good first issue*.
- Sign the contributor license agreement (CLA).

The project continues to receive contributions with a wide range of complexity—from small documentation improvements, to new connectors or other plug-ins, all the way to improvements deep in the internals of Trino.

Of course, any work you do with and around Trino is welcome in the community. This certainly includes seemingly unrelated work such as writing blog posts, presenting at user group meetings or conferences, or writing and managing a plug-in on your own, maybe to a database system you use.

Overall, we encourage you to work with the team and get involved. The project grows and thrives with contributions from everyone. We are ready to help. You can do it!

Book Repository

We provide resources related to this book—such as configuration file examples, SQL queries, data sets and more—in a Git repository for your convenience.

Find it at *https://github.com/trinodb/trino-the-definitive-guide*, and download the content as an archive file or clone the repository with `git`.

Feel free to create a pull request for any corrections, desired additions, or file issues if you encounter any problems.

Iris Data Set

In later sections of this book, you are going to encounter example queries and use cases that talk about iris flowers (*https://en.wikipedia.org/wiki/Iris_(plant)*) and the iris data set. The reason is a famous data set, commonly used in data science classification examples, which is all about iris flowers.

The data set consists of one simple table of 150 records and columns with values for sepal length, sepal width, petal length, petal width, and species.

The small size allows users to test and run queries easily and perform a wide range of analyses. This makes the data set suitable for learning, including for use with Trino. You can find out more about the data set on the Wikipedia page about it (*https://en.wikipedia.org/wiki/Iris_flower_data_set*).

Our book repository contains the directory *iris-data-set* with the data in comma-separated values (CSV) format, as well as an SQL file to create a table and insert it. After reading Chapter 2 and "Trino Command-Line Interface" on page 27, the following instructions are easy to follow.

You can use the data set by first copying the *etc/catalog/brain.properties* file into the same location as your Trino installation and restarting Trino.

Now you can use the Trino CLI to get the data set into the `iris` table in the `default` schema of the `brain` catalog:

```
$ trino -f iris-data-set/iris-data-set.sql
USE
CREATE TABLE
INSERT: 150 rows
```

Confirm that the data can be queried:

```
$ trino --execute 'SELECT * FROM brain.default.iris;'
"5.1","3.5","1.4","0.2","setosa"
"4.9","3.0","1.4","0.2","setosa"
"4.7","3.2","1.3","0.2","setosa"
...
```

Alternatively, you can run the queries in any SQL management tool connected to Trino; for example, with the Java Database Connectivity (JDBC) driver described in "Trino JDBC Driver" on page 32.

Later sections include example queries to run with this data set in Chapters 8 and 9, as well as information about the memory connector used in the `brain` catalog in "Memory Connector" on page 117.

Flight Data Set

Similar to the iris data set, the flight data set is used later in this book for example queries and usage. The data set is a bit more complex than the iris data set, consisting of lookup tables for carriers, airports, and other information, as well as transactional data about specific flights. This makes the data set suitable for more complex queries using joins and for use in federated queries, where different tables are located in different data sources.

The data is collected from the Federal Aviation Administration (FAA) and curated for analysis. The `flights` table schema is fairly large, with a subset of the available columns shown in Table 1-1.

Table 1-1. Subset of available columns

flightdate	airlineid	origin	dest	arrtime	deptime

Each row in the data set represents either a departure or an arrival of a flight at an airport in the United States.

The book repository—see "Book Repository" on page 15—contains a separate folder, *flight-data-set*. It contains instructions on how to import the data into different database systems, so that you can hook them up to Trino and run the example queries.

A Brief History of Trino

In 2008, Facebook made Hive (later to become Apache Hive) open source. Hive became widely used within Facebook for running analytics against data in HDFS on its very large Apache Hadoop cluster.

Data analysts at Facebook used Hive to run interactive queries on its large data warehouse. Before Presto existed at Facebook, all data analysis relied on Hive, which was not suitable for interactive queries at Facebook's scale. In 2012, its Hive data warehouse was 250 petabytes in size and needed to handle hundreds of users issuing tens of thousands of queries each day. Hive started to hit its limit within Facebook and did not provide the ability to query other data sources within Facebook.

Presto was designed from the ground up to run fast queries at Facebook scale. Rather than create a new system to move the data to, Presto was designed to read the data from where it is stored via its pluggable connector system. One of the first connectors developed for Presto was the Hive connector; see "Hive Connector for Distributed Storage Data Sources" on page 102. This connector queries data stored in a Hive data warehouse directly.

In 2012, four Facebook engineers started Presto development to address the performance, scalability, and extensibility needs for analytics at Facebook. From the beginning, the intent was to build Presto as an open source project. At the beginning of 2013, the initial version of Presto was rolled out in production at Facebook. By the fall of 2013, Presto was officially offered as open source. Seeing the success at Facebook, other large web-scale companies started to adopt Presto, including Netflix, LinkedIn, Treasure Data, and others. Many companies continued to follow.

In 2015, Teradata announced a large commitment of 20 engineers contributing to Presto, focused on adding enterprise features such as security enhancements and ecosystem tool integration. Later in 2015, Amazon added Presto to its AWS Elastic MapReduce (EMR) offering. In 2016, Amazon announced Athena, in which Presto serves as a major foundational piece. And 2017 saw the creation of Starburst, a company dedicated to driving the success of Presto everywhere.

At the end of 2018, the original creators left Facebook and founded the Presto Software Foundation to ensure that the project remains collaborative and independent. The project came to be known as *PrestoSQL*. The whole community of contributors and users moved to the PrestoSQL codebase with the founders and maintainers of the project. Since then, the innovation and growth of the project has accelerated even more.

The end of 2020 saw another milestone of the project. To reduce confusion between PrestoSQL, the legacy PrestoDB project, and other versions, the community decided to rename the project. After a long search for a suitable name, Trino was chosen (*https://trino.io/blog/2020/12/27/announcing-trino.html*). The code, website, and everything surrounding the project was updated to use *Trino*. The foundation was renamed the Trino Software Foundation. The last release under the PrestoSQL banner was 350. Versions 351 and later use Trino. The community welcomed and celebrated the change, moved with the project, and chose a name for the new mascot, Commander Bun Bun.

Today, the Trino community thrives and grows, and Trino continues to be used at large scale by many well-known companies (*https://trino.io/users.html*). The core maintainers and the wider community around Trino constantly drive innovation with new SQL support, updated runtime usage of Java 17, modernized code and architecture to support fault-tolerant execution and increased performance, and integrations with client tools for reporting and data platform needs. The project is maintained by a flourishing community of developers and contributors from many companies across the world, including Amazon, Bloomberg, Eventbrite, Gett, Google, Line, LinkedIn, Lyft, Netflix, Pinterest, Red Hat, Salesforce, Shopify, Starburst, Treasure Data, Zuora, and the many customers of these users.

Conclusion

In this chapter, we introduced you to Trino. You learned more about some of its features, and we explored possible use cases together.

In Chapter 2, you get Trino up and running, connect a data source, and see how you can query the data.

Installing and Configuring Trino

In Chapter 1, you learned about Trino and its possible use cases. Now you are ready to try it out. In this chapter, you learn how to install Trino, configure a data source, and query the data.

Trying Trino with the Docker Container

The Trino project provides a Docker container. It allows you to easily start up a configured demo environment of Trino for a first glimpse and exploration.

To run Trino in Docker, you must have Docker installed on your machine. You can download Docker from the Docker website (*https://www.docker.com*), or use the packaging system of your operating system.

Use docker to download the container image, save it with the name **trino-trial**, start it to run in the background, and map the port 8080 from inside the container to port 8080 on your workstation:

```
docker run -d -p 8080:8080 --name trino-trial trinodb/trino
```

Now let's connect to the container and run the Trino command-line interface (CLI), trino, on it. It connects to the Trino server running on the same container. In the prompt, you then execute a query on a table of the tpch benchmark data:

```
$ docker exec -it trino-trial trino
trino> select count(*) from tpch.sf1.nation;
 _col0
-------
    25
(1 row)

Query 20181105_001601_00002_e6r6y, FINISHED, 1 node
```

```
Splits: 21 total, 21 done (100.00%)
0:06 [25 rows, 0B] [4 rows/s, 0B/s]
```

 If you try to run Docker and see an error message resembling
`Query xyz failed: Trino server is still initializing`, try
waiting a bit and then retrying your last command.

You can continue to explore the data set with your SQL knowledge and use the `help`
command to learn about the Trino CLI.

Alternatively, you can use the Trino CLI installed directly on your workstation. The
default server URL in the CLI of *http://localhost:8080* matches the port used in the
command to start the container. More information about using the CLI can be found
in "Trino Command-Line Interface" on page 27. You can also connect with any
other client application, such as DBeaver, to Trino on the container.

The image already contains a default configuration to get started, and some catalogs
to allow you to explore Trino. You can also use the container with your custom
configuration files in a local *etc* directory structure as created in the "Installing from
the Archive File" on page 21. If you mount this directory as a volume in the path
etc/trino when starting the container, your configuration is used instead of the default
in the image:

```
$ docker run -d -p 8080:8080 --volume $PWD/etc:/etc/trino  trinodb/trino
```

Once you are done with your exploration, just type the command **quit**.

To stop the container, simply execute the following:

```
$ docker stop trino-trial
trino-trial
```

You can start it again if you want to experiment further:

```
$ docker start trino-trial
trino-trial
```

If you have learned enough and do not need the Docker images anymore, you can
remove the image and delete all related Docker resources:

```
$ docker rm trino-trial
trino-trial
$ docker rmi trinodb/trino
Untagged: trinodb/trino:latest
...
Deleted: sha256:877b494a9f...
```

Installing from the Archive File

After trying Trino with Docker, or even as a first step, you can install Trino on your local workstation or a server of your choice from the archive file.

Trino works on most modern Linux distributions. For local testing, you can also use macOS. It requires a Java Virtual Machine (JVM) and a Python installation.

Java Virtual Machine

Trino is written in Java and requires a JVM to be installed on your system. Trino requires the long-term support version Java 17, specifically 17.0.3 or newer. Trino does not support older versions of Java. Newer major releases might work, but Trino is not well tested on these.

Confirm that `java` is installed and available on the PATH:

```
$ java --version
openjdk version "17.0.3" 2022-04-19 LTS
OpenJDK Runtime Environment Zulu17.34+19-CA (build 17.0.3+7-LTS)
OpenJDK 64-Bit Server VM Zulu17.34+19-CA (build 17.0.3+7-LTS, mixed mode, sharing)
```

If you do not have Java 17 installed, Trino fails to start.

Python

Python version 2.6 or higher is required by the launcher script included with Trino.

Confirm that `python` is installed and available on the PATH:

```
$ python --version
Python 3.9.13
```

Installation

The Trino release binaries are distributed on the Maven Central Repository. The server is available as a *tar.gz* archive file.

You can see the list of available versions at *https://repo.maven.apache.org/maven2/io/trino/trino-server*.

Determine the largest number, which represents the latest release, and navigate into the folder and download the *tar.gz* file. You can also download the archive on the command line; for example, with `wget` for version 392:

```
$ wget https://repo.maven.apache.org/maven2/\
    io/trino/trino-server/392/trino-server-392.tar.gz
```

As a next step, extract the archive:

```
$ tar xvzf trino-server-*.tar.gz
```

The extraction creates a single top-level directory, named identical to the base file-name without an extension. This directory is referred to as the *installation* directory.

The installation directory contains these directories:

lib

Contains the Java archives (JARs) that make up the Trino server and all required dependencies.

plugins

Contains the Trino plug-ins and their dependencies, in separate directories for each plug-in. Trino includes many plug-ins by default, and third-party plug-ins can be added as well. Trino allows for pluggable components to integrate with Trino, such as connectors, functions, and security access controls.

bin

Contains launch scripts for Trino. These scripts are used to start, stop, restart, kill, and get the status of a running Trino process. Learn more about the use of these scripts in "Launcher" on page 83.

etc

This is the configuration directory. It is created by the user and provides the necessary configuration files needed by Trino. You can find out more about the configuration in "Configuration Details" on page 79.

var

Finally, this is a data directory, the place where logs are stored. It is created the first time the Trino server is launched. By default, it is located in the installation directory. We recommend configuring it outside the installation directory to allow for the data to be preserved across upgrades.

Configuration

Before you can start Trino, you need to provide a set of configuration files:

- Trino logging configuration
- Trino node configuration
- JVM configuration

By default, the configuration files are expected in the *etc* directory inside the installation directory.

With the exception of the JVM configuration, the configurations follow the Java properties standards. As a general description for Java properties, each configuration parameter is stored as a pair of strings in the format `key=value` per line.

Inside the Trino installation directory you created in the previous section, you need to create the basic set of Trino configuration files. You can find ready-to-go configuration files in the Git repository for the book, detailed in "Book Repository" on page 15. Here is the content of the three configuration files:

etc/config.properties:

```
coordinator=true
node-scheduler.include-coordinator=true
http-server.http.port=8080
discovery.uri=http://localhost:8080
```

etc/node.properties:

```
node.environment=demo
```

etc/jvm.config:

```
-server
-Xmx4G
-XX:InitialRAMPercentage=80
-XX:MaxRAMPercentage=80
-XX:G1HeapRegionSize=32M
-XX:+ExplicitGCInvokesConcurrent
-XX:+ExitOnOutOfMemoryError
-XX:+HeapDumpOnOutOfMemoryError
-XX:-OmitStackTraceInFastThrow
-XX:ReservedCodeCacheSize=512M
-XX:PerMethodRecompilationCutoff=10000
-XX:PerBytecodeRecompilationCutoff=10000
-Djdk.attach.allowAttachSelf=true
-Djdk.nio.maxCachedBufferSize=2000000
-XX:+UnlockDiagnosticVMOptions
-XX:+UseAESCTRIntrinsics
```

With the preceding configuration files in place, Trino is ready to be started. You can find a more detailed description of these files in Chapter 5.

Adding a Data Source

Although our Trino installation is ready, you are not going to start it just yet. After all, you want to be able to query some sort of external data in Trino. That requires you to add a data source configured as a catalog.

Trino *catalogs* define the data sources available to users. The data access is performed by a Trino connector configured in the catalog with the connector.name property. Catalogs expose all the schemas and tables inside the data source to Trino.

For example, the Hive connector maps each Hive database to a schema. If a Hive database web contains a table clicks and the catalog is named sitehive, the Hive connector exposes that table. The Hive connector has to be specified in the catalog file. You can access the table in the catalog and schema with the fully qualified name syntax `catalog.schema.table` so, in this example, `sitehive.web.clicks`.

Catalogs are registered by creating a catalog properties file in the *etc/catalog* directory. The basename of the file sets the name of the catalog. For example, let's say you create catalog properties files *etc/catalog/cdh-hadoop.properties*, *etc/catalog/sales.properties*, *etc/catalog/web-traffic.properties*, and *etc/catalog/mysql-dev.properties*. Then the catalogs exposed in Trino are `cdh-hadoop`, `sales`, `web-traffic`, and `mysql-dev`.

You can use the TPC-H connector for your first exploration of a Trino example. The TPC-H connector is built into Trino and provides a set of schemas to support the TPC Benchmark H (TPC-H). You can learn more about it in "Trino TPC-H and TPC-DS Connectors" on page 100.

To configure the TPC-H connector, create a catalog properties file, *etc/catalog/tpch.properties* with the `tpch` connector configured:

```
connector.name=tpch
```

Every catalog file requires the `connector.name` property. Additional properties are determined by the Trino connector implementations. These are documented in the Trino documentation, and you can start to learn more in Chapters 6 and 7.

Our book repository contains a collection of other catalog files that can be very useful for your learning with Trino.

Running Trino

Now you are truly ready to go, and we can proceed to start Trino. The installation directory contains the launcher scripts. You can use them to start Trino:

```
$ bin/launcher run
```

The `run` command starts Trino as a foreground process. Logs and other output of Trino are written to `stdout` and `stderr`. A successful start is logged, and you should see the following line after a while:

```
INFO main io.trino.server.Server ======== SERVER STARTED ========
```

Running Trino in the foreground can be useful for first testing and quickly verifying whether the process starts up correctly and that it is using the expected configuration settings. You can stop the server with Ctrl-C.

You can learn more about the launcher script in "Launcher" on page 83, and about logging in "Logging" on page 80.

Conclusion

Now you know how simple it is to get Trino installed and configured. It is up and running and ready to be used.

In Chapter 3, you learn how to interact with Trino and use it to query the data sources with the configured catalogs. You can also jump ahead to Chapters 6 and 7 to learn more about other connectors and how to include the additional catalogs in your next steps.

Using Trino

Congratulations! In the prior chapters, you were introduced to Trino and learned how to get it installed, configured, and started. Now you get to use it.

Trino Command-Line Interface

The *Trino command-line interface* (*CLI*) provides a terminal-based, interactive shell for running queries and for interacting with the Trino server to inspect its metadata.

Getting Started

Just like the Trino server itself, the Trino CLI release binaries are distributed on the Maven Central Repository. The CLI application is available as an executable JAR file, which allows you to use it like a normal Unix executable.

You can see the list of available versions at *https://repo.maven.apache.org/maven2/io/trino/trino-cli*.

Locate the version of the CLI that is identical to the Trino server version you are running, or a newer version. Download the **-executable.jar* file from the versioned directory, and rename it to **trino**; for example, with **wget** and version 392:

```
$ wget -O trino \
https://repo.maven.apache.org/maven2/\
io/trino/trino-cli/392/trino-cli-392-executable.jar
```

Ensure that the file is set to be executable. For convenience, make it available on the PATH—for example, by copying it to *~/bin* and adding that folder to the PATH:

```
$ chmod +x trino
$ mv trino ~/bin
$ export PATH=~/bin/:$PATH
```

You can now run the Trino CLI and confirm the version:

```
$ trino --version
Trino CLI 392
```

Documentation for all available options and commands is available with the help option:

```
$ trino --help
```

Before you start using the CLI, you need to determine which Trino server you want to interact with. By default, the CLI connects to the Trino server running on *http://localhost:8080*. If your server is running locally for testing or development, or you access the server with SSH, or you're using the Docker container with exec and the CLI is installed there, you are ready to go:

```
$ trino
trino>
```

If Trino is running at a different server, you have to specify the URL:

```
$ trino --server http://trino.example.com:8080
```

A Trino deployment that uses any authentication system is required to use Transport Layer Security (TLS), and therefore HTTPS. In that case, the port is typically set to use the default HTTPS port of 443, so you can omit it:

```
$ trino --server https://trino.example.com
```

The trino> prompt shows that you are using the interactive console accessing the Trino server. Type **help** to get a list of available commands:

```
trino> help
Supported commands:
QUIT
EXIT
CLEAR
EXPLAIN [ ( option [, ...] ) ] <query>
    options: FORMAT { TEXT | GRAPHVIZ | JSON }
             TYPE { LOGICAL | DISTRIBUTED | VALIDATE | IO }
DESCRIBE <table>
SHOW COLUMNS FROM <table>
SHOW FUNCTIONS
SHOW CATALOGS [LIKE <pattern>]
SHOW SCHEMAS [FROM <catalog>] [LIKE <pattern>]
SHOW TABLES [FROM <schema>] [LIKE <pattern>]
USE [<catalog>.]<schema>
```

Most commands, and especially all SQL statements, in the CLI need to end with a semicolon. You can find much more information in "SQL with Trino" on page 39. For now, you can just explore a few simple things to get started.

First, you can check what data sources are configured as catalogs. At a minimum, you find the internal metadata catalog—system. In our case, you also find tpch and a few other catalogs:

```
SHOW CATALOGS;
 Catalog
---------
 abyss
 brain
 monitor
 system
 tpcds
 tpch
(6 rows)

Query 20220618_163043_00000_9ftag, FINISHED, 1 node
Splits: 11 total, 11 done (100.00%)
0.70 [0 rows, 0B] [0 rows/s, 0B/s]
```

You can easily display available schemas as well as tables in the schemas. Each time you query Trino, query processing statistics are returned, together with the result. You see them just as in the preceding code. We are going to omit them in the following listings:

```
trino> SHOW SCHEMAS FROM tpch;
       Schema
--------------------
 information_schema
 sf1
 sf100
 sf1000
 sf10000
 sf100000
 sf300
 sf3000
 sf30000
 tiny
(10 rows)

trino> SHOW TABLES FROM tpch.sf1;
  Table
----------
 customer
 lineitem
 nation
 orders
 part
 partsupp
```

```
region
supplier
(8 rows)
```

Now you are ready to query some actual data:

```
trino> SELECT count(name) FROM tpch.sf1.nation;
 _col0
-------
    25
(1 row)
```

Alternatively, you can select a catalog and schema to work with, and then omit the qualifier from the query:

```
trino> USE tpch.sf1;
USE
trino:sf1> SELECT count(name) FROM nation:
```

If you know that you are going to work with a specific catalog and schema, before you start the CLI, you can specify both at startup:

```
$ trino --catalog tpch --schema sf1
```

Now you are ready to exercise all your SQL knowledge and the power of Trino to query the configured data sources.

To exit the CLI, you can simply type **quit** or **exit**, or press Ctrl-D.

Pagination

By default, the results of queries are paginated using the less program, which is configured with a carefully selected set of options. This behavior can be overridden by setting the environment variable TRINO_PAGER to the name of a different program such as more, or set it to an empty value to completely disable pagination.

History and Completion

The Trino CLI keeps a history of the previously used commands. You can use the up and down arrows to scroll through the history as well as Ctrl-S and Ctrl-R to search through the history. If you want to execute a query again, press Enter to execute the query.

By default, the Trino history file is located in ~/.trino_history. You can change the default with the TRINO_HISTORY_FILE environment variable.

The history is also used to show possible completion of your commands and queries while you type. Use the right arrow key to choose a displayed command and press Enter to run the query.

Additional Diagnostics

The Trino CLI provides the --debug option to enable debug information when running queries:

```
$ trino --debug

trino> SELECT count(*) FROM tpch.sf1.foo;
Query 20181103_201856_00022_te3wy failed:
 line 1:22: Table tpch.sf1.foo does not exist
io.trino.sql.analyzer.SemanticException:
 line 1:22: Table tpch.sf1.foo does not exist
...
at java.lang.Thread.run(Thread.java:748)
```

Executing Queries

It is possible to execute a query directly with the trino command and have the Trino CLI exit after query completion. This is often desirable if you are scripting execution of multiple queries or are automating a more complex workflow with another system. The execution returns the query results from Trino.

To run a query with the Trino CLI, use the --execute option. It is also important to fully qualify the table (for example, catalog.schema.table):

```
$ trino --execute 'SELECT nationkey, name, regionkey FROM tpch.sf1.nation LIMIT 5'
"0","ALGERIA","0"
"1","ARGENTINA","1"
"2","BRAZIL","1"
"3","CANADA","1"
"4","EGYPT","4"
```

Alternatively, use the --catalog and --schema options:

```
$ trino --catalog tpch --schema sf1 \
   --execute 'select nationkey, name, regionkey from nation limit 5'
```

You can execute multiple queries by separating the queries with a semicolon.

The Trino CLI also supports executing commands and SQL queries in a file, like *nations.sql*:

```
USE tpch.sf1;
SELECT name FROM nation;
```

When you use the CLI with the -f option, it returns the data on the command line and then exits:

```
$ trino -f nations.sql
USE
"ALGERIA"
"ARGENTINA"
"BRAZIL"
"CANADA"
...
```

Output Formats

The Trino CLI provides the option --output-format to control how the output is displayed when running in noninteractive mode. The available options are ALIGNED, VERTICAL, TSV, TSV_HEADER, CSV, CSV_HEADER, CSV_UNQUOTED, CSV_HEADER_UNQUOTED, JSON, and NULL. The default value is CSV.

Ignoring Errors

The Trino CLI provides the option --ignore-error, if you want to skip any errors encountered while executing the queries in a file. The default behavior is to stop execution of the script upon encountering the first error.

Trino JDBC Driver

Trino can be accessed from any Java application using the Trino Java Database Connectivity (JDBC) driver. JDBC is a standard API that provides the necessary methods such as querying, inserting, deleting, and updating data in a relational database. Many client and server-side applications running on the JVM implement features for database management, reporting, and other aspects, and use JDBC to access the underlying database. All of these applications can use Trino with the JDBC driver.

The Trino JDBC driver allows you to connect to Trino and interact with Trino via SQL statements.

 If you're familiar with the different implementations of JDBC drivers, the Trino JDBC driver is a Type 4 driver. This simply means it talks to the Trino native protocol.

Using the JDBC driver enables you to use powerful SQL client and database administration tools, such as the open source tools DBeaver (*https://dbeaver.io*) or SQuirreL SQL Client (*http://www.squirrelsql.org*) and many others. Report generation, dashboard, and analytics tools using JDBC can also be used with Trino.

The steps to use any of these tools with Trino are similar:

1. Download the JDBC driver.
2. Make the JDBC driver available on the classpath of the application.
3. Configure the JDBC driver.
4. Configure the connection to Trino.
5. Connect to Trino and use it.

For example, the open source database management tool DBeaver makes this process simple. After installing and starting DBeaver, follow these steps:

1. From the File menu, select New.
2. From the DBeaver section, select Database Connection and then click Next.
3. Type **trino** in the input field, select the Trino icon, and click Next. Type **prestosql**, and select the PrestoSQL icon to connect to a Trino cluster version 350 and older.
4. Configure the connection to Trino and click Finish. Note that a username value is *required*. You can provide a random name on a default installation of Trino without authentication.

Now you see the connection in the Database Navigator on the left and can inspect the schemas and tables, with an example displayed in Figure 3-1. You can also start the SQL Editor and start writing your queries and working with Trino.

SQuirreL SQL Client (*http://www.squirrelsql.org*) and many other tools use a similar process. Some steps, such as downloading the JDBC driver, and configuring the database driver and connection, are more manual. Let's look at the details.

Figure 3-1. DBeaver user interface displaying `tpch.sf1.customer` *table columns*

Downloading and Registering the Driver

The Trino JDBC driver is distributed on the Maven Central Repository. The driver is available as a JAR file.

You can see the list of available versions at *https://repo.maven.apache.org/maven2/io/trino/trino-jdbc*.

Determine the largest number, which represents the latest release, and navigate into the folder and download the *.jar* file. You can also download the archive on the command line—for example, with `wget` for version 392:

```
$ wget https://repo.maven.apache.org/maven2/\
io/trino/trino-jdbc/392/trino-jdbc-392.jar
```

To use the Trino JDBC driver in your application, add it to the classpath of the Java application. This differs for each application but often uses a folder named *lib*, as is the case for SQuirreL SQL Client. Some applications include a dialog to add libraries to the classpath, which can be used as an alternative to copying the file into place manually.

Loading the driver typically requires a restart of the application.

Now you are ready to register the driver. In SQuirreL SQL Client, you can do that with the + button to create a new driver in the Drivers tab on the left of the user interface.

When configuring the driver, you need to ensure that you configure the following parameters:

- Class name: `io.trino.jdbc.TrinoDriver`
- Example JDBC URL: `jdbc:trino://host:port/catalog/schema`
- Name: `Trino`
- Website: `https://trino.io`

Only the class name, JDBC URL, and the JAR on the classpath are truly required for the driver to operate. Other parameters are optional and depend on the application.

Establishing a Connection to Trino

With the driver registered and Trino up and running, you can now connect to it from your application.

In SQuirreL SQL Client, this connection configuration is called an *alias*. You can use the Alias tab on the left of the user interface and the + button to create a new alias with the following parameters:

Name
A descriptive name for the Trino connection. The name is more important if you end up connecting to multiple Trino instances, or different schemas and databases. Choosing a meaningful name allows you to distinguish the connections.

Driver
Select the Trino driver you created earlier.

URL
The JDBC URL uses the pattern *jdbc:trino://host:port/catalog/schema*, with catalog and schema values optional. You can connect to Trino, installed earlier on your machine and running on *http://localhost:8080*, with the JDBC URL *jdbc:trino://localhost:8080*. The host parameter is the host where the Trino coordinator is running. It is the same hostname you use when connecting via the Trino CLI. This can be in the form of an IP address or DNS hostname. The port parameter is the HTTP port to connect to Trino on the host. The optional catalog and schema parameters are used to establish a connection by using the catalog and schema specified. When you specify these, you do not have to fully qualify the table names in the queries.

Username

A username value is *required*, even when no authentication is configured on Trino. This allows Trino to report the initiator for any queries.

Password

The password is associated with the user and used for authentication. No password is required for a default installation of Trino without configured authentication.

The JDBC driver can receive further parameters as properties. The mechanism for providing these values depends on the application. Both DBeaver and SQuirreL SQL Client include a user interface to specify properties as part of the connection configuration:

SSL

Enable SSL usage of the connection, `true` or `false`. You must set this to `true` if your cluster is available via HTTPS.

`SSLTrustStorePath`

Path to the SSL truststore.

`SSLTrustStorePassword`

Password for the SSL truststore.

`user` *and* `password`

Equivalent to the username and password parameters.

`applicationNamePrefix`

Property used to identify the application to Trino. This is used to set the source name for the Trino query. This name is displayed in the Trino Web UI so that administrators can see where the query originated. Furthermore, it can be used in conjunction with resource groups in which you can use the `ApplicationName` to decide how to assign resources in Trino. This is discussed in "Resource Groups" on page 272.

The full list of available parameters for the JDBC drivers can be found in the Trino documentation; see "Documentation" on page 14.

Once you have configured the connection, you can use it to connect to Trino. This enables you to query Trino itself and all configured schemas and databases. The specific features available for query execution or report generation or any other functionality depend on the application connected to Trino. Figure 3-2 shows a successful connection to Trino in SQuirreL SQL Client with example queries and a result set.

Figure 3-2. SQuirreL SQL Client user interface displaying queries and result set

Trino and ODBC

Similar to the connection to Trino with the JDBC driver—"Trino JDBC Driver" on page 32—Open Database Connectivity (ODBC) allows any application supporting ODBC to use Trino. It provides an API for typically C-based applications.

Currently, no open source ODBC driver for Trino is available. However, commercial drivers can be purchased from Starburst (*https://www.starburst.io*) and Simba (*https:// www.simba.com*).

This enables several popular applications from the database administration, business intelligence, and reporting and analytics space, such as Microsoft Power BI, Tableau, SAS, Quest Toad, and others. ODBC also enables Microsoft Excel usage.

Client Libraries

Besides the Trino CLI and the JDBC driver, the Trino team directly maintains trino-python-client and trino-go-client. In addition, numerous members of the larger Trino community have created client libraries for Trino.

You can find libraries for C, Node.js, R, Ruby, and others. A list is maintained on the Trino website, as discussed in "Website" on page 13.

These libraries can be used to integrate Trino with applications in these language ecosystems, including your own applications.

Trino Web UI

Every Trino server provides a web interface, commonly referred to as the *Trino Web UI*. The Trino Web UI, shown in Figure 3-3, exposes details about the Trino server and query processing on the server.

The Trino Web UI is accessible at the same address as the Trino server, using the same HTTP port number. By default, this port is 8080; for example, *http://trino.example.com:8080*. So on your local installation, you can check out the Web UI at *http://localhost:8080*.

You are required to provide a username and login. By default, no authentication is configured, and you can therefore supply a random username.

The main dashboard shows details about the Trino utilization and a list of queries. Further details are available in the UI. All this information is of great value for operating Trino and managing the running queries.

Using the Web UI is very useful for monitoring Trino and tuning performance, as explained in more detail in "Monitoring with the Trino Web UI" on page 251. As a beginner user, it is mostly useful to confirm that the server is up and running and is processing your queries.

Figure 3-3. Trino Web UI display of high-level information about the cluster

SQL with Trino

Trino is an ANSI SQL-compliant query engine. It allows you to query and manipulate data in any connected data source with the same SQL statements, functions, and operators.

Trino strives to be compliant with existing SQL standards. One of the main design principles of Trino is to neither invent another SQL-like query language nor deviate too much from the SQL standard. Every new functionality and language feature attempts to comply with the standard.

Extending the SQL feature set is considered only when the standard does not define an equivalent functionality. And even then, great care is taken to design the feature by considering similar features in the standard and other existing SQL implementations as a sign of what can become standard in the future.

> In rare cases, when the standard does not define an equivalent functionality, Trino extends the standard. A prominent example is lambda expressions; see "Lambda Expressions" on page 204.

Trino does not define any particular SQL standard version it complies with. Instead, the standard is treated as a living document, and the newest standard version is always considered important. On the other hand, Trino does not yet implement all the mandatory features defined in the SQL standard. As a rule, if an existing functionality is found to be noncompliant, it is deprecated and later replaced with a standard compliant one.

Querying Trino can be done with the Trino CLI as well as any database management tool connected with JDBC or ODBC, as discussed earlier.

Concepts

Trino enables SQL-based access to external *data sources* such as relational databases, key-value stores, and object storage. The following concepts are important to understand in Trino:

Connector
> Adapts Trino to a data source. Every catalog is associated with a specific connector.

Catalog
> Defines details for accessing a data source; contains schemas and configures a specific connector to use.

Schema

A way to organize tables. A catalog and schema together define a set of tables that can be queried.

Table

A set of unordered rows, which are organized into named columns with data types.

First Examples

This section presents a short overview of supported SQL and Trino statements, with much more detail available in Chapters 8 and 9.

Trino metadata is contained in the `system` catalog. Specific statements can be used to query that data and, in general, find out more about the available catalogs, schemas, information schemas, tables, functions, and more.

Use the following to list all catalogs:

```
SHOW CATALOGS;
 Catalog
---------
 abyss
 brain
 monitor
 system
 tpcds
 tpch
(6 rows)
```

Show all schemas in the `tpch` catalog as follows:

```
SHOW SCHEMAS FROM tpch;
       Schema
------------------
 information_schema
 sf1
 sf100
 sf1000
 sf10000
 sf100000
 sf300
 sf3000
 sf30000
 tiny
(10 rows)
```

Here's how to list the tables in the `sf1` schema:

```
SHOW TABLES FROM tpch.sf1;
  Table
  ---------
  customer
  lineitem
  nation
  orders
  part
  partsupp
  region
  supplier
(8 rows)
```

Find out about the data in the `region` table as follows:

```
DESCRIBE tpch.sf1.region;
  Column   |    Type     | Extra | Comment
----------+-------------+-------+---------
 regionkey | bigint      |       |
 name      | varchar(25) |       |
 comment   | varchar(152)|       |
(3 rows)
```

Other useful statements, such as `USE` and `SHOW FUNCTIONS`, are available. More information about the system catalog and Trino statements is available in "Trino Statements" on page 142.

With the knowledge of the available catalogs, schemas, and tables, you can use standard SQL to query the data.

You can check what regions are available:

```
SELECT name FROM tpch.sf1.region;
    name
-------------
 AFRICA
 AMERICA
 ASIA
 EUROPE
 MIDDLE EAST
(5 rows)
```

You can return a subset and order the list:

```
SELECT name FROM tpch.sf1.region
WHERE name like 'A%' ORDER BY name DESC;
  name
---------
 ASIA
 AMERICA
 AFRICA
(3 rows)
```

Joining multiple tables and other parts of the SQL standard is supported as well:

```
SELECT nation.name AS nation, region.name AS region
FROM tpch.sf1.region, tpch.sf1.nation
WHERE region.regionkey = nation.regionkey
AND region.name LIKE 'AFRICA'
ORDER by nation;
   nation   | region
------------+--------
 ALGERIA    | AFRICA
 ETHIOPIA   | AFRICA
 KENYA      | AFRICA
 MOROCCO    | AFRICA
 MOZAMBIQUE | AFRICA
(5 rows)
```

Trino supports operators like || for string concatenation. You can also use mathematical operators such as plus (+) and minus (–).

You can change the preceding query to use JOIN and concatenate the result string to one field:

```
SELECT nation.name || ' / ' || region.name AS Location
FROM tpch.sf1.region JOIN tpch.sf1.nation
ON region.regionkey = nation.regionkey
AND region.name LIKE 'AFRICA'
ORDER BY Location;
      Location
--------------------
 ALGERIA / AFRICA
 ETHIOPIA / AFRICA
 KENYA / AFRICA
 MOROCCO / AFRICA
 MOZAMBIQUE / AFRICA
(5 rows)
```

In addition to the operators, Trino supports a large variety of functions. They range from simple use cases to very complex functionality. You can display a list in Trino by using SHOW FUNCTIONS.

A simple example is to calculate the average prices of all orders and display the rounded integer value:

```
SELECT cast(round(avg(totalprice)) AS integer) AS average_price
FROM tpch.sf1.orders;
 average_price
--------------
        151220
(1 row)
```

More details about SQL usage are available in the Trino documentation and in Chapter 8. Information about functions and operators is also available on the website, and you can find a good overview with more examples in Chapter 9.

Conclusion

Trino is up and running. You connected a data source and used SQL to query it. You can use the Trino CLI or applications connected to Trino with JDBC.

With this powerful combination in place, you are ready to dive deeper. In the next chapters, we are going to do exactly that: learn how to install Trino for a larger production deployment, understand the architecture of Trino, and get into the details about SQL usage.

PART II
Diving Deeper into Trino

After learning about Trino and various use cases, installing it, and starting to use it, you are now ready to dive deeper and find out more.

In this second part of the book, you learn about the internal workings of Trino in preparation for installing it for production-ready usage, running it, tuning the setup, and more.

In the following chapters, we discuss details about connecting data sources, and then querying them with the Trino support for SQL statements, operators, functions, and more.

Trino Architecture

After the introduction to Trino, and an initial installation and usage in the earlier chapters, we now discuss the Trino architecture. We dive deeper into related concepts, so you can learn about the Trino query execution model, query planning, and cost-based optimizations.

In this chapter, we first discuss the Trino high-level architectural components. It is important to have a general understanding of the way Trino works, especially if you intend to install and manage a Trino cluster yourself, as discussed in Chapter 5.

In the later part of the chapter, we dive deeper into those components when we talk about the query execution model of Trino. This is most important if you need to diagnose or tune a slow performance query, all discussed in Chapter 8, or if you plan to contribute to the Trino open source project.

Coordinator and Workers in a Cluster

When you first installed Trino, as discussed in Chapter 2, you used only a single machine to run everything. For the desired scalability and performance, this deployment is not suitable.

Trino is a distributed SQL query engine resembling massively parallel processing (MPP) style databases and query engines. Rather than relying on vertical scaling of the server running Trino, it is able to distribute all processing across a cluster of servers horizontally. This means that you can add more nodes to gain more processing power.

Leveraging this architecture, the Trino query engine is able to process SQL queries on large amounts of data in parallel across a cluster of computers, or nodes. Trino runs as a single-server process on each node. Multiple nodes running Trino, which are configured to collaborate with each other, make up a Trino cluster.

Figure 4-1 displays a high-level overview of a Trino cluster composed of one coordinator and multiple worker nodes. A Trino user connects to the coordinator with a client, such as a tool using the JDBC driver or the Trino CLI. The coordinator then collaborates with the workers, which access the data sources.

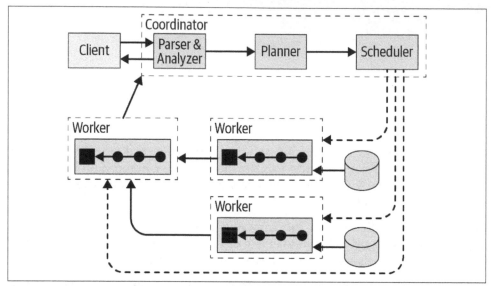

Figure 4-1. Trino architecture overview with coordinator and workers

A *coordinator* is a Trino server that handles incoming queries and manages the *workers* to execute the queries.

A *worker* is a Trino server responsible for executing tasks and processing data.

The *discovery service* runs on the coordinator and allows workers to register to participate in the cluster.

All communication and data transfer between clients, coordinator, and workers uses REST-based interactions over HTTP/HTTPS.

Figure 4-2 shows how the communication within the cluster happens between the coordinator and the workers, as well as from one worker to another. The coordinator talks to workers to assign work, update status, and fetch the top-level result set to return to the users. The workers talk to each other to fetch data from upstream tasks, running on other workers. And the workers retrieve result sets from the data source.

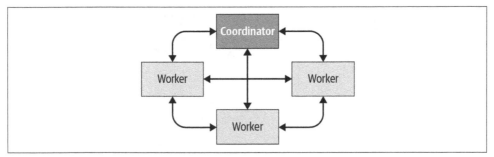

Figure 4-2. Communication between coordinator and workers in a Trino cluster

Coordinator

The Trino *coordinator* is the server responsible for receiving SQL statements from the users, parsing these statements, planning queries, and managing worker nodes. It's the brain of a Trino installation and the node to which a client connects. Users interact with the coordinator via the Trino CLI, applications using the JDBC or ODBC drivers, the Trino Python client, or any other client library for a variety of languages. The coordinator accepts SQL statements from the client such as SELECT queries for execution.

Every Trino installation must have a coordinator alongside one or more workers. For development or testing purposes, a single instance of Trino can be configured to perform both roles.

The coordinator keeps track of the activity on each worker and coordinates the execution of a query. The coordinator creates a logical model of a query involving a series of stages.

Once the coordinator receives an SQL statement, it is responsible for parsing, analyzing, planning, and scheduling the query execution across the Trino worker nodes. The statement is translated into a series of connected tasks running on a cluster of workers. As the workers process the data, the results are retrieved by the coordinator and exposed to the clients on an output buffer. When an output buffer is completely read by the client, the coordinator requests more data from the workers on behalf of the client. The workers, in turn, interact with the data sources to get the data from them. As a result, data is continuously requested by the client and supplied by the workers from the data source until the query execution is completed.

Coordinators communicate with workers and clients by using an HTTP-based protocol. Figure 4-3 displays the communication between client, coordinator, and workers.

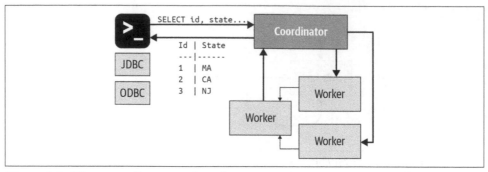

Figure 4-3. Client, coordinator, and worker communication processing an SQL statement

Discovery Service

Trino uses a *discovery service* to find all nodes in the cluster. Every Trino instance registers with the discovery service on startup and periodically sends a heartbeat signal. This allows the coordinator to have an up-to-date list of available workers and use that list for scheduling query execution.

If a worker fails to report heartbeat signals, the discovery service triggers the failure detector, and the worker becomes ineligible for further tasks.

The Trino coordinator runs the discovery service. It shares the HTTP server with Trino and thus uses the same port. Worker configuration of the discovery service therefore points at the hostname and port of the coordinator.

Workers

A Trino *worker* is a server in a Trino installation. It is responsible for executing tasks assigned by the coordinator, including retrieving data from the data sources and for processing data. Worker nodes fetch data from data sources by using connectors and then exchange intermediate data with each other. The final resulting data is passed on to the coordinator. The coordinator is responsible for gathering the results from the workers and providing the final results to the client.

During installation, workers are configured to know the hostname or IP address of the discovery service for the cluster. When a worker starts up, it advertises itself to the discovery service, which makes it available to the coordinator for task execution.

Workers communicate with other workers and the coordinator by using an HTTP-based protocol.

Figure 4-4 shows how multiple workers retrieve data from the data sources and collaborate to process the data, until one worker can provide the data to the coordinator.

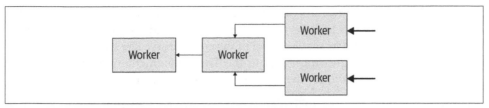

Figure 4-4. Workers in a cluster collaborate to process SQL statements and data

Connector-Based Architecture

At the heart of the separation of storage and compute in Trino is the connector-based architecture. A *connector* provides Trino an interface to access an arbitrary data source.

Each connector provides a table-based abstraction over the underlying data source. As long as data can be expressed in terms of tables, columns, and rows by using the data types available to Trino, a connector can be created and the query engine can use the data for query processing.

Trino provides a *service provider interface* (*SPI*), which defines the functionality a connector has to implement for specific features. By implementing the SPI in a connector, Trino can use standard operations internally to connect to any data source and perform operations on any data source. The connector takes care of the details relevant to the specific data source.

Every connector implements the three parts of the API:

- Operations to fetch table/view/schema metadata
- Operations to produce logical units of data partitioning, so that Trino can parallelize reads and writes
- Data sources and sinks that convert the source data to/from the in-memory format expected by the query engine

Let's clarify the SPI with an example. Any connector in Trino that supports reading data from the underlying data source needs to implement the listTables SPI. As a result, Trino can use the same method to ask any connector to check the list of available tables in a schema. Trino does not have to know that some connectors have to get that data from an information schema, others have to query a metastore, and still others have to request that information via an API of the data source. For the core Trino engine, those details are irrelevant. The connector takes care of the details. This approach clearly separates the concerns of the core query engine from the specifics of any underlying data source. This simple, yet powerful approach provides large benefits for the ability to read, expand, and maintain the code over time.

Trino provides many connectors to systems such as HDFS/Hive, Iceberg, Delta Lake, MySQL, PostgreSQL, MS SQL Server, Kafka, Cassandra, Redis, and many more. In Chapters 6 and 7, you learn about several of the connectors. The list of available connectors is continuously growing. Refer to the Trino documentation (*https://trino.io/docs/current/connector.html*) for the latest list of supported connectors.

Trino's SPI also gives you the ability to create your own custom connectors. This may be necessary if you need to access a data source without a compatible connector. If you end up creating a connector, we strongly encourage you to learn more about the Trino open source community, use our help, and contribute your connector. Check out "Trino Resources" on page 13 for more information. A custom connector may also be needed if you have a unique or proprietary data source within your organization. This is what allows Trino users to query any data source by using SQL—truly SQL-on-Anything.

Figure 4-5 shows how the Trino SPI includes separate interfaces for metadata, data statistics, and data location used by the coordinator, and for data streaming used by the workers.

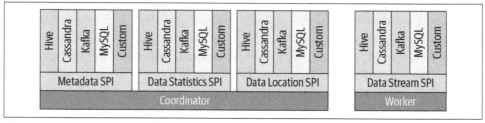

Figure 4-5. Overview of the Trino SPI

Trino connectors are plug-ins loaded by each server at startup. They are configured by specific parameters in the catalog properties files and loaded from the plug-ins directory. We explore this more in Chapter 6.

Trino uses a plug-in-based architecture for numerous aspects of its functionality. Besides connectors, plug-ins can provide implementations for event listeners, access controls, and function and type providers.

Catalogs, Schemas, and Tables

The Trino cluster processes all queries by using the connector-based architecture described earlier. Each catalog configuration uses a connector to access a specific data source. The data source exposes one or more schemas in the catalog. Each schema contains tables that provide the data in table rows, with columns using different data types. For more details, see Chapter 8: specifically "Catalogs" on page 146, "Schemas" on page 147, and "Tables" on page 150.

Query Execution Model

Now that you understand how any real-world deployment of Trino involves a cluster with a coordinator and many workers, we can look at how an actual SQL query statement is processed.

> Check out Chapters 8 and 9 to learn details about the SQL support of Trino.

Understanding the execution model provides you the foundational knowledge necessary to tune Trino's performance for your particular queries.

Recall that the coordinator accepts SQL statements from the end user, from the CLI or applications using the ODBC or JDBC driver or other client libraries. The coordinator then triggers the workers to get all the data from the data source, creates the result data set, and makes it available to the client.

Let's take a closer look into what happens inside the coordinator first. When a SQL statement is submitted to the coordinator, it is received in textual format. The coordinator takes that text and parses and analyzes it. It then creates a plan for execution by using an internal data structure in Trino called the *query plan*. This flow is displayed in Figure 4-6. The query plan broadly represents the needed steps to process the data and return the results per the SQL statement.

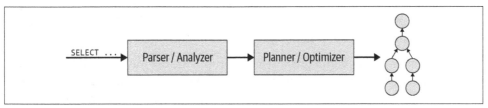

Figure 4-6. Processing an SQL query statement to create a query plan

As you can see in Figure 4-7, the query plan generation uses the metadata SPI and the data statistics SPI to create the query plan. So the coordinator uses the SPI to gather information about tables and other metadata connecting to the data source directly.

Figure 4-7. The SPIs for query planning and scheduling

The coordinator uses the *metadata SPI* to get information about tables, columns, and types. These are used to validate that the query is semantically valid and to perform type checking of expressions in the original query and security checks.

The *statistics SPI* is used to obtain information about row counts and table sizes to perform cost-based query optimizations during planning.

The *data location SPI* is then facilitated in the creation of the distributed query plan. It is used to generate logical splits of the table contents. Splits are the smallest unit of work assignment and parallelism.

> The various SPIs are more of a conceptual separation; the actual lower-level Java API is separated by multiple Java packages in a more fine-grained manner.

The distributed query plan is an extension of the simple query plan consisting of one or more stages. The simple query plan is split into *plan fragments*. A *stage* is the runtime incarnation of a plan fragment, and it encompasses all the tasks of the work described by the stage's plan fragment.

The coordinator breaks up the plan to allow processing on clusters facilitating workers in parallel to speed up the overall query. Having more than one stage results in the creation of a dependency tree of stages. The number of stages depends on the complexity of the query. For example, queried tables, returned columns, JOIN statements, WHERE conditions, GROUP BY operations, and other SQL statements all impact the number of stages created.

Figure 4-8 shows how the *logical query plan* is transformed into a *distributed query plan* on the coordinator in the cluster.

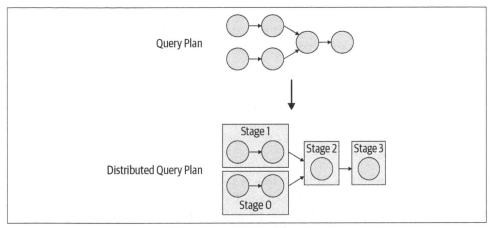

Figure 4-8. Transformation of the query plan to a distributed query plan

The distributed query plan defines the stages and the way the query is to execute on a Trino cluster. It's used by the coordinator to further plan and schedule *tasks* across the workers. A stage consists of one or more tasks. Typically, many tasks are involved, and each task processes a piece of the data.

The coordinator assigns the tasks from a stage out to the workers in the cluster, as displayed in Figure 4-9.

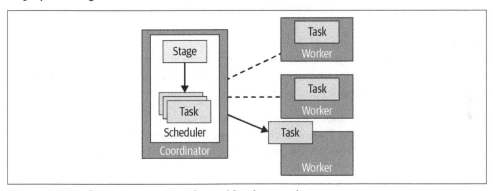

Figure 4-9. Task management performed by the coordinator

The unit of data that a task processes is called a *split*. A split is a descriptor for a segment of the underlying data that can be retrieved and processed by a worker. It is the unit of parallelism and work assignment.

The specific operations on the data performed by the connector depend on the underlying data source. For example, the Hive connector describes splits in the form of a path to a file with offset and length that indicate which part of the file needs to be processed.

Tasks at the source stage produce data in the form of *pages*, which are a collection of rows in columnar format. These pages flow to other intermediate downstream stages. Pages are transferred between stages by exchange operators, which read the data from tasks within an upstream stage.

The *source* tasks use the data source SPI to fetch data from the underlying data source with the help of a connector. This data is presented to Trino and flows through the engine in the form of pages. Operators process and produce pages according to their semantics. For example, filters drop rows, projections produce pages with new derived columns, and so on.

The sequence of operators within a task is called a *pipeline*. The last operator of a pipeline typically places its output pages in the task's output buffer. Exchange operators in downstream tasks consume the pages from an upstream task's output buffer. All these operations occur in parallel on different workers, as seen in Figure 4-10.

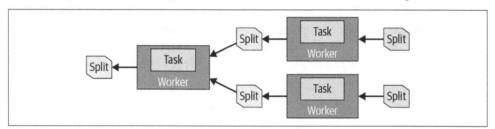

Figure 4-10. Data in splits is transferred between tasks and processed on different workers

So a task is the runtime incarnation of a plan fragment when assigned to a worker. After a task is created, it instantiates a *driver* for each split. Each driver is an instantiation of a pipeline of operators and performs the processing of the data in the split.

A task may use one or more drivers, depending on the Trino configuration and environment, as shown in Figure 4-11. Once all drivers are finished and the data is passed to the next split, the drivers and the task are finished with their work and are destroyed.

Figure 4-11. Parallel drivers in a task with input and output splits

An *operator* processes input data to produce output data for a downstream operator. Example operators are table scans, filters, joins, and aggregations. A series of these operators form an operator pipeline. For example, you may have a pipeline that first scans and reads the data, and then filters the data, and finally partially aggregates the data.

To process a query, the coordinator creates the list of splits with the metadata from the connector. Using the list of splits, the coordinator starts scheduling tasks on the workers to gather the data in the splits. During query execution, the coordinator tracks all splits available for processing and the locations where tasks are running on workers and processing splits.

As tasks finish processing and are producing more splits for downstream processing, the coordinator continues to schedule tasks until no splits remain for processing. Once all splits are processed on the workers, all data is available, and the coordinator can make the result available to the client.

Query Planning

Before diving into how the Trino query planner and cost-based optimizations work, let's set up a stage that frames our considerations in a certain context. We present an example query as context for our exploration to help you understand the process of query planning.

Example 4-1 uses the TPC-H data set—see "Trino TPC-H and TPC-DS Connectors" on page 100—to sum up the value of all orders per nation and list the top five nations.

Example 4-1. Example query to explain query planning

```
SELECT
    (SELECT name FROM region r WHERE regionkey = n.regionkey) AS region_name,
    n.name AS nation_name,
    sum(totalprice) orders_sum
FROM nation n, orders o, customer c
WHERE n.nationkey = c.nationkey
  AND c.custkey = o.custkey
GROUP BY n.nationkey, regionkey, n.name
ORDER BY orders_sum DESC
LIMIT 5;
```

Let's try to understand the SQL constructs used in the query and their purpose:

- A SELECT query using three tables in the FROM clause, implicitly defining a CROSS JOIN between the nation, orders, and customer tables

- A WHERE condition to retain the matching rows from the nation, orders, and customer tables

- An aggregation using GROUP BY to aggregate values of orders for each nation

- A subquery (`SELECT name FROM region WHERE regionkey = n.regionkey`) to pull the region name from the `region` table; note that this query is correlated, as if it was supposed to be executed independently for each row of the containing result set

- An ordering definition, `ORDER BY orders_sum DESC`, to sort the result before returning

- A limit of five rows defined to return only nations with the highest order sums and filter out all others

Parsing and Analysis

Before a query can be planned for execution, it needs to be parsed and analyzed. Details about SQL and the related syntactic rules for building the query can be found in Chapters 8 and 9. Trino verifies the text for these syntax rules when parsing it. As a next step, Trino analyses the query:

Identifying tables used in a query
Tables are organized within catalogs and schemas, so multiple tables can have the same name. For example, TPC-H data provides `orders` tables of various sizes in the different schemas as `sf10.orders`, `sf100.orders`, etc.

Identifying columns used in a query
A qualified column reference `orders.totalprice` unambiguously refers to a `totalprice` column within the `orders` table. Typically, however, an SQL query refers to a column by name only—`totalprice`, as seen in Example 4-1. The Trino analyzer can determine which table a column originates from.

Identifying references to fields within ROW values
A dereference expression `c.bonus` may refer to a `bonus` column in the table named `c` or aliased with `c`. Or, it may refer to a `bonus` field in a `c` column of row type (a struct with named fields). It is the job of the analyzer in Trino to decide which is applicable, with a table-qualified column reference taking precedence in case of ambiguity. Analysis needs to follow SQL language's scoping and visibility rules. The information collected, such as identifier disambiguation, is later used during planning, so that the planner does not need to understand the query language scoping rules again.

As you see, the query analyzer has complex, cross-cutting duties. Its role is very technical, and it remains invisible from the user perspective as long as the queries are correct. The analyzer manifests its existence whenever a query violates SQL language rules, exceeds the user's privileges, or is unsound for some other reason.

Once the query is analyzed and all identifiers in the query are processed and resolved, Trino proceeds to the next phase, which is query planning.

Initial Query Planning

A query plan defines a program that produces query results. Recall that SQL is a declarative language: the user writes an SQL query to specify the data they want from the system. Unlike an imperative program, the user does not specify how to process the data to get the result. This part is left to the query planner and optimizer to determine the sequence of steps to process the data for the desired result.

This sequence of steps is often referred to as the *query plan*. Theoretically, an exponential number of query plans could yield the same query result. The performance of the plans varies dramatically, and this is where the Trino planner and optimizer try to determine the optimal plan. Plans that always produce the same results are called *equivalent plans*.

Let's consider the query shown previously in Example 4-1. The most straightforward query plan for this query is the one that most closely resembles the query's SQL syntactical structure. This plan is shown in Example 4-2. For the purposes of this discussion, the listing should be self-explanatory. You just need to know that the plan is a tree, and its execution starts from leaf nodes and proceeds up along the tree structure.

Example 4-2. Manually condensed, straightforward textual representation of the query plan for the example query

```
- Limit[5]
  - Sort[orders_sum DESC]
    - LateralJoin[2]
      - Aggregate[by nationkey...; orders_sum := sum(totalprice)]
        - Filter[c.nationkey = n.nationkey AND c.custkey = o.custkey]
          - CrossJoin
            - CrossJoin
              - TableScan[nation]
              - TableScan[orders]
            - TableScan[customer]
      - EnforceSingleRow[region_name := r.name]
        - Filter[r.regionkey = n.regionkey]
          - TableScan[region]
```

Each element of the query plan can be implemented in a straightforward, imperative fashion. For example, TableScan accesses a table in its underlying storage and returns a result set containing all rows within the table. Filter receives rows and applies a filtering condition on each, retaining only the rows that satisfy the condition. CrossJoin operates on two data sets that it receives from its child nodes. It produces all combinations of rows in those data sets, probably storing one of the data sets in memory, so that the underlying storage does not have to be accessed multiple times.

 The latest Trino releases have changed the names of the operations in a query plan. For example, TableScan is equivalent to ScanProject with a table specification. The Filter operation has been renamed to FilterProject. The ideas presented, however, remain the same.

Let's now consider the computational complexity of this query plan. Without knowing all the nitty-gritty details of the actual implementation, we cannot fully reason about the complexity. However, we can assume that the lower bound for the complexity of a query plan node is the size of the data set it produces. Therefore, we describe complexity by using Big Omega notation, which describes the asymptotic lower bound. If N, O, C, and R represent the number of rows in nation, orders, customer, and region tables, respectively, we can observe the following:

- TableScan[orders] reads the orders table, returning O rows, so its complexity is $\Omega(O)$. Similarly, the other two TableScan operations return N and C rows; thus their complexity is $\Omega(N)$ and $\Omega(C)$, respectively.

- CrossJoin above TableScan[nation] and TableScan[orders] combines the data from nation and orders tables; therefore, its complexity is $\Omega(N \times O)$.

- The CrossJoin above combines the earlier CrossJoin, which produced $N \times O$ rows, with TableScan[customer], so with data from the customer table; therefore, its complexity is $\Omega(N \times O \times C)$.

- TableScan[region] at the bottom has complexity $\Omega(R)$. However, because of the LateralJoin, it is invoked N times, with N as the number of rows returned from the aggregation. Thus, in total, this operation incurs $\Omega(R \times N)$ computational cost.

- The Sort operation needs to order a set of N rows, so it cannot take less time than is proportional to $N \times \log(N)$.

Disregarding other operations for a moment as no more costly than the ones we have analyzed so far, the total cost of the preceding plan is at least $\Omega[N + O + C + (N \times O) + (N \times O \times C) + (R \times N) + (N \times \log(N))]$. Without knowing the relative table sizes, this can be simplified to $\Omega[(N \times O \times C) + (R \times N) + (N \times \log(N))]$. Adding a reasonable assumption that region is the smallest table and nation is the second smallest, we can neglect the second and third parts of the result and get the simplified result of $\Omega(N \times O \times C)$.

Enough of algebraic formulas. It's time to see what this means in practice! Let's consider an example of a popular shopping site with 100 million customers from 200 nations who placed 1 billion orders in total. The `CrossJoin` of these two tables needs to materialize 20 quintillion (20,000,000,000,000,000,000) rows. For a moderately beefy 100-node cluster, processing 1 million rows a second on each node, it would take over 63 centuries to compute the intermediate data for our query.

Of course, Trino does not even try to execute such a naive plan. But this initial plan serves as a bridge between two worlds: the world of SQL language and its semantic rules, and the world of query optimizations. The role of query optimization is to transform and evolve the initial plan into an equivalent plan that can be executed as fast as possible, at least in a reasonable amount of time, given finite resources of the Trino cluster. Let's talk about how query optimizations attempt to reach this goal.

Optimization Rules

In this section, you get to take a look at a handful of the many important optimization rules implemented in Trino.

Predicate Pushdown

Predicate pushdown is probably the single most important optimization and easiest to understand. Its role is to move the filtering condition as close to the source of the data as possible. As a result, data reduction happens as early as possible during query execution. In our case, it transforms a `Filter` into a simpler `Filter` and an `InnerJoin` above the same `CrossJoin` condition, leading to a plan shown in Example 4-3. Portions of the plan that didn't change are excluded for readability.

Example 4-3. Transformation of a `CrossJoin` and `Filter` into an `InnerJoin`

```
- Aggregate[by nationkey...; orders_sum := sum(totalprice)]
  - Filter[c.nationkey = n.nationkey AND c.custkey = o.custkey]  // original filter
    - CrossJoin
      - CrossJoin
        - TableScan[nation]
        - TableScan[orders]
      - TableScan[customer]
...
- Aggregate[by nationkey...; orders_sum := sum(totalprice)]
  - Filter[c.nationkey = n.nationkey]               // transformed simpler filter
    - InnerJoin[o.custkey = c.custkey]              // added inner join
      - CrossJoin
        - TableScan[nation]
        - TableScan[orders]
      - TableScan[customer]
...
```

The "bigger" join that was present is now converted into `InnerJoin` on an equality condition. Without going into details, let's assume for now that such a join can be efficiently implemented in a distributed system, with computational complexity equal to the number of produced rows. This means that predicate pushdown replaced an "at least" $\Omega(N \times O \times C)$ `CrossJoin` with a `Join` that is "exactly" $\Theta(N \times O)$.

However, predicate pushdown could not improve the `CrossJoin` between the `nation` and `orders` tables because no immediate condition is joining these tables. This is where cross join elimination comes into play.

Cross Join Elimination

In the absence of the cost-based optimizer, Trino joins the tables contained in the `SELECT` query in the order of their appearance in the query text. The one important exception to this occurs when the tables to be joined have no joining condition, which results in a *cross join*. In almost all practical cases, a cross join is unwanted, and all the multiplied rows are later filtered out, but the cross join itself has so much work to do that it may never complete.

Cross join elimination reorders the tables being joined to minimize the number of cross joins, ideally reducing it to zero. In the absence of information about relative table sizes, other than the cross join elimination, table join ordering is preserved, so the user remains in control. The effect of cross join elimination on our example query can be seen in Example 4-4. Now both joins are inner joins, bringing overall computational cost of joins to $\Theta(C + O) = \Theta(O)$. Other parts of the query plan did not change since the initial plan, so the overall query computation cost is at least $\Omega[O + (R \times N) + (N \times \log(N))]$—of course, the O component representing the number of rows in the `orders` table is the dominant factor.

Example 4-4. Reordering the joins to eliminate the cross join

```
- Aggregate[by nationkey...; orders_sum := sum(totalprice)]
  - Filter[c.nationkey = n.nationkey]              // filter on nationkey first
    - InnerJoin[o.custkey = c.custkey]             // then inner join custkey
      - CrossJoin
        - TableScan[nation]
        - TableScan[orders]
      - TableScan[customer]
...
- Aggregate[by nationkey...; orders_sum := sum(totalprice)]
  - InnerJoin[c.custkey = o.custkey]               // reordered to custkey first
    - InnerJoin[n.nationkey = c.nationkey]         // then nationkey
      - TableScan[nation]
      - TableScan[customer]
    - TableScan[orders]
```

TopN

Typically, when a query has a LIMIT clause, it is preceded by an ORDER BY clause. Without the ordering, SQL does not guarantee which result rows are returned. The combination of ORDER BY followed by LIMIT is also present in our query.

When executing such a query, Trino could sort all the rows produced and then retain just the first few of them. This approach would have $\Theta(row\_count \times \log(row\_count))$ computational complexity and $\Theta(row\_count)$ memory footprint. However, it is not optimal and is wasteful to sort the entire results only to keep a much smaller subset of the sorted results. Therefore, an optimization rule rolls ORDER BY followed by LIMIT into a *TopN* plan node. During query execution, TopN keeps the desired number of rows in a heap data structure, updating the heap while reading input data in a streaming fashion. This brings computational complexity down to $\Theta(row\_count \times \log(limit))$ and memory footprint to $\Theta(limit)$. Overall query computation cost is now $\Omega[O + (R \times N) + N]$.

Partial Aggregations

Trino does not need to pass all rows from the orders table to the join because we are not interested in individual orders. Our example query computes an aggregate, the sum over totalprice for each nation, so it is possible to pre-aggregate the rows as shown in Example 4-5. We reduce the amount of data flowing into the downstream join by aggregating the data. The results are not complete, which is why this is referred to as a *pre-aggregation*. But the amount of data is potentially reduced, significantly improving query performance.

Example 4-5. Partial pre-aggregation can significantly improve performance

```
- Aggregate[by nationkey...; orders_sum := sum(totalprice)]
  - InnerJoin[c.custkey = o.custkey]
    - InnerJoin[n.nationkey = c.nationkey]
      - TableScan[nation]
      - TableScan[customer]
    - Aggregate[by custkey; totalprice := sum(totalprice)]
      - TableScan[orders]
```

For improved parallelism, this kind of pre-aggregation is implemented differently, as a so-called *partial aggregation*. Here, we are presenting simplified plans, but in an actual EXPLAIN plan, this is represented differently than the final aggregation.

The kind of pre-aggregation shown in Example 4-5 is not always an improvement. It is detrimental to query performance when partial aggregation does not reduce the amount of data. For this reason, the optimization is currently disabled by default and can be enabled with the `push_partial_aggregation_through_join` session property or the `optimizer.push-partial-aggregation-through-join` configuration property. By default, Trino uses partial aggregations and places them above the join to reduce the amount of data transmitted over the network between Trino nodes. To fully appreciate the role of these partial aggregations, we would need to consider nonsimplified query plans.

Implementation Rules

The rules we have covered so far are *optimization rules*—rules with a goal to reduce query processing time, a query's memory footprint, or the amount of data exchanged over the network. However, even in the case of our example query, the initial plan contained an operation that is not implemented at all: the lateral join. In the next section, we look at how Trino handles these kinds of operations.

Lateral Join Decorrelation

The *lateral join* could be implemented as a for-each loop that traverses all rows from a data set and executes another query for each of them. Such an implementation is possible, but this is not how Trino handles the cases like our example. Instead, Trino *decorrelates* the subquery, pulling up all the correlated conditions and forming a regular left join. In SQL terms, this corresponds to transformation of a query:

```
SELECT
    (SELECT name FROM region r WHERE regionkey = n.regionkey)
        AS region_name,
    n.name AS nation_name
FROM nation n
```

into

```
SELECT
    r.name AS region_name,
    n.name AS nation_name
FROM nation n LEFT OUTER JOIN region r ON r.regionkey = n.regionkey
```

Even though we may use such constructs interchangeably, a cautious reader familiar with SQL semantics immediately realizes that they are not fully equivalent. The first query fails if duplicate entries in the `region` table have the same `regionkey`, whereas the second query does not fail. Instead, it produces more result rows. For this reason, lateral join decorrelation uses two additional components besides the join. First, it "numbers" all the source rows so that they can be distinguished. Second, after the join, it checks whether any row was duplicated, as shown in Example 4-6. If duplication is detected, the query processing is failed in order to preserve the original query semantics.

Example 4-6. Lateral join decompositions require additional checks

```
- TopN[5; orders_sum DESC]
  - MarkDistinct & Check
    - LeftJoin[n.regionkey = r.regionkey]
      - AssignUniqueId
        - Aggregate[by nationkey...; orders_sum := sum(totalprice)]
          - ...
      - TableScan[region]
```

Semi-Join (IN) Decorrelation

A subquery can be used within a query not only to pull information, as we just saw in the lateral join example, but also to filter rows by using the IN predicate. In fact, an IN predicate can be used in a filter (the WHERE clause), or in a projection (the SELECT clause). When you use IN in a projection, it becomes apparent that it is not a simple Boolean-valued operator like EXISTS. Instead, the IN predicate can evaluate to true, false, or null.

Let's consider a query designed to find orders for which the customer and item suppliers are from the same country, as shown in Example 4-7. Such orders may be interesting. For example, we may want to save shipping costs or reduce shipping environmental impact by shipping directly from the supplier to the customer, bypassing our own distribution centers.

Example 4-7. Semi-join (IN) example query

```
SELECT DISTINCT o.orderkey
FROM lineitem l
  JOIN orders o ON o.orderkey = l.orderkey
  JOIN customer c ON o.custkey = c.custkey
WHERE c.nationkey IN (
    -- subquery invoked multiple times
    SELECT s.nationkey
    FROM part p
      JOIN partsupp ps ON p.partkey = ps.partkey
      JOIN supplier s ON ps.suppkey = s.suppkey
    WHERE p.partkey = l.partkey
);
```

As with a lateral join, this could be implemented with a loop over rows from the outer query, where the subquery to retrieve all nations for all suppliers of an item gets invoked multiple times.

Instead of doing this, Trino decorrelates the subquery—the subquery is evaluated once, with the correlation condition removed, and then is joined back with the outer query by using the correlation condition. The tricky part is ensuring that the join does not multiply result rows (so a deduplicating aggregation is used) and that the transformation correctly retains the IN predicate's three-valued logic.

In this case, the deduplicating aggregation uses the same partitioning as the join, so it can be executed in a streaming fashion, without data exchange over the network and with minimal memory footprint.

Cost-Based Optimizer

In "Query Planning" on page 57, you learned how the Trino planner converts a query in textual form into an executable and optimized query plan. You learned about various optimization rules in "Optimization Rules" on page 61, and their importance for query performance at execution time. You also saw implementation rules in "Implementation Rules" on page 64, without which a query plan would not be executable at all.

We walked the path from the beginning, where query text is received from the user, to the end, where the final execution plan is ready. Along the way, we saw selected plan transformations, which are critical because they make the plan execute orders of magnitude faster, or make the plan executable at all.

Now let's take a closer look at plan transformations that make their decisions based not only on the shape of the query but also, and more importantly, on the shape of the data being queried. This is what the Trino state-of-the-art *cost-based optimizer* (*CBO*) does.

The Cost Concept

Earlier, we used an example query as our work model. Let's use a similar approach, again for convenience and to aid understanding. As you can see in Example 4-8, certain query clauses, which are not relevant for this section, are removed. This allows you to focus on the cost-based decisions of the query planner.

Example 4-8. Example query for cost-based optimization

```
SELECT
    n.name AS nation_name,
    avg(extendedprice) as avg_price
FROM nation n, orders o, customer c, lineitem l
```

```
WHERE n.nationkey = c.nationkey
  AND c.custkey = o.custkey
  AND o.orderkey = l.orderkey
GROUP BY n.nationkey, n.name
ORDER BY nation_name;
```

Without cost-based decisions, the query planner rules optimize the initial plan for this query to produce a plan, as shown in Example 4-9. This plan is determined solely by the lexical structure of the SQL query. The optimizer used only the syntactic information; hence it is sometimes called the *syntactic optimizer*. The name is meant to be humorous, highlighting the simplicity of the optimizations. Since the query plan is based only on the query, you can hand-tune or optimize the query by adjusting the syntactic order of the tables in the query.

Example 4-9. Query join order from the syntactic optimizer

```
- Aggregate[by nationkey...; orders_sum := sum(totalprice)]
  - InnerJoin[o.orderkey = l.orderkey]
  - InnerJoin[c.custkey = o.custkey]
    - InnerJoin[n.nationkey = c.nationkey]
      - TableScan[nation]
      - TableScan[customer]
    - TableScan[orders]
  - TableScan[lineitem]
```

Now let's say the query was written differently, changing only the order of the WHERE conditions:

```
SELECT
    n.name AS nation_name,
    avg(extendedprice) as avg_price
FROM nation n, orders o, customer c, lineitem l
WHERE c.custkey = o.custkey
  AND o.orderkey = l.orderkey
  AND n.nationkey = c.nationkey
GROUP BY n.nationkey, n.name;
```

The plan ends up with a different join order as a result:

```
- Aggregate[by nationkey...; orders_sum := sum(totalprice)]
  - InnerJoin[n.nationkey = c.nationkey]
  - InnerJoin[o.orderkey = l.orderkey]
    - InnerJoin[c.custkey = o.custkey]
      - TableScan[customer]
      - TableScan[orders]
    - TableScan[lineitem]
  - TableScan[nation]
```

The fact that a simple change of ordering conditions affects the query plan, and therefore the performance of the query, is cumbersome for the SQL analyst. Creating efficient queries then requires internal knowledge of the way Trino processes the queries. A query author should not be required to have this knowledge to get the best performance out of Trino. In addition, tools with Trino, such as Apache Superset, Tableau, Qlick, or Metabase, typically support many different databases and query engines and do not write optimized queries for Trino.

The cost-based optimizer ensures that the two variants of the query produce the same optimal query plan for processing by Trino's execution engine.

From a time-complexity perspective, it does not matter whether you join, for example, the `nation` table with `customer`—or, vice versa, the `customer` table with `nation`. Both tables need to be processed, and in the case of hash-join implementation, total running time is proportional to the number of output rows. However, time complexity is not the only thing that matters. This is generally true for programs working with data, but it is especially true for large database systems. Trino needs to be concerned about memory usage and network traffic as well. To reason about memory and network usage of the join, Trino needs to better understand how the join is implemented.

CPU time, memory requirements, and network bandwidth usage are the three dimensions that contribute to query execution time, both in single-query and concurrent workloads. These dimensions constitute the cost in Trino.

Cost of the Join

When joining two tables over the equality condition (=), Trino implements an extended version of the algorithm known as a *hash join* (*https://en.wikipedia.org/wiki/Hash_join*). One of the joined tables is called the *build* side. This table is used to build a lookup hash table with the join condition columns as the key. Another joined table is called the *probe* side. Once the lookup hash table is ready, rows from the probe side are processed, and the hash table is used to find matching build-side rows in constant time. By default, Trino uses three-level hashing in order to parallelize processing as much as possible:

1. Both joined tables are distributed across the worker nodes, based on the hash values of the join condition columns. Rows that should be matched have the same values on join condition columns, so they are assigned to the same node. This reduces the size of the problem by the number of nodes being used at this stage. This *node-level data assignment* is the first level of hashing.

2. At a node level, the build side is further scattered across build-side worker threads, again using a hash function. Building a hash table is a CPU-intensive process, and using multiple threads to do the job greatly improves throughput.

3. Each worker thread ultimately produces one partition of the final lookup hash table. Each partition is a hash table itself. The partitions are combined into a

two-level lookup hash table so that we avoid scattering the probe side across multiple threads as well. The probe side is still processed in multiple threads, but the threads get their work assigned in batches, which is faster than partitioning the data by using a hash function.

As you can see, the build side is kept in memory to facilitate fast, in-memory data processing. Of course, a memory footprint is also associated, proportional to the size of the build side. This means that the build side must fit into the memory available on the node. This also means that less memory is available to other operations and to other queries. This is the memory cost associated with the join. There is also the network cost. In the algorithm described previously, both joined tables are transferred over the network to facilitate node-level data assignment.

The cost-based optimizer can select which table should be the build table, controlling the memory cost of the join. Under certain conditions, the optimizer can also avoid sending one of the tables over the network, thus reducing network bandwidth usage (reducing the network cost). To do its job, the cost-based optimizer needs to know the size of the joined tables, which is provided as the table statistics.

Table Statistics

In "Connector-Based Architecture" on page 51, you learned about the role of connectors. Each table is provided by a connector. Besides table schema information and access to actual data, the connector can provide table and column statistics:

- Number of rows in a table
- Number of distinct values in a column
- Fraction of NULL values in a column
- Minimum and maximum values in a column
- Average data size for a column

Of course, if some information is missing—for example, the average text length in a varchar column is not known—a connector can still provide other information, and the cost-based optimizer uses what is available.

With an estimation of the number of rows in the joined tables and, optionally, average data size for columns, the cost-based optimizer already has sufficient knowledge to determine the optimal ordering of the tables in our example query. The CBO can start with the biggest table (lineitem) and subsequently join the other tables— orders, then customer, then nation:

```
- Aggregate[by nationkey...; orders_sum := sum(totalprice)]
  - InnerJoin[l.orderkey = o.orderkey]
    - InnerJoin[o.custkey = c.custkey]
```

```
    - InnerJoin[c.nationkey = n.nationkey]
      - TableScan[lineitem]
     - TableScan[orders]
    - TableScan[customer]
  - TableScan[nation]
```

Such a plan is good and should be considered because every join has the smaller relation as the build side, but it is not necessarily optimal. If you run the example query, using a connector that provides table statistics, you can enable the CBO with the session property:

```
SET SESSION join_reordering_strategy = 'AUTOMATIC';
```

With the table statistics available from the connector, Trino may come up with a different plan:

```
  - Aggregate[by nationkey...; orders_sum := sum(totalprice)]
    - InnerJoin[l.orderkey = o.orderkey]
      - TableScan[lineitem]
     - InnerJoin[o.custkey = c.custkey]
        - TableScan[orders]
       - InnerJoin[c.nationkey = n.nationkey]
          - TableScan[customer]
         - TableScan[nation]
```

This plan was chosen because it avoids sending the biggest table (`lineitem`) three times over the network. The table is scattered across the nodes only once.

The final plan depends on the actual sizes of joined tables and the number of nodes in a cluster, so if you're trying this out on your own, you may get a different plan than the one shown here.

Cautious readers notice that the join order is selected based only on the join conditions, the links between tables, and the data size of the tables, including number of rows and average data size for each column. Other statistics are critical for optimizing more involved query plans, which contain intermediate operations between table scans and the joins—for example, filters, aggregations, and non-inner joins.

Filter Statistics

As you just saw, knowing the sizes of the tables involved in a query is fundamental to properly reordering the joined tables in the query plan. However, knowing just the table sizes is not enough. Consider a modification of our example query, in which the user added another condition like `l.partkey = 638`, in order to drill down in their data set for information about orders for a particular item:

```
SELECT
    n.name AS nation_name,
    avg(extendedprice) as avg_price
FROM nation n, orders o, customer c, lineitem l
```

```
WHERE n.nationkey = c.nationkey
  AND c.custkey = o.custkey
  AND o.orderkey = l.orderkey
  AND l.partkey = 638
GROUP BY n.nationkey, n.name
ORDER BY nation_name;
```

Before the condition was added, lineitem was the biggest table, and the query was planned to optimize handling of that table. But now, the filtered lineitem is one of the smallest joined relations.

Looking at the query plan shows that the filtered lineitem table is now small enough. The CBO puts the table on the build side of the join, so that it serves as a filter for other tables:

```
- Aggregate[by nationkey...; orders_sum := sum(totalprice)]
  - InnerJoin[l.orderkey = o.orderkey]
    - InnerJoin[o.custkey = c.custkey]
      - TableScan[customer]
      - InnerJoin[c.nationkey = n.nationkey]
        - TableScan[orders]
        - Filter[partkey = 638]
          - TableScan[lineitem]
    - TableScan[nation]
```

To estimate the number of rows in the filtered lineitem table, the CBO again uses statistics provided by a connector: the number of distinct values in a column and fraction of NULL values in a column. For the partkey = 638 condition, no NULL value satisfies the condition, so the optimizer knows that the number of rows gets reduced by the fraction of NULL values in the partkey column. Further, if you assume roughly uniform distribution of values in the column, you can derive the final number of rows:

```
filtered rows = unfiltered rows * (1 - null fraction)
    / number of distinct values
```

Obviously, the formula is correct only when the distribution of values is uniform. However, the optimizer does not need to know the number of rows; it just needs to know the estimation of it, so in general being somewhat off is not a problem. Of course, if an item is bought much more frequently than others—say, Starburst candies—the estimation may be too far off, and the optimizer may choose a bad plan. Currently, when this happens, you have to disable the CBO.

In the future, connectors will be able to provide information about the data distribution to handle cases like this. For example, if a histogram were available for the data, then the CBO could more accurately estimate the filtered rows.

Table Statistics for Partitioned Tables

One special type of filtered table deserves special mention: partitioned tables. Data may be organized into *partitioned tables* in a Hive/HDFS warehouse accessed by the Hive connector or a modern lakehouse using the Iceberg or Delta Lake table formats and connectors; see "Hive Connector for Distributed Storage Data Sources" on page 102 and "Modern Distributed Storage Management and Analytics" on page 112. When the data is filtered by a condition on partitioning keys, only matching partitions are read during query executions. Furthermore, since the table statistics are stored on a per partition basis, the CBO gets statistics information only for partitions that are read, so it's more accurate.

Of course, every connector can provide this kind of improved stats for filtered relations. We are referring only to the way the Hive connector provides statistics here.

Join Enumeration

So far, we've discussed how the CBO leverages data statistics, in order to come up with an optimal plan for executing a query. In particular, it chooses an optimal join order, which affects the query performance substantially for two primary reasons:

Hash join implementation
> The hash join implementation is asymmetric. It is important to carefully choose which input is the build side and which input is the probe side.

Distributed join type
> It is important to carefully choose whether to broadcast or redistribute the data to the join inputs.

Broadcast Versus Distributed Joins

In the previous section, you learned about the hash join implementation and the importance of the build and probe sides. Because Trino is a distributed system, joins can be done in parallel across a cluster of workers, where each worker processes a fraction of the join. For a distributed join to occur, the data may need to be distributed across the network, and different strategies are available that vary in efficiency, depending on the data shape.

Broadcast join strategy

In a *broadcast join strategy*, the build side of the join is broadcast to all the worker nodes that are performing the join in parallel. In other words, each join gets a complete copy of the data for the build side, as displayed in Figure 4-12. This is semantically correct only if the probe side remains distributed across the workers without duplication. Otherwise, duplicate results are created.

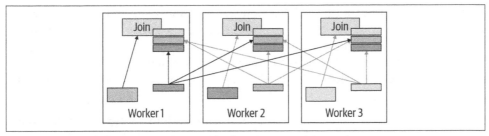

Figure 4-12. Broadcast join strategy visualization

The broadcast join strategy is advantageous when the build side is small, allowing for cost-effective transmission of data. The advantage is also greater when the probe side is very large because it avoids having to redistribute the data as is necessary in the distributed join.

Distributed join strategy

In a *distributed join strategy*, the input data to both the build side and the probe side is redistributed across the cluster such that the workers perform the join in parallel. The difference in data transmission over the network is that each worker receives a unique fraction of the data set, rather than a copy of the data as performed in the broadcast join. The data redistribution must use a partitioning algorithm such that the matching join key values are sent to the same node. For example, say we have the following data sets of join keys on a particular node:

```
Probe: {4, 5, 6, 7, 9, 10, 11, 14}
Build: {4, 6, 9, 10, 17}
```

Consider a simple partitioning algorithm:

```
if joinkey mod 3 == 0 then send to Worker 1
if joinkey mod 3 == 1 then send to Worker 2
if joinkey mod 3 == 2 then send to Worker 3
```

The partitioning results in these probes and builds on Worker 1:

```
Probe:{6, 9}
Build:{6, 9}
```

Worker 2 deals with different probes and builds:

```
Probe: {4, 7, 10}
Build: {4, 10}
```

And, finally, Worker 3 deals with a different subset:

```
Probe:{5, 11, 14}
Build: {17}
```

By partitioning the data, the CBO guarantees that the joins can be computed in parallel without having to share information during the processing. The advantage of a distributed join is that it allows Trino to compute a join whereby both sides are very large and there is not enough memory on a single machine to hold the entirety of the probe side in memory. The disadvantage is the extra data being sent over the network.

The decision between a broadcast join and distributed join strategy must be costed. Each strategy has trade-offs, and we must take into account the data statistics in order to cost the optimal one. Furthermore, this also needs to be decided during the join reordering process. Depending on the join order and where filters are applied, the data shape changes. This could lead to cases in which a distributed join between two data sets may work best in one join order scenario, but a broadcast join may work better in a different scenario. The join enumeration algorithm takes this into consideration.

 The join enumeration algorithm used by Trino is rather complex and beyond the scope of this book. It is documented in detail on a Starburst blog post (*https://www.starburst.io/blog/presto-join-enumeration/*). It breaks the problem into subproblems with smaller partitions, finds the correct join usage with recursions, and aggregates the results to a global result.

Working with Table Statistics

In order to leverage the CBO in Trino, your data must have statistics. Without data statistics, the CBO cannot do much; it requires data statistics to estimate rows and costs of the different plans.

Because Trino does not store data, producing statistics for Trino is connector-implementation dependent. As of the time of this writing, the Hive, Delta Lake, and Iceberg connectors for object storage systems, as well as a number of RDBMS connectors including PostgreSQL and others, provide data statistics to Trino. We expect that, over time, more connectors will support statistics, and you should continue to refer to the Trino documentation for up-to-date information.

Table statistics gathering and maintenance depend on the underlying data source. Let's look at the Hive connector as an example of ways to collect statistics:

- Use Trino's ANALYZE command to collect statistics.
- Enable Trino to gather statistics when writing data to a table.
- Use Hive's ANALYZE command to collect statistics.

It is important to note that Trino and the Hive connector stores statistics in the Hive metastore, the same place that Hive uses to store statistics. Other connectors use the metadata storage as used by the connected data source—for example, metadata files in the Iceberg table format or the information schema in some relational databases. So if you're sharing the same tables between Hive and Trino, they overwrite each other's statistics. This is something you should consider when determining how to manage statistics collection.

Trino ANALYZE

Trino provides an ANALYZE command to collect statistics for a connector (for example, the Hive connector). When run, Trino computes column-level statistics by using its execution engine and stores the statistics in the Hive metastore. The syntax is as follows:

```
ANALYZE table_name [ WITH ( property_name = expression [, ...] ) ]
```

For example, if you want to collect and store statistics from the flights table, you can run this:

```
ANALYZE datalake.ontime.flights;
```

In the partitioned case, we can use the WITH clause if we want to analyze only a particular partition:

```
ANALYZE datalake.ontime.flights WITH (partitions = ARRAY[ARRAY['01-01-2019']])
```

The nested array is needed when you have more than one partition key and you'd like each key to be an element in the next array. The topmost array is used if you have multiple partitions you want to analyze. The ability to specify a partition is very useful in Trino. For example, you may have some type of ETL process that creates new partitions. As new data comes in, statistics could become stale, as they do not incorporate the new data. However, by updating statistics for the new partition, you don't have to reanalyze all the previous data.

Gathering Statistics When Writing to Disk

If you have tables for which the data is always written through Trino, statistics can be collected during write operations. For example, if you run a CREATE TABLE AS, or an INSERT SELECT query, Trino collects the statistics as it is writing the data to disk (HDFS or S3, for example) and then stores the statistics in the Hive metastore.

This is a useful feature, as it does not require you to run the manual step of ANALYZE. The statistics are never stale. However, for this to work properly and as expected, the data in the table must always be written by Trino.

The overhead of this process has been extensively benchmarked and tested, and it shows negligible impact to performance. To enable the feature, you can add the following property into your catalog properties file by using the Hive connector:

```
hive.collect-column-statistics-on-write=true
```

Hive ANALYZE

Outside of Trino, you can still use the Hive `ANALYZE` command to collect the statistics for Trino. The computation of the statistics is performed by the Hive execution engine and not the Trino execution engine, so the results may vary, and there is always the risk of Trino behaving differently when using statistics generated by Hive versus Trino. It's generally recommended to use Trino to collect statistics. But there may be reasons for using Hive, such as if the data lands as part of a more complex pipeline and is shared with other tools that may want to use the statistics. To collect statistics by using Hive, you can run the following commands:

```
hive> ANALYZE TABLE datalake.ontime.flights COMPUTE STATISTICS;
hive> ANALYZE TABLE datalake.ontime.flights COMPUTE STATISTICS FOR COLUMNS;
```

For complete information on the Hive `ANALYZE` command, you can refer to the official Hive documentation (*https://cwiki.apache.org/confluence/display/Hive/StatsDev*).

Displaying Table Statistics

Once you have collected the statistics, it is often useful to view them. You may want to do this to confirm that statistics have been collected, or perhaps you are debugging a performance issue and want to see the statistics being used.

Trino provides a `SHOW STATS` command:

```
SHOW STATS FOR datalake.ontime.flights;
```

Alternatively, if you want to see the statistics on a subset of data, you can provide a filtering condition. For example:

```
SHOW STATS FOR (SELECT * FROM datalake.ontime.flights WHERE year > 2010);
```

Conclusion

Now you understand the Trino architecture, with a coordinator receiving user requests and then using workers to assemble all the data from the data sources.

Each query is translated into a distributed query plan of tasks in numerous stages. The data is returned by the connectors in splits and processed in multiple stages until the final result is available and provided to the user by the coordinator.

If you are interested in the Trino architecture in even more detail, you can dive into the paper "Trino: SQL on Everything" by the Trino creators, published at the IEEE International Conference on Data Engineering (ICDE) and available on the Trino website (*https://trino.io*).

Next, you are going to learn more about deploying a Trino cluster in Chapter 5, hooking up more data sources with different connectors in Chapters 6 and 7, and writing powerful queries in Chapter 8.

Production-Ready Deployment

Following the installation of Trino from the *tar.gz* archive in Chapter 2, and your new understanding of the Trino architecture from Chapter 4, you are now ready to learn more about the details of installing a Trino cluster. You can then take that knowledge and work toward a production-ready deployment of a Trino cluster with a coordinator and multiple worker nodes.

Configuration Details

The Trino configuration is managed in multiple files discussed in the following sections. These files are all in the *etc* directory located within the installation directory by default.

The default location of this folder, as well as of each individual configuration file, can be overridden with parameters passed to the launcher script, discussed in "Launcher" on page 83.

Server Configuration

The file *etc/config.properties* provides the configuration for the Trino server. A Trino server can function as a coordinator, or a worker, or both at the same time. A cluster must be set up with only one coordinator. Dedicating a single server to perform only coordinator work, and adding a number of other servers as dedicated workers, provides the best performance and creates a Trino *cluster*.

The contents of the file are critical, specifically since they determine the role of the server as a worker or coordinator, which in turn affects resource usage and configuration.

All worker configurations in a Trino cluster should be identical.

The following are the basic allowed Trino server configuration properties. In later chapters, as we discuss features such as authentication, authorization, and resource groups, we cover additional optional properties.

`coordinator=true|false`
: Allows this Trino instance to function as a coordinator and therefore accept queries from clients and manage query execution. Defaults to `true`. Setting the value to `false` dedicates the server as a worker.

`node-scheduler.include-coordinator=true|false`
: Allows scheduling work on the coordinator. Defaults to `true`. For larger clusters, we suggest setting this property to `false`. Processing work on the coordinator can impact query performance because the server resources are not available for the critical task of scheduling, managing, and monitoring query execution.

`http-server.http.port=8080` *and* `http-server.https.port=8443`
: Specifies the ports used for the server for the HTTP/HTTPS connection. Trino uses HTTP for all internal and external communication.

`discovery.uri=http://localhost:8080`
: The URI to the discovery server, equivalent to the coordinator, including the correct port. This URI can be local to the network of the coordinator and cluster nodes, and it must not end in a slash.

Logging

The optional Trino logging configuration file, *etc/log.properties*, allows setting the minimum log level for named logger hierarchies. Every logger has a name, which is typically the fully qualified name of the Java class that uses the logger. Loggers use the Java class hierarchy. The packages used for all components of Trino can be seen in the source code, discussed in "Source Code, License, and Version" on page 14.

For example, consider the following log levels file:

```
io.trino=INFO
io.trino.plugin.postgresql=DEBUG
```

The first line sets the minimum level to `INFO` for all classes inside `io.trino`, including nested packages such as `io.trino.spi.connector` and `io.trino.plugin.hive`. The default level is `INFO`, so the preceding example does not actually change logging for any packages in the first line. Having the default level in the file just makes the configuration more explicit. However, the second line overrides the logging configuration for the PostgreSQL connector to debug-level logging.

Four levels, DEBUG, INFO, WARN, and ERROR, are sorted by decreasing verbosity. Throughout the book, we may refer to setting logging when discussing topics such as troubleshooting in Trino.

 When setting the logging levels, keep in mind that DEBUG levels can be verbose. Set DEBUG on only specific lower-level packages that you are actually troubleshooting to avoid creating large numbers of log messages, negatively impacting system performance.

After starting Trino, you find the various log files in the *var/log* directory within the installation directory, unless you specified another location in the *etc/node.properties* file:

launcher.log
    This log, created by the launcher (see "Launcher" on page 83), is connected to standard out (stdout) and standard error (stderr) streams of the server. It contains a few log messages from the server initialization and any errors or diagnostics produced by the JVM.

server.log
    This is the main log file used by Trino. It typically contains the relevant information if the server fails during initialization, as well as most information concerning the actual running of the application, connections to data sources, and more.

http-request.log
    This is the HTTP request log, which contains every HTTP request received by the server. These include all usage of the Web UI, Trino CLI, as well as the JDBC or ODBC connection discussed in Chapter 3, since all of them operate using HTTP connections. It also includes authentication and authorization logging.

All log files are automatically rotated and can also be configured in more detail in terms of size and compression.

Node Configuration

The node properties file, *etc/node.properties*, contains configuration specific to a single installed instance of Trino on a server—a node in the overall Trino cluster.

The following is a small example file:

```
node.environment=production
node.id=ffffffff-ffff-ffff-ffff-ffffffffffff
node.data-dir=/var/trino/data
```

The following parameters are the allowed Trino configuration properties:

`node.environment=demo`
> The *required* name of the environment. All Trino nodes in a cluster must have the same environment name. The name shows up in the Trino Web UI header.

`node.id=some-random-unique-string`
> An optional unique identifier for this installation of Trino. This must be unique for every node. This identifier should remain consistent across reboots or upgrades of Trino, and therefore be specified. If omitted, a random identifier is created with each restart.

`node.data-dir=/var/trino/data`
> The optional filesystem path of the directory, where Trino stores log files and other data. Defaults to the *var* folder inside the installation directory.

JVM Configuration

The JVM configuration file, *etc/jvm.config*, contains a list of command-line options used for starting the JVM running Trino.

The format of the file is a list of options, one per line. These options are not interpreted by the shell, so options containing spaces or other special characters should not be quoted.

The following provides a good starting point for creating *etc/jvm.config*:

```
-server
-Xmx4G
-XX:InitialRAMPercentage=80
-XX:MaxRAMPercentage=80
-XX:G1HeapRegionSize=32M
-XX:+ExplicitGCInvokesConcurrent
-XX:+ExitOnOutOfMemoryError
-XX:+HeapDumpOnOutOfMemoryError
-XX:-OmitStackTraceInFastThrow
-XX:ReservedCodeCacheSize=512M
-XX:PerMethodRecompilationCutoff=10000
-XX:PerBytecodeRecompilationCutoff=10000
-Djdk.attach.allowAttachSelf=true
-Djdk.nio.maxCachedBufferSize=2000000
-XX:+UnlockDiagnosticVMOptions
-XX:+UseAESCTRIntrinsics
```

Because an `OutOfMemoryError` typically leaves the JVM in an inconsistent state, we write a heap dump for debugging and forcibly terminate the process when this occurs.

The `-Xmx` option is an important property in this file. It sets the maximum heap space for the JVM. This determines how much memory is available for the Trino process.

The configuration to allow the JDK/JVM to attach to itself is required for Trino usage.

More information about memory and other JVM settings is discussed in Chapter 12.

Launcher

As mentioned in Chapter 2, Trino includes scripts to start and manage Trino in the *bin* directory. These scripts require Python.

The `run` command can be used to start Trino as a foreground process.

In a production environment, you typically start Trino as a background daemon process:

```
$ bin/launcher start
Started as 48322
```

The number 48322 you see in this example is the assigned process ID (PID). It differs at each start.

You can `stop` a running Trino server, which causes it to shut down gracefully:

```
$ bin/launcher stop
Stopped 48322
```

When a Trino server process is locked or experiences other problems, it can be useful to forcefully stop it with the `kill` command:

```
$ bin/launcher kill
Killed 48322
```

You can obtain the status and PID of Trino with the `status` command:

```
$ bin/launcher status
Running as 48322
```

If Trino is not running, the `status` command returns that information:

```
$ bin/launcher status
Not running
```

Besides the commands noted previously, the launcher script supports numerous options that can be used to customize the configuration file locations and other parameters. The `--help` option can be used to display the full details:

```
$ bin/launcher --help
Usage: launcher [options] command

Commands: run, start, stop, restart, kill, status

Options:
  -h, --help                 show this help message and exit
  -v, --verbose              Run verbosely
  --etc-dir=DIR              Defaults to INSTALL_PATH/etc
  --launcher-config=FILE     Defaults to INSTALL_PATH/bin/launcher.properties
  --node-config=FILE         Defaults to ETC_DIR/node.properties
  --jvm-config=FILE          Defaults to ETC_DIR/jvm.config
  --config=FILE              Defaults to ETC_DIR/config.properties
  --log-levels-file=FILE     Defaults to ETC_DIR/log.properties
  --data-dir=DIR             Defaults to INSTALL_PATH
  --pid-file=FILE            Defaults to DATA_DIR/var/run/launcher.pid
  --launcher-log-file=FILE Defaults to DATA_DIR/var/log/launcher.log (only in
                             daemon mode)
  --server-log-file=FILE     Defaults to DATA_DIR/var/log/server.log (only in
                             daemon mode)
  -J OPT                     Set a JVM option
  -D NAME=VALUE              Set a Java system property
```

Other installation methods use these options to modify paths. For example, the RPM package, discussed in "RPM Installation" on page 86, adjusts the path to better comply with Linux filesystem hierarchy standards and conventions. You can use them for similar needs, such as complying with enterprise-specific standards, using specific mount points for storage, or simply using paths outside the Trino installation directory to ease upgrades.

Cluster Installation

In Chapter 2, we discussed installing Trino on a single machine, and in Chapter 4, you learned more about how Trino is designed and intended to be used in a distributed environment.

For any real use, other than for demo purposes, you need to install Trino on a cluster of machines. Fortunately, the installation and configuration are similar to those operations on a single machine. It requires a Trino installation on each machine, either by installing manually or by using a deployment automation system like Ansible.

So far, you've deployed a single Trino server process to act as both a coordinator and a worker. For the cluster installation, you need to install and configure one coordinator and multiple workers. Simply copy the downloaded *tar.gz* archive to all machines in the cluster and extract it.

As before, you have to add the *etc* folder with the relevant configuration files. A set of example configuration files for the coordinator and the workers is available in the *cluster-installation* directory of the support repository of the book; see "Book Repository" on page 15. The configuration files need to exist on every machine you want to be part of the cluster.

The configurations are the same as the simple installation for the coordinator and workers, with some important differences:

- The `coordinator` property in *config.properties* is set to `true` on the coordinator and set to `false` on the workers.

- The `node-scheduler` is set to exclude the coordinator.

- The `discovery.uri` property has to point to the IP address or hostname of the coordinator on all workers and the coordinator itself.

The main configuration file, *etc/config.properties*, is suitable for the coordinator:

```
coordinator=true
node-scheduler.include-coordinator=false
http-server.http.port=8080
discovery.uri=http://<coordinator-ip-or-host-name>:8080
```

Note the difference of the configuration file, *etc/config.properties*, suitable for the workers:

```
coordinator=false
http-server.http.port=8080
discovery.uri=http://<coordinator-ip-or-host-name>:8080
```

With Trino installed and configured on a set of nodes, you can use the launcher to start Trino on every node. Generally, it is best to start the Trino coordinator first, followed by the Trino workers:

```
$ bin/launcher start
```

As before, you can use the Trino CLI to connect to the Trino server. In the case of a distributed setup, you need to specify the address of the Trino coordinator by using the `--server` option. If you are running the Trino CLI on the Trino coordinator node directly, you do not need to specify this option, as it defaults to `localhost:8080`:

```
$ trino --server <coordinator-ip-or-host-name>:8080
```

You can now verify that the Trino cluster is running correctly. The `nodes` system table contains the list of all the active nodes that are currently part of the cluster. You can query it with an SQL query:

```
trino> SELECT * FROM system.runtime.nodes;
 node_id |        http_uri        | node_version | coordinator | state
---------+------------------------+--------------+-------------+-------------------
 c00367d | http://<http_uri>:8080 | 392          | true        | active
 9408e07 | http://<http_uri>:8080 | 392          | false       | active
 90dfc04 | http://<http_uri>:8080 | 392          | false       | active
(3 rows)
```

The list includes the coordinator and all connected workers in the cluster. The coordinator and each worker expose status and version information by using the REST API at the endpoint */v1/info*; for example, *http://worker-or-coordinator-hostname/v1/info*.

You can also confirm the number of active workers by using the Trino Web UI.

RPM Installation

Trino can be installed using the RPM Package Manager (RPM) on various Linux distributions such as CentOS, Red Hat Enterprise Linux, and others.

The RPM package is available on the Maven Central Repository at *https://repo.maven.apache.org/maven2/io/trino/trino-server-rpm*. Locate the RPM in the folder with the desired version and download it.

You can download the archive with wget; for example, for version 392:

```
$ wget https://repo.maven.apache.org/maven2/ \
io/trino/trino-server-rpm/392/trino-server-rpm-392.rpm
```

With administrative access, you can install Trino with the archive in single-node mode:

```
$ sudo rpm -i trino-server-rpm-*.rpm --nodeps
```

Using the --no-deps option causes rpm to install the package even if declared dependencies are not installed or available. This is typically necessary since the packaged versions of Python and Java are often not suitable. You can initially try an installation without the option, but for most distributions you need to use the flag and separately install the required Python and Java versions.

The rpm installation creates the basic Trino configuration files and a service control script to control the server. The script is configured so that the service is started automatically on the operating system boot. After installing Trino from the RPM, you can manage the Trino server with the service command:

```
service trino [start|stop|restart|status]
```

Installation Directory Structure

When using the RPM-based installation method, Trino is installed in a directory structure more consistent with the Linux filesystem hierarchy standards. This means that not everything is contained within the single Trino installation directory structure as we have seen so far. The service is configured to pass the correct paths to Trino with the launcher script:

/usr/lib/trino/
> The directory contains the various libraries needed to run the product. Plug-ins are located in a nested *plugin* directory.

/etc/trino
> This directory contains the general configuration files such as *node.properties*, *jvm.config*, and *config.properties*. Catalog configurations are located in a nested *catalog* directory.

/etc/trino/env.sh
> This file sets the Java installation path used.

/var/log/trino
> This directory contains the log files.

/var/lib/trino/data
> This is the data directory.

/etc/rc.d/init.d/trino
> This directory contains the service scripts for controlling the server process.

The *node.properties* file is automatically configured to set the following two additional properties, since our directory structure is different from the defaults used by Trino:

```
catalog.config-dir=/etc/trino/catalog
plugin.dir=/usr/lib/trino/plugin
```

Configuration

The RPM package installs Trino acting as coordinator and worker out of the box, identical to the *tar.gz* archive. To create a working cluster, you can update the configuration files on the nodes in the cluster manually, or use a generic configuration management and provisioning tool such as Ansible.

Uninstall Trino

If Trino is installed using RPM, you can uninstall it the same way you remove any other RPM package:

```
$ rpm -e trino
```

When removing Trino, all files and configurations, apart from the logs directory */var/log/trino*, are deleted. Create a backup copy if you wish to keep anything.

Installation in the Cloud

A typical installation of Trino involves running at least one cluster with a coordinator and multiple workers. Over time, the number of workers in the cluster, as well as the number of clusters, can change based on the demand from users.

The number and type of connected data sources, as well as their location, also has a major impact on choosing where to install and run your Trino cluster. Typically, it is desirable that the Trino cluster has a high-bandwidth, low-latency network connectivity to the data sources.

The simple requirements of Trino, discussed in Chapter 2, allow you to run Trino in many situations. You can run it on different machines such as physical servers or virtual machines, as well as Docker containers.

Trino is known to work on private cloud deployments as well as on many public cloud providers including Amazon Web Services (AWS), Google Cloud, Microsoft Azure, and others.

Using containers allows you to run Trino on Kubernetes (K8s) clusters such as Amazon Elastic Kubernetes Service (Amazon EKS), Microsoft Azure Kubernetes Service (AKS), Google Kubernetes Engine (GKE), Red Hat Open Shift, and any other Kubernetes deployments.

An advantage of these cloud deployments is the potential for a highly dynamic cluster, where workers are created and destroyed on demand. Tooling for such use cases has been created by different users, including cloud vendors embedding Trino in their offerings and other vendors offering Trino tooling and support.

Organizations typically create their own packages, configuration management setups, container images, K8s operators, or whatever is necessary, and they use tools such as Concord (*https:// concord.walmartlabs.com*) or Terraform (*https://www.terraform.io*) to create and manage the clusters. Alternatively, you can consider relying on the support and offerings from a company like Starburst.

Helm Chart for Kubernetes Deployment

Kubernetes is an increasingly popular, and for some use cases even the default, method to deploy any software with container images in cloud environments. Helm is the widely adopted package manager for Kubernetes. The Trino project provides a simple Helm chart (*https://github.com/trinodb/charts*) suitable for managing your clusters.

After installing the necessary client tools, including `helm` and `kubectl`, the following high-level steps are necessary to start a Trino cluster on Kubernetes. Specific details vary based on the chosen Kubernetes version and platform.

- Create a Kubernetes cluster in your preferred Kubernetes platform from a cloud provider. Keep in mind that the typical requirements for Trino include higher CPU and memory amounts than a typical stateless application often deployed on Kubernetes.

- Configure `kubectl` to point at the new cluster.

- Add the Trino Helm chart repository to your configuration:

```
helm repo add trino https://trinodb.github.io/charts/
```

- Create a custom YAML file *myvalues.yaml* with the configuration for your cluster. This includes specific configuration for memory, `config.properties`, catalog properties files, number of workers, and any other configuration supported by the Helm chart. You can start by copying the template supplied with the charts and modifying values as desired.

- Install the chart into the cluster with your custom configuration:

```
helm upgrade --install \
  --values myvalues.yaml \
  mycluster \
  trino/trino \
  --version 0.8.0
```

- Expose the coordinator and the default port 8080 outside the Kubernetes cluster by configuring a port-forwarding or using methods such as `loadBalancer` or `ingress`.

At this stage, the cluster is up and running, and you can connect and query with the Trino CLI or any other client tool. You can also access the Trino Web UI at the coordinator URL.

The following simple YAML file configures usage of Trino 392, a cluster with five workers, and an additional abyss catalog with the black hole connector, as used in the archive installation:

```
image:
  tag: "392"
server:
  workers: 5
additionalCatalogs:
  abyss: |-
    connector.name=blackhole
```

Any following changes to the cluster are performed by updating the YAML configuration file, and running the `helm upgrade` command again.

You can see that Kubernetes and the Helm chart provide a very versatile and efficient method to install and manage Trino clusters. The Kubernetes platform manages all the underlying infrastructure aspects like hardware, networking, and many others for you, allowing you to concentrate on configuring catalogs for data source connections and writing SQL queries.

Cluster Sizing Considerations

An important part of getting Trino deployed is sizing the cluster. In the longer run, you might even work toward multiple clusters for different use cases. Sizing the Trino cluster is a complex task and follows the same patterns and steps as other applications:

1. Decide on an initial size, based on rough estimates and available infrastructure.

2. Ensure that the tooling and infrastructure for the cluster are able to scale the cluster.

3. Start the cluster and ramp up usage.

4. Monitor utilization and performance.

5. React to the findings by changing cluster scale and configuration.

Understanding the architecture of Trino is critical for initial sizing. Specifically, you need to know that Trino is not a typical horizontally scaled application that relies on many small stateless server nodes in a cluster. The Trino coordinator and the workers are stateful parts of the overall query processing architecture. Large amounts of data are transferred from the data sources to the workers, between the workers, and to the coordinator. All of this transfer and the related data processing happen in parallel on all the workers, and also in many threads within the JVM on each node.

As a result of these demands, the initial recommended size of a typical node is much larger than in a stateless architecture. It is common for a node to have 16 vCPUs and

64 GiB memory or more. Typically, it is also better to have a smaller number of larger nodes, as compared to many smaller nodes. A static production deployment should start with at least four workers and a dedicated coordinator.

The feedback loop around monitoring, adapting, and continued use allows you to get a good understanding of the behavior of your Trino deployment.

Many factors influence your cluster performance, and the combination of these is specific to each Trino deployment:

- Resources like CPU and memory for each node
- Network performance within the cluster and to data sources and storage
- Number and characteristics of connected data sources
- Queries run against the data sources and their scope, complexity, number, and resulting data volume
- Storage read/write performance of the data sources
- Active users and their usage patterns

Once you have your initial cluster deployed, make sure you take advantage of using the Trino Web UI for monitoring. Chapter 12 provides more tips.

Conclusion

As you've now learned, Trino installation and running a cluster requires just a handful of configuration files and properties. Depending on your actual infrastructure and management system, you can achieve a powerful setup of one or even multiple Trino clusters. Check out real-world examples in Chapter 13.

Of course, you are still missing a major ingredient of configuring Trino. And that is the connections to the external data sources that your users can then query with Trino and SQL. In Chapters 6 and 7, you get to learn all about the various data sources, the connectors to access them, and the configuration of the catalogs that point at specific data sources using the connectors.

Connectors

In Chapter 3, you configured a catalog to use a connector to access a data source in Trino—specifically, the TPC-H benchmark data—and then learned a bit about how to query that data with SQL.

Catalogs are an important aspect of using Trino. They define the connection to the underlying data source and storage system, and they use concepts such as connector, schema, and table. These fundamental concepts are described in Chapter 4, and their use with SQL is discussed in more detail in Chapter 8.

A *connector* translates the query and storage concepts of an underlying data source, such as a RDBMS, object storage, or a key-value store, to the SQL and Trino concepts of tables, columns, rows, and data types. These can be simple SQL-to-SQL translations and mappings, but can also be much more complicated translations from SQL to object storage or NoSQL systems. These can also be user defined.

You can think of a connector the same way you think of a driver for a database. It translates the user input into operations that the underlying database can execute. Every connector implements the connector-related aspects of the Trino SPI. This enables Trino to allow you to use the same SQL tooling to work with whatever underlying data source the connector exposes and makes Trino a SQL-on-Anything system.

Query performance is also influenced by the connector implementation. The most basic connector makes a single connection to the data source and provides the data to Trino. However, a more advanced connector can break a statement into multiple connections, performing operations in parallel to allow for better performance. Another advanced feature of a connector is to provide table statistics, which can then be used by the cost-based optimizer to create highly performant query plans. Such a connector is, however, more complex to implement.

Trino provides numerous connectors:

- Connectors for RDBMS systems such as PostgreSQL or MySQL—see "RDBMS Connector Example: PostgreSQL" on page 95

- A Hive connector suitable for querying systems by using the HDFS and similar object storage systems—see "Hive Connector for Distributed Storage Data Sources" on page 102

- Connectors for the modern object storage systems and table formats used for lakehouse systems—see "Modern Distributed Storage Management and Analytics" on page 112

- Numerous connectors to non-relational data sources—see "Non-Relational Data Sources" on page 114

- `tpch` and `tpcds` connectors designed to serve TPC benchmark data—see "Trino TPC-H and TPC-DS Connectors" on page 100

- A connector for Java Management Extensions, or JMX—see "Trino JMX Connector" on page 115

In this chapter, you learn more about some of these connectors, available from the Trino project. More than two dozen connectors are shipped in Trino today, and more are created by the Trino team and the user community. Commercial, proprietary connectors are also available to extend the reach and performance of Trino. Finally, if you have a custom data source, or one with no suitable connector available, you can implement your own connector by implementing the necessary SPI calls and drop it into the `plugin` directory in Trino.

One important aspect of the catalog and connector usage is that they all become available to SQL statements and queries in Trino at the same time. This means you can create queries that span data sources. For example, you can combine data from a relational database with the data in files stored in your object storage backend. These *federated queries* are discussed in more detail in "Query Federation in Trino" on page 133.

Configuration

As discussed in "Adding a Data Source" on page 23, every data source you want to access needs to be configured as a catalog by creating a catalog properties file. The name of the file determines the name of the catalog when writing queries.

The mandatory property `connector.name` indicates which connector is used for the catalog. The same connector can be used multiple times in different catalogs—for example, to access different RDBMS server instances with different databases all using the same technology such as PostgreSQL. Or if you have two Hive clusters, you can configure two catalogs in a single Trino cluster that both use the Hive connector, allowing you to query data from both Hive clusters.

RDBMS Connector Example: PostgreSQL

Trino contains connectors to both open source and proprietary RDBMSs, including MySQL, PostgreSQL, Oracle, Amazon Redshift, Microsoft SQL Server, and others. Trino queries these data sources with the connectors by using each system's respective JDBC drivers.

Let's look at a simple example using PostgreSQL. A PostgreSQL instance may consist of several databases. Each database contains schemas, which contain objects such as tables and views. When configuring Trino with PostgreSQL, you choose the database that is exposed as a catalog in Trino.

After creating a simple catalog file pointing at a specific database in the server, *etc/catalog/postgresql.properties* shown next, and restarting Trino, you can find out more information. You also can see that the postgresql connector is configured with the required connector.name:

```
connector.name=postgresql
connection-url=jdbc:postgresql://db.example.com:5432/database
connection-user=root
connection-password=secret
```

 The user and password in the catalog properties file determines the access rights to the underlying data source. This can be used to, for example, restrict access to read-only operations or to restrict available tables.

You can list all catalogs to confirm that the new catalog is available and inspect details with the Trino CLI, or a database management tool using the JDBC driver (as explained in "Trino Command-Line Interface" on page 27 and "Trino JDBC Driver" on page 32):

```
SHOW CATALOGS;
  Catalog
-----------
 system
 postgresql
(2 rows)

SHOW SCHEMAS IN postgresql;
  Catalog
-----------
 public
 airline
```

```
(2 rows)

USE postgresql.airline
SHOW TABLES;
  Table
---------
  airport
  carrier
(2 rows)
```

In this example, you see we connected to a PostgreSQL database that contains two schemas: public and airline. And then within the airline schema are two tables, airport and carrier. Let's try running a query. In this example, we issue an SQL query to Trino, where the table exists in a PostgreSQL database. Using the PostgreSQL connector, Trino is able to retrieve the data for processing, returning the results to the user:

```
SELECT code, name FROM airport WHERE code = 'ORD';
  code |                name
 ------+-------------------------------
  ORD  | Chicago OHare International
(1 row)
```

As displayed in Figure 6-1, the client submits the query to the Trino coordinator. It offloads the work to a worker, which sends the entire SQL query statement to PostgreSQL using JDBC. The PostgreSQL JDBC driver is contained within the PostgreSQL connector. PostgreSQL processes the query and returns the results over JDBC. The connector reads the results and writes them to the Trino internal data format. Trino continues the processing on the worker, provides it to the coordinator, and then returns the results to the user.

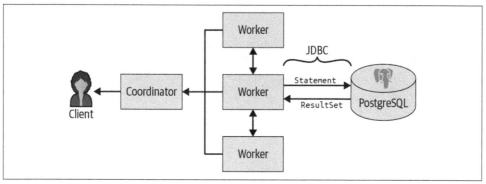

Figure 6-1. Trino cluster interaction with PostgreSQL using JDBC in the connector

Query Pushdown

As we saw in the previous example, Trino is able to offload processing by pushing the SQL statement down into the underlying data source. This is known as *query pushdown*, or *SQL pushdown*. This is advantageous, as the underlying system can reduce the amount of data returned to Trino, avoiding unnecessary memory, CPU, and network costs. Furthermore, systems like PostgreSQL typically have indexes on certain filter columns, allowing for faster processing. However, it is not always possible to push the entire SQL statement down into the data source. Currently, the Trino Connector SPI limits the types of operations that can be pushed down to filter and column projections:

```
SELECT state, count(*)
FROM airport
WHERE country = 'US'
GROUP BY state;
```

Given the preceding Trino query, the PostgreSQL connector constructs the SQL query to push down to PostgreSQL:

```
SELECT state
FROM airport
WHERE country = 'US';
```

There are two important places to look when queries are pushed by a RDBMS connector. The columns in the SELECT list are specifically set to what is needed by Trino. In this case, we need only the state column for processing the GROUP BY in Trino. We also push the filter country = 'US', which means we do not need to perform further processing of the country column in Trino. You notice that the aggregations are not pushed down to PostgreSQL. This is because Trino is not able to push any other form of queries down, and the aggregations must be performed in Trino. This can be advantageous because Trino is a distributed query processing engine, whereas PostgreSQL is not.

If you do want to push additional processing down to the underlying RDBMS source, you can accomplish this by using views. If you encapsulate the processing in a view in PostgreSQL, it is exposed as a table to Trino, and the processing occurs within PostgreSQL. For example, let's say you create the view in PostgreSQL:

```
CREATE view airline.airports_per_us_state AS
SELECT state, count(*) AS count_star
FROM airline.airport
WHERE country = 'US'
GROUP BY state;
```

When you run SHOW TABLES in Trino, you see this view:

```
SHOW TABLES IN postgresql.airline;
  Table
- - - - - - - - -
 airport
 carrier
 airports_per_us_state
(3 rows)
```

Now you can just query the view, and all processing is pushed down to PostgreSQL, since the view appears as an ordinary table to Trino:

```
SELECT * FROM airports_per_us_state;
```

Parallelism and Concurrency

Currently, all RDBMS connectors use JDBC to make a single connection to the underlying data source. The data is not read in parallel, even if the underlying data source is a parallel system. For parallel systems, like Teradata or Vertica, you have to write parallel connectors that can take advantage of how those systems store the data in a distributed fashion.

When accessing multiple tables from the same RDBMS, a JDBC connection is created and used for each table in the query. For example, if the query is performing a join between two tables in PostgreSQL, Trino creates two different connections over JDBC to retrieve the data, as displayed in Figure 6-2. They run in parallel, send their results back, and then the join is performed in Trino. The PostgreSQL connector does support join pushdown, so depending on the specifics of the join and the data type of the column used in the join, the join operation can be pushed down to be processed by the database itself.

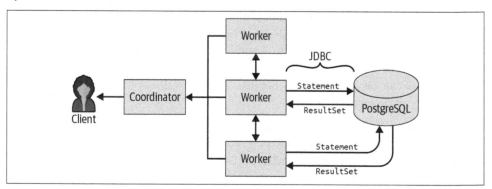

Figure 6-2. Multiple JDBC connections used to access different tables in PostgreSQL

If you want to force the usage of the query processing in the underlying PostgreSQL system, you can create a view in PostgreSQL and even add native indices for further improvements.

Other RDBMS Connectors

The Trino open source project includes other RDBMS connectors such as MySQL, MariaDB, Oracle, PostgreSQL, Amazon Redshift, and Microsoft SQL Server. These connectors are already included in the plugin directory of Trino and are ready to be configured. If you have multiple servers or want to separate access, you can configure multiple catalogs in Trino for each instance. You just need to name the *.properties* file differently. As usual, the name of the properties file determines the name of the catalog:

```
SHOW CATALOGS;
  Catalog
-----------
 system
 mysql-dev
 mysql-prod
 mysql-site
(2 rows)
```

Nuances exist among different RDBMSs. Let's take a look at how some are configured in their catalog configuration files.

In MySQL, there is no difference between a database and a schema, and the catalog file and the JDBC connection string basically point at the specific MySQL server instance:

```
connector.name=mysql
connection-url=jdbc:mysql://example.net:3306
connection-user=root
connection-password=secret
```

PostgreSQL makes a clear distinction, and a server instance can contain multiple databases that contain schemas. The JDBC connection points at a specific database:

```
connector.name=postgresql
connection-url=jdbc:postgresql://example.net:5432/database
connection-user=root
connection-password=secret
```

The Amazon Redshift catalog looks similar to PostgreSQL's. In fact, Redshift used the PostgreSQL JDBC driver in the past, since it is based on the open source PostgreSQL code:

```
connector.name=redshift
connection-url=jdbc:redshift://example.net:5439/database
connection-user=root
connection-password=secret
```

Microsoft SQL Server connection strings look similar to the MySQL string. However, SQL Server does have the notion of databases and schemas, and the example simply connects to the default database:

```
connector.name=sqlserver
connection-url=jdbc:sqlserver://example.net:1433
connection-user=root
connection-password=secret
```

Using a different database like `sales` has to be configured with a property:

```
connection-url=jdbc:sqlserver://example.net:1433;databaseName=sales
```

Security

The easiest way to authenticate to RDBMS connectors is by storing the username and password in the catalog configuration file. Since the machines in the Trino cluster are designed to be a trusted system, this should be sufficient for most uses. In order to keep Trino and the connected data sources secure, it's important to secure access to the machines and configuration files. It should be treated the same way as a private key. All users of Trino use the same connection to the RDBMS.

If you do not want to store a password in clear text, there are ways to pass through the username and password from the Trino client. You can also use username and password values that are injected into an environment variable by the provisioning system, and Trino can then pick up these secrets. We discuss this further in Chapter 10.

In conclusion, using Trino with RDBMSs is easy and allows you to expose all the systems in one place and query them all at the same time. This use case alone is already providing a significant benefit for Trino users. Of course, it gets much more interesting when you add more data sources with other connectors. So let's continue to learn more.

Query Pass-Through

Another powerful feature available in some RDBMS connectors is the query pass-through table function. It takes advantage of the support for polymorphic table functions in Trino. These functions are SQL statements that return a table as result. In the case of query pass-through, these table functions are query statements that Trino itself ignores and passes through the connector to the underlying data source. It parses and processes this query statement and returns a table as result. Trino can then return this table or use it for further processing in a Trino SQL query.

In practice, this means that you can embed native query language code (for example, an Oracle-specific SQL snippet) that returns a table within a Trino SQL statement. This allows you to access features of the underlying data source for legacy migration usage. It can also unlock further performance or query methods, such as support for other query languages.

Trino TPC-H and TPC-DS Connectors

You have already discovered the TPC-H connector usage in Chapter 2. Let's have a closer look.

The TPC-H and the TPC-DS connectors are built into Trino and provide a set of schemas to support the TPC Benchmark H (TPC-H) and the TPC Benchmark DS (TPC-DS). These database benchmark suites from the Transaction Processing Performance Council (*http://tpc.org*) are industry standard benchmarks for database systems, used to measure the performance of highly complex decision support databases.

The connectors can be used to test Trino's capabilities and query syntax without configuring access to an external data source. When you query a TPC-H or TPC-DS schema, the connector generates data on the fly by using a deterministic algorithm.

Create a catalog properties file (for example, named *etc/catalog/tpch.properties*) to use the TPC-H connector:

```
connector.name=tpch
```

Configuration is similar for the TPC-DS connector—for example, with *etc/catalog /tpcdsdata.properties*:

```
connector.name=tpcds
```

Both connectors expose schemas that include the same data sets in terms of structure:

```
SHOW SCHEMAS FROM tpch;
        Schema
-------------------
 information_schema
 sf1
 sf100
 sf1000
 sf10000
 sf100000
 sf300
 sf3000
 sf30000
 tiny
(10 rows)
```

Table 6-1 shows how the different schemas contain increasingly larger numbers of records in transactional tables such as orders.

Table 6-1. Example record counts for the orders table in different tpch schemas

Schema	Count
tiny	15000
sf1	1500000
sf3	4500000
sf100	150000000

You can use these data sets for learning more about SQL supported by Trino, as discussed in Chapters 8 and 9, without the need to connect another database (for example, also using the Docker container).

Another important use case of these connectors is the simple availability of the data. You can use the connectors for development and testing, or even on a production Trino deployment. With the huge data amounts easily available, you can build queries that put a significant load on your Trino cluster.

If you want to test your object storage or RDBMS performance with the TPC data sets, you can run CREATE TABLE AS SELECT queries that copy the data from the connectors into another catalog. Then you can use the same TPC test queries against the data in your specific infrastructure.

This allows you to better understand the performance of your cluster, tune and optimize it, and ensure that it performs over time and across version updates and other changes.

Hive Connector for Distributed Storage Data Sources

As you learned in "A Brief History of Trino" on page 17, Trino is designed to run fast queries at Facebook scale. Given that Facebook had massive storage in its Hive data warehouse, it is only natural that the Hive connector is one of the first connectors that was developed with Trino.

Apache Hadoop and Hive

Before you read about the Hive connector and its suitability for numerous object storage formats, you need to brush up a bit on your knowledge of Apache Hadoop (*https://hadoop.apache.org*) and Apache Hive (*https://hive.apache.org*).

If you're not that familiar with Hadoop and Hive and want to learn more, we recommend the official websites of the projects, videos and other resources on the web, and some of the great books available. For example, *Programming Hive* (*https:// oreil.ly/liekE*) by Edward Capriolo et al. (O'Reilly) has been a great guide for us.

For now, we need to discuss certain Hadoop and Hive concepts to provide enough context for the Trino usage.

At its very core, Hadoop consists of the Hadoop Distributed File System (HDFS) and application software, such a Hadoop MapReduce, to interact with the data stored in HDFS. Apache YARN is used to manage the resources needed by Hadoop applications. *Hadoop* is the leading system for distributed processing of large data sets across clusters of computers. It is capable of scaling the system while maintaining a highly available service on top of a cluster of computers.

Originally, data processing was performed by writing MapReduce programs. They followed a specific programming model that enables the data processing to be naturally distributed across the cluster. This model works well and is robust. However, writing MapReduce programs for analytical questions is cumbersome. It also does not transfer well for existing infrastructure, tooling, and users that rely on SQL and data warehousing.

Hive provides an alternative to using MapReduce. It was created as a method to provide an SQL layer of abstraction on top of Hadoop, to interact with data in HDFS by using an SQL-like syntax. Now the large set of users who know and understand SQL can interact with data stored in HDFS.

Hive data is stored as files, often referred to as *objects*, in HDFS. These files use various formats, such as ORC, Parquet, and others. The files are stored using a particular directory and file layout that Hive understands (for example, partitioned and bucketed tables). We refer to the layout as a *Hive-style table format*.

Hive metadata describes how data stored in HDFS maps to schemas, tables, and columns to be queried via the Hive query language, and indirectly with Trino and SQL. This metadata information is persisted in a database such as MySQL or PostgreSQL and is accessible via the *Hive Metastore Service* (*HMS*).

The Hive runtime provides the SQL-like Hive query language and distributed execution layer to execute the queries. The Hive runtime translates the query into a set of MapReduce programs that can run on a Hadoop cluster. Over time, Hive has evolved to provide other execution engines such as Apache Tez and Spark that the query is translated to.

Hadoop and Hive are widely used across the industry. With their use, the HDFS format has become a supported format for many other distributed storage systems such as Amazon S3 and S3-compatible stores, Azure Data Lake Storage, Azure Blob Storage, Google Cloud Storage, and many others.

Hive Connector

The *Hive connector* for Trino allows you to connect to an HDFS object storage cluster. It leverages the metadata in HMS and queries and processes the data stored in HDFS.

Probably the most common use case of Trino is to leverage the Hive connector to read data from distributed storage such as HDFS or cloud storage.

 Trino and the Trino Hive connector do not use the Hive runtime at all. Trino is a high-performance replacement for it and is suitable for running interactive queries. It works directly with the files, rather than using the Hive runtime and execution engine.

The Hive connector allows Trino to read and write from distributed storage such as HDFS. However, it is not constrained to HDFS but designed to work with distributed storage in general. Currently, you can configure the Hive connector to work with HDFS, S3, Azure Blob Storage, Azure Data Lake Storage, Google Cloud Storage, and S3-compatible storage. S3-compatible storage may include MinIO, Ceph, IBM Cloud Object Storage, SwiftStack, Cloudian, Riak CS, LeoFS, OpenIO, and others. As long as they implement the S3 API and behave the same way, for the most part, Trino does not need to know the difference.

Because of the widespread use of Hadoop and other compatible systems using HDFS and the expanded feature set of the Hive connector to support them, it can be considered the main connector for querying object storage with Trino and is therefore critical for many, if not most, Trino users.

Architecturally, the Hive connector is a bit different from RDBMS and other connectors since it does not use the Hive engine itself at all. It therefore cannot push SQL processing to Hive. Instead, it simply uses the metadata in HMS and accesses the data directly on HDFS, using the HDFS client provided with the Hadoop project. It also assumes the Hive table format in the way the data is organized in the distributed storage.

In all cases, the schema information is accessed from HMS, and the data layout is the same as with a Hive data warehouse. The concepts are the same, but the data is simply stored in a location other than HDFS. However, unlike Hadoop, these non-Hadoop distributed filesystems do not always have an HMS equivalent to store the metadata for use by Trino. To leverage the Hive-style table format, you must configure Trino to use HMS from an existing Hadoop cluster or to your own standalone HMS. This can mean that you use a replacement for HMS such as AWS Glue or run a minimal Hadoop deployment with HMS only.

Using HMS to describe data in blob storage other than HDFS allows the Hive connector to be used to query these storage systems. This unlocks the data stored in these systems to all the power of SQL usage via Trino and any tool capable of using SQL.

Configuring a catalog to use the Hive connector requires you to create a catalog properties file with the desired name—for example, *etc/catalog/s3.properties*, *etc/catalog/gcs.properties*, *etc/catalog/minio.properties*, or even just *etc/catalog/hdfs.properties* or *etc/catalog/objectstorage.properties*. In the following, we assume the use of *etc/catalog/datalake.properties*. At a minimum, you need to configure the connector name and the URL for HMS:

```
connector.name=hive
hive.metastore.uri=thrift://example.net:9083
```

Numerous other configuration properties apply for different use cases, some of which you learn more about soon. When in doubt, always check out the documentation; see "Documentation" on page 14. Let's get into some of those details next.

Hive-Style Table Format

Once the connector is configured, you can create a schema from Trino—for example, in HDFS:

```
CREATE SCHEMA datalake.web
WITH (location = 'hdfs://starburst-oreilly/web')
```

The schema, sometimes still called a *database*, can contain multiple tables. You can read more about them in the next section. The schema creation typically creates only the metadata about the schema in the HMS:

```
...
hdfs://starburst-oreilly/web/customers
hdfs://starburst-oreilly/web/clicks
hdfs://starburst-oreilly/web/sessions
...
```

Using Amazon S3 is not much different. You just use a different protocol string:

```
CREATE SCHEMA datalake.web
WITH (location = 's3://example-org/web')

...
s3://example-org/web/customers
s3://example-org/web/clicks
s3://example-org/web/sessions
...
```

If you notice a similarity to paths in a directory structure, you are not mistaken. Database, schema, and table can be inspected just like nested directories in the user interface of the object storage, even though the underlying setup may or may not use directories.

Managed and External Tables

After the schema, we need to learn more about the content in the schema, organized as tables. Hive distinguishes between managed tables and external tables. A *managed table* is managed by Hive, and therefore also by Trino potentially, and is created along with its data under the location of the database's directory. An *external table* is not managed by Hive and explicitly points to another location outside the directory that Hive manages.

The main difference between a managed table and an external table is that Hive, and therefore Trino, owns the data in the managed table. If you drop a managed table, the metadata in the HMS and the data are deleted. If you drop an external table, the data remains, and only the metadata about the table is deleted.

The types of tables you use really comes down to the way you plan to use Trino. You may be using Trino for data federation, your data warehouse or data lake, both, or some other mix. You need to decide who owns the data. It could be Trino working with the HMS, or it could be Hadoop and HMS, or Spark, or other tools in an ETL pipeline. In all cases, the metadata is managed in HMS.

The decision about which system owns and manages HMS and the data is typically based on your data architecture. In the early use cases of Trino, Hadoop often controlled the data life cycle. But as more use cases leverage Trino as the central tool, many users shift their pattern, and Trino takes over control.

Some new Trino users start by querying an existing Hadoop deployment. In this case, it starts as more of a data federation use, and Hadoop owns the data. You then configure the Hive connector to expose the existing tables in Hadoop to Trino for querying. You use external tables. Typically, you do not allow Trino to write to these tables in this case.

Other Trino users may start to migrate away from Hadoop and completely toward Trino, or they may start new with another object storage system, specifically, often a cloud-based system. In this case, it is best to start creating the data definition language (DDL) via Trino to let Trino own the data.

Let's consider the following DDL for a Trino table:

```
CREATE TABLE datalake.web.page_views (
  view_time timestamp,
  user_id bigint,
  page_url varchar,
  view_date date,
  country varchar
)
```

In this example, the table page_views stores data under a directory also named page_views. This page_views directory is either a subdirectory under the directory defined by hive.metastore.warehouse.dir or is a different directory if you defined the schema location when creating the schema.

Here is an HDFS example:

```
hdfs://user/hive/warehouse/web/page_views/...
```

And here's an Amazon S3 example:

```
s3://example-org/web/page_views/...
```

Next, let's consider DDL for a Trino table that points to existing data. This data is created and managed by another means, such as by Spark or an ETL process where the data lands in storage. In this case, you may create an external table via Trino pointing to the external location of this data:

```
CREATE TABLE datalake.web.page_views (
  view_time timestamp,
  user_id bigint,
  page_url varchar,
  view_date date,
  country varchar
)
WITH (
  external_location = 's3://starburst-external/page_views'
)
```

This inserts the metadata about the table into the HMS, including the external path and a flag that signals to Trino and HMS that the table is external and therefore managed by another system.

As a result, the data, located in *s3://example-org/page_views*, may already exist. Once the table is created in Trino, you can start querying it. When you configure the Hive connector to an existing Hive warehouse, you see the existing tables and are able to query from them immediately.

Alternatively, you could create the table in an empty directory and expect the data to be loaded later, either by Trino or by an external source. In either case, Trino expects that the directory structure is already created; otherwise, the DDL errors. The most common case for creating an external table is when data is shared with other tools.

Partitioned Data

So far, you have learned how the data for a table, whether managed or external, is stored as one or more files in a directory. *Data partitioning* is an extension of this and is a technique used to horizontally divide a logical table into smaller pieces of data known as *partitions.*

The concept itself derives from partitioning schemes in RDBMSs. Hive introduced this technique for data in HDFS as a way to achieve better query performance and data manageability.

Partitioning is now a standard data organization strategy in distributed filesystems, such as HDFS, and in object storage, such as S3.

Let's use this table example to demonstrate partitioning:

```
CREATE TABLE datalake.web.page_views (
  view_time timestamp,
  user_id bigint,
  page_url varchar,
  view_date date
)
```

```
WITH (
  partitioned_by = ARRAY['view_date']
)
```

 The columns listed in the `partitioned_by` clause must be the last columns as defined in the DDL. Otherwise, you get an error from Trino.

As with nonpartitioned tables, the data for the `page_views` table is located within *…/page_views*. Using partitioning changes the way the table layout is structured. With partitioned tables, additional subdirectories are added within the table subdirectory. In the following example, you see the directory structure as defined by the partition keys:

```
...
.../page_views/view_date=2019-01-14/...
.../page_views/view_date=2019-01-15/...
.../page_views/view_date=2019-01-16/...
...
```

Trino uses this same Hive-style table format. Additionally, you can choose to partition on multiple columns:

```
CREATE TABLE datalake.web.page_views (
  view_time timestamp,
  user_id bigint,
  page_url varchar,
  view_date date,
  country varchar
)
WITH (
  partitioned_by = ARRAY['view_date', 'country']
)
```

When choosing multiple partitioned columns, Trino creates a hierarchical directory structure:

```
...
.../page_views/view_date=2019-01-15/country=US…
.../page_views/view_date=2019-01-15/country=PL…
.../page_views/view_date=2019-01-15/country=UA...
.../page_views/view_date=2019-01-16/country=US…
.../page_views/view_date=2019-01-17/country=AR...
...
```

Partitioning gives you improved query performance, especially as your data grows in size. For example, let's take the following query:

```
SELECT DISTINCT user_id
FROM page_views
WHERE view_date = DATE '2019-01-15' AND country = 'US';
```

When this query is submitted, Trino recognizes the partition columns in the `WHERE` clause and uses the associated value to read only the *view_date=2019-01-15/country=US* subdirectory. By reading only the partition you need, potentially large performance savings can result. If your data is small today, the performance gain might not be noticeable. But as your data grows, the improved performance is significant.

Loading Data

So far, you've learned about the Hive-style table format, including partitioned data. How do you get the data into the tables? It really depends on who owns the data. Let's start under the assumption that you are creating the tables in Trino and loading the data with Trino:

```
CREATE TABLE datalake.web.page_views (
  view_time timestamp,
  user_id bigint,
  page_url varchar,
  view_date date,
  country varchar
)
WITH (
  partitioned_by = ARRAY['view_date', 'country']
)
```

To load data via Trino, Trino supports `INSERT INTO ... VALUES`, `INSERT INTO ... SELECT`, and `CREATE TABLE AS SELECT`. Although `INSERT INTO` exists, it has limited use, since it creates a single file and single row for each statement. It is often good to use as you learn Trino.

`INSERT SELECT` and `CREATE TABLE AS` perform the same function. Which one you use is a matter of whether you want to load into an existing table or create the table as you're loading. Let's take, for example, `INSERT SELECT`, where you may be querying data from a nonpartitioned external table and loading into a partitioned table in Trino:

```
trino:web> INSERT INTO page_views_ext SELECT * FROM page_views;
INSERT: 16 rows
```

The preceding example inserts new data into an external table. By default, Trino disallows writing to an external table. To enable it, you need to set `hive.non-managed-table-writes-enabled` to `true` in your catalog configuration file.

If you're familiar with Hive, Trino does what is known as *dynamic partitioning*: the partitioned directory structure is created the first time Trino detects a partition column value that doesn't have a directory.

You can also create an external partitioned table in Trino. Say we have this directory structure with data in S3:

```
...
s3://example-org/page_views/view_date=2019-01-14/...
s3://example-org/page_views/view_date=2019-01-15/...
s3://example-org/page_views/view_date=2019-01-16/...
...
```

We create the external table definition:

```
CREATE TABLE datalake.web.page_views (
  view_time timestamp,
  user_id bigint,
  page_url varchar,
  view_date date
)
WITH (
  partitioned_by = ARRAY['view_date']
)
```

Now let's query from it:

```
trino:web> SELECT * FROM page_views;
 view_time | user_id | page_url | view_date
-----------+---------+----------+-----------
(0 rows)
```

What happened? Even though we know there is data in it, the HMS does not recognize the partitions. If you're familiar with Hive, you know about the MSCK REPAIR TABLE command to autodiscover all the partitions. Fortunately, Trino has its own command as well to autodiscover and add the partitions:

```
CALL system.sync_partition_metadata(
  'web',
  'page_views',
  'FULL'
)
...
```

Now that you have added the partitions, let's try again:

```
trino:web> SELECT * FROM page_views;
        view_time        | user_id | page_url | view_date
-------------------------+---------+----------+------------
 2019-01-25 02:39:09.987 |     123 | ...      | 2019-01-14
 ...
 2019-01-25 02:39:11.807 |     123 | ...      | 2019-01-15
 ...
```

Alternatively, Trino provides the ability to create partitions manually. This is often cumbersome because you have to use the command to define each partition separately:

```
CALL system.create_empty_partition(
  'web',
  'page_views',
  ARRAY['view_date'],
  ARRAY['2019-01-14']
)
...
```

Adding empty partitions is useful when you want to create the partitions outside Trino via an ETL process, and then want to expose the new data to Trino.

Trino also supports dropping partitions simply by specifying the partition column value in the WHERE clause of a DELETE statement. And in this example, the data stays intact because it is an external table:

```
DELETE FROM datalake.web.page_views
WHERE view_date = DATE '2019-01-14'
```

It is important to emphasize that you do not have to manage your tables and data with Trino, but you can if desired. Many users leverage Hive, or other tools, to create and manipulate data, and use Trino only to query the data.

File Formats and Compression

Trino supports many of the common file formats used in Hadoop/HDFS, including:

- ORC
- PARQUET
- AVRO
- JSON
- TEXTFILE
- RCTEXT
- RCBINARY
- CSV
- SEQUENCEFILE

The three most common file formats used by Trino are ORC, Parquet, and Avro data files. The readers for ORC, Parquet, RC Text, and RC Binary formats are heavily optimized in Trino for performance.

The metadata in HMS contains the file format information so that Trino knows what reader to use when reading the data files. When creating a table in Trino, the default file format is set to ORC. However, the default can be overridden in the CREATE TABLE statement as part of the WITH properties:

```
CREATE TABLE datalake.web.page_views (
  view_time timestamp,
  user_id bigint,
  page_url varchar,
  ds_date,
  country varchar
)
WITH (
  format = 'PARQUET'
)
```

The default storage format for all table creation in the catalog can be set with the hive.storage-format configuration in the catalog properties file.

By default, Trino uses the GZIP compression codec for writing files. You can change the codec to use SNAPPY or NONE by setting the hive.compression-codec configuration in the catalog properties file.

MinIO Example

MinIO (*https://min.io*) is an S3-compatible, lightweight distributed storage system you can use with Trino and the Hive connector. You can install it on your local workstation and experiment with it and Trino locally. If you want to explore its use in more detail, check out the example project from Brian Olsen (*https://github.com/bit sondatadev/trino-getting-started/tree/main/hive/trino-minio*).

Modern Distributed Storage Management and Analytics

As discussed in "Hive Connector for Distributed Storage Data Sources" on page 102, a core use case of Trino enables fast analytics and other SQL-based workloads on data lakes. These systems are based on Hadoop object storage systems and other compatible solutions for the data with a Hive Metastore Service for the metadata. The Hive connector interacts with both systems. Data lakes have proven to be an excellent solution for storing large amounts of structured and semi-structured data since the original creation.

However, time and innovation have not stood still. The large adoption of data lakes quickly also exposed many problems. ACID compatibility was missed by everyone accustomed to relational databases. Schema evolution was discovered to be critical for many use cases, and also very hard or impossible to implement with large data volumes. From the many troubled users, a few initiatives emerged and resulted in newer solutions that solve these and a number of other problems:

- Delta Lake, developed by Databricks, emerged from the Apache Spark ecosystem.
- Apache Hudi was originally developed at Uber.
- Apache Iceberg was started at Netflix.

All three systems implement new mechanisms to improve data lakes and make them suitable for analytics and other more demanding use cases beyond simple data storage. A deployment of these new table formats and systems is typically called a *data lakehouse*. It combines the successful traits of data warehouses and data lakes.

Iceberg leads these table formats with numerous powerful features, including the following:

- Support for ACID transactions
- Schema evolution without large operational burden
- Snapshots, time travel support, and transaction rollbacks
- Efficient data storage with file formats such as ORC, Parquet, and Avro
- Access and data management improvements with advanced partitioning, bucketing, compacting, cleaning, and indexing
- Built-in and highly efficient metadata management
- Support for change data capturing, stream ingestion, and audit history

Iceberg also includes a full open specification of the table format, which in fact has already evolved to version 2. Delta Lake also offers many of these features, while Hudi is architecturally more limited.

All of these features address problems with Hadoop/Hive that were often impossible to overcome. In other cases, they were operationally so difficult or expensive in terms of time, performance, or storage that users decided to drop the related use cases and sought alternatives or accepted the large drawbacks.

The Iceberg connector was created first and is developed in close collaboration with the Iceberg community. It is included in every Trino release. It is very feature-rich and supports many advanced features such as time travel and materialized views.

The Delta Lake connector was created as part of the commercial Trino distribution Starburst Enterprise and donated to the Trino community by Starburst in 2022. Databricks and Starburst continue to improve the connector with the community. The connector is available with every Trino release and supports full read-and-write operations and numerous advanced features.

The Hudi connector is currently in active development with the creators of Hudi. It is likely that the initial implementation is completed, and the connector is available with every Trino release by the time you read this book.

The configuration and usage of the connectors is similar to the Hive connector. All you need is an object storage filesystem like S3, a metastore, and a catalog properties file to configure the details. Following is a simple example for a catalog using the Iceberg connector:

```
connector.name=iceberg
hive.metastore.uri=thrift://metastore.example.com:9083
```

With these alternatives available, any new data lake creation should be avoided and replaced with a lakehouse. Trino supports all three formats. Migration from an existing lake with Hive connector access is also possible and worth considering.

Non-Relational Data Sources

Trino includes connectors to query variants of non-relational data sources. These data sources are often referred to as *NoSQL systems* and can be key-value stores, column stores, stream processing systems, document stores, and other systems.

Some of these data sources provide SQL-like query languages such as CQL for Apache Cassandra (*https://cassandra.apache.org*). Others provide only specific tools or APIs to access the data, or include entirely different query languages such as the Query Domain Specific Language used in Elasticsearch. The completeness of these languages is often limited and not standardized.

Trino connectors for these NoSQL data sources allow you to run SQL queries for these systems as if they were relational. This allows you to use applications such as business intelligence tools or allows those who know SQL to query these data sources. This includes use of joins, aggregations, subqueries, and other advanced SQL capabilities against these data sources.

In the next chapter, you learn more about some of these connectors:

- NoSQL systems such as Elasticsearch or MongoDB—"Document Store Connector Example: Elasticsearch" on page 130
- Streaming systems such as Apache Kafka—"Streaming System Connector Example: Kafka" on page 128
- Key-value store systems such as Apache Accumulo—"Key-Value Store Connector Example: Accumulo" on page 120 and Apache Cassandra—"Apache Cassandra Connector" on page 127

- Apache HBase with Apache Phoenix connector—"Connecting to HBase with Phoenix" on page 119

Let's skip over these for now and first talk about some simpler connectors and related aspects.

Trino JMX Connector

The JMX connector can easily be configured for use in a catalog properties file such as *etc/catalog/monitor.properties*:

```
connector.name=jmx
```

The JMX connector exposes runtime information about the JVMs running the Trino coordinator and workers. It uses Java Management Extensions (JMX) and allows you to use SQL in Trino to access the available information. It is especially useful for monitoring and troubleshooting.

The connector exposes a history schema for historic, aggregate data, a current schema with up-to-date information, and the information_schema schema for metadata.

The easiest way to learn more is to use SQL statements in Trino to investigate the available tables:

```
SHOW TABLES FROM monitor.current;
                  Table
------------------------------------------------------------------
 com.sun.management:type=diagnosticcommand
 com.sun.management:type=hotspotdiagnostic
 io.airlift.discovery.client:name=announcer
 io.airlift.discovery.client:name=serviceinventory
 io.airlift.discovery.store:name=dynamic,type=distributedstore
 io.airlift.discovery.store:name=dynamic,type=httpremotestore
 ....
```

As you can see, the table names use the Java classpath for the metrics emitting classes and parameters. This means you need to use quotes when referring to the table names in SQL statements. Typically, it is useful to find out about the available columns in a table:

```
DESCRIBE monitor.current."java.lang:type=runtime";
        Column          | Type    | Extra | Comment
------------------------+---------+-------+---------
 bootclasspath          | varchar |       |
 bootclasspathsupported | boolean |       |
 classpath              | varchar |       |
 inputarguments         | varchar |       |
 librarypath            | varchar |       |
 managementspecversion  | varchar |       |
```

```
...
vmname                  | varchar |        |
vmvendor                | varchar |        |
vmversion               | varchar |        |
node                    | varchar |        |
object_name             | varchar |        |
(20 rows)
```

This allows you to get information nicely formatted:

```
SELECT vmname, uptime, node FROM  monitor.current."java.lang:type=runtime";
         vmname            | uptime  |      node
--------------------------+---------+--------------
 OpenJDK 64-Bit Server VM | 1579140 | ffffffff-ffff
(1 row)
```

Notice that only one node is returned in this query since this is a simple installation of a single coordinator/worker node, as described in Chapter 2.

The JMX connector exposes information about the JVM as well as Trino-specific aspects. You can start exploring by looking at the tables starting with `trino` —for example, with DESCRIBE monitor.current."trino.execution:name=query execution";.

Here are a few other describe statements worth checking out:

```
DESCRIBE monitor.current."trino.execution:name=querymanager";
DESCRIBE monitor.current."trino.memory:name=clustermemorymanager";
DESCRIBE monitor.current."trino.failuredetector:name=heartbeatfailuredetector";
```

To learn more about monitoring Trino by using the Web UI and other related aspects, you can head over to Chapter 12.

Black Hole Connector

The *black hole connector* can easily be configured for use in a catalog properties file such as *etc/catalog/abyss.properties*:

```
connector.name=blackhole
```

It acts as a sink for any data, similar to the null device in Unix operating systems, */dev/null*. This allows you to use it as a target for any insert queries reading from other catalogs. Since it does not actually write anything, you can use this to measure read performance from those catalogs.

For example, you can create a test schema in `abyss` and create a table from the `tpch.tiny` data set. Then you read a data set from the `tpch.sf3` data and insert it into the `abyss` catalog:

```
CREATE SCHEMA abyss.test;
CREATE TABLE abyss.test.orders AS SELECT * from tpch.tiny.orders;
INSERT INTO abyss.test.orders SELECT * FROM tpch.sf3.orders;
```

This operation essentially measures read performance from the tpch catalog, since it reads 4.5 million order records and then sends them to abyss. Using other schemas like tcph.sf100 increases the data-set size. This allows you to assess the performance of your Trino deployment.

A similar query with a RDBMS, object storage, or a key-value store catalog can be helpful for query development and performance testing and improvements.

Memory Connector

The *memory connector* can be configured for use in a catalog properties file—for example, *etc/catalog/brain.properties*:

```
connector.name=memory
```

You can use the memory connector like a temporary database. All data is stored in memory in the cluster. Stopping the cluster destroys the data. Of course, you can also actively use SQL statements to remove data in a table or even drop the table altogether.

Using the memory connector is useful for testing queries or temporary storage. For example, we use it as a simple replacement for the need to have an external data source configured when using the iris data set; see "Iris Data Set" on page 15.

 While useful for testing and small tasks, the memory connector is *not* suitable for large data sets and production usage, especially when distributed across a cluster. For example, the data might be distributed across different worker nodes, and a crash of a worker results in loss of that data. Use the memory connector only for temporary data.

Other Connectors

As you now know, the Trino project includes many connectors, yet sometimes you end up in a situation where you need just one more connector for that one specific data source.

The good news is that you are not stuck. The Trino team, and the larger Trino community, are constantly expanding the list of available connectors, so by the time you read this book, the list is probably longer than it is now.

Connectors are also available from parties outside the Trino project itself. This includes other community members and users of Trino who wrote their own connectors and have not yet contributed them back, or who cannot contribute for one reason or another.

Connectors are also available from commercial vendors of database systems, so asking the owner or creator of the system you want to query is a good idea. And the Trino community includes commercial vendors, such as Starburst, which bundle Trino with support and extensions, including additional or improved connectors.

Last, but not least, you have to keep in mind that Trino is a welcoming community around the open source project. So you can, and are encouraged to, look at the code of the existing connectors and create new connectors as desired. Ideally, you can even work with the project and contribute a connector back to the project to enable simple maintenance and usage going forward. This will expose you to the help from other users and contributors in the community, and expose your connector to other use cases and probably improve the quality of the connector overall.

Conclusion

Now you know a lot more about the power of Trino to access a large variety of data sources. No matter what data source you access, Trino makes the data available to you for querying with SQL and SQL-powered tools. In particular, you learned about the crucial Hive connector, used to query distributed storage such as HDFS or cloud storage systems. In the next chapter, Chapter 7, you can learn more details about a few other connectors in wide use.

Detailed documentation for all the connectors is available on the Trino website (*https://trino.io*). And if you do not find what you are looking for, you can even work with the community to create your own connector or enhance existing connectors.

Advanced Connector Examples

Now you know what functionality connectors provide to Trino and how to configure them from Chapter 6. Let's expand that knowledge to some of the more complex usage scenarios and connectors. These are typically connectors that need to be smart enough to translate storage patterns and ideas from the underlying data source, which do not easily map to the table-oriented model from SQL and Trino.

Learn more by jumping right to the section about the system you want to connect to with Trino and query with SQL:

Then you can round out your understanding by learning about query federation and the related ETL usage in "Query Federation in Trino" on page 133.

Connecting to HBase with Phoenix

The distributed, scalable, big data store Apache HBase (*http://hbase.apache.org*) builds on top of HDFS. Users are, however, not restricted to using low-level HDFS and accessing it with the Hive connector. The Apache Phoenix project (*https://phoenix.apache.org*) provides a SQL layer to access HBase, and thanks to the Trino Phoenix connector, you can therefore access HBase databases from Trino just like any other data source.

As usual, you simply need a catalog file like *etc/catalog/bigtables.properties*:

```
connector.name=phoenix5
phoenix.connection-url=jdbc:phoenix:zookeeper1,zookeeper2:2181:/hbase
```

The connection URL is a JDBC connection string to the database. It includes a list of the Apache ZooKeeper nodes, used for the discovery of the HBase nodes.

Phoenix schemas and tables are mapped to Trino schemas and tables, and you can inspect them with the usual Trino statements:

```
SHOW SCHEMAS FROM bigtable;
SHOW TABLES FROM bigtable.example;
SHOW COLUMNS FROM bigtable.examples.user;
```

Now you are ready to query any HBase tables and use them in the downstream tooling, just like the data from any other data source connected to Trino.

Using Trino allows you to query HBase with the performance benefits of a horizontally scaled Trino. Any queries you create have access to HBase and any other catalog, allowing you to combine HBase data with other sources into federated queries.

Key-Value Store Connector Example: Accumulo

Trino includes connectors for several key-value data stores. A *key-value store* is a system for managing a dictionary of records stored and retrieved by using a unique key. Imagine a hash table for which a record is retrieved by a key. This record may be a single value, multiple values, or even a collection.

Several key-value store systems exist that have a range of functionality. One widely used system is the open source, wide column store database Apache Cassandra (*https://cassandra.apache.org*), for which a Trino connector is available. You can find more information in "Apache Cassandra Connector" on page 127.

Another example we will now discuss in more detail is Apache Accumulo (*https://accumulo.apache.org*). It is a highly performant, widely used, open source key-value store that can be queried with a Trino connector. The general concepts translate to other key-value stores. We use the Accumulo connector as an example to show what a connector needs to achieve to map the context of a different system to the concepts of Trino.

Inspired by Google's BigTable, Apache Accumulo is a sorted, distributed key-value store for scalable stores and retrieval. Accumulo stores key-value data on HDFS sorted by the key.

Figure 7-1 shows how a key in Accumulo consists of a triplet of row ID, column, and timestamp. The key is sorted first by the row ID and the column in ascending lexicographic order, and then timestamps in descending order.

Figure 7-1. A key-value pair in Accumulo

Accumulo can be further optimized by utilizing column families and locality groups. Most of this is transparent to Trino, but knowing the access patterns of your SQL queries may help you optimize your creation of Accumulo tables. This is identical to optimizing the tables for any other application using Accumulo.

Let's take a look at the logical representation of a relational table in Table 7-1.

Table 7-1. Relational or logic view of the data in Accumulo

rowid	flightdate	flightnum	origin	dest
1234	2019-11-02	2237	BOS	DTW
5678	2019-11-02	133	BOS	SFO
...	...	...	...	...

Because Accumulo is a key-value store, it stores this representation of data on disk differently from the logic view, as shown in Table 7-2. This non-relational storage makes it less straightforward to determine how Trino can read from it.

Table 7-2. View of how Accumulo stores data

rowid	column	value
1234	flightdate:flightdate	2019-11-02
1234	flightnum:flightnum	2237
1234	origin:origin	BOS
1234	dest:dest	DTW
5678	flightdate:flightdate	2019-11-02
5678	flightnum:flightnum	133
5678	origin:origin	BOS
5678	dest:dest	SFO
...	...	...

The Trino Accumulo connector handles mapping the Accumulo data model into a relational one that Trino can understand.

Figure 7-2 shows that Accumulo uses HDFS for storage and ZooKeeper to manage metadata about the tables.

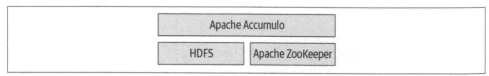

Figure 7-2. Basic Accumulo architecture consisting of distributed Accumulo, HDFS, and Apache ZooKeeper

At its core, Accumulo is a distributed system that consists of a master node and multiple tablet servers, as displayed in Figure 7-3. Tablet servers contain and expose tablets, which are horizontally partitioned pieces of a table. Clients connect directly to the tablet server to scan the data that is needed.

Figure 7-3. Accumulo architecture with master node and multiple tablet servers

Just like Accumulo itself, the Trino Accumulo connector uses ZooKeeper. It reads all information such as tables, views, table properties, and column definitions from the ZooKeeper instance used by Accumulo.

Let's take a look at how to scan data in Accumulo from Trino. In Accumulo, key pairs can be read from a table by using the Scanner object. The scanner starts reading from the table at a particular key and ends at another key, or at the end of the table. The scanners can be configured to read only the exact columns needed. Recall from the RDBMS connectors that only the columns needed are added to the SQL query generated to push into the database.

Accumulo also has the notion of a BatchScanner object. This is used when reading from Accumulo over multiple ranges. This is more efficient because it is able to use multiple workers to communicate with Accumulo, as displayed in Figure 7-4.

The user first submits the query to the coordinator, and the coordinator communicates with Accumulo to determine the splits from the metadata. It determines the splits by looking for the ranges from the available index in Accumulo. Accumulo returns the row IDs from the index, and Trino stores these ranges in the split. If an index cannot be used, one split is used for all the ranges in a single tablet. Last, the worker uses the information to connect to the specific tablet servers and pulls the data in parallel from Accumulo. This pulls the database by using the BatchScanner utility from Accumulo.

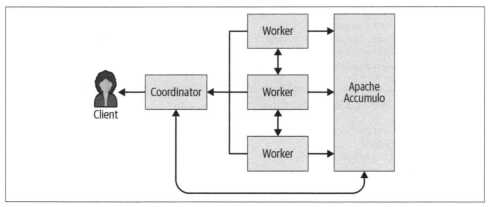

Figure 7-4. Multiple workers accessing Accumulo in parallel

Once the data is pulled back from the workers, the data is put into a relational format that Trino understands, and the remainder of the processing is completed by Trino. In this case, Accumulo is being used for the data storage. Trino provides the higher-level SQL interface for access to the data in Accumulo.

If you were writing an application program yourself to retrieve the data from Accumulo, you'd write something similar to the following Java snippet. You set the ranges to be scanned and define which columns to fetch:

```
ArrayList<Range> ranges = new ArrayList<Range>();
ranges.add(new Range("1234"));
ranges.add(new Range("5678"));

BatchScanner scanner = client.createBatchScanner("flights", auths, 10);
scanner.setRangers(ranges);
scanner.fetchColumn("flightdate");
scanner.fetchColumn("flightnum");
scanner.fetchColumn("origin");

  for (Entry<Key,Value> entry : scanner) {
    // populate into Trino format
  }
}
```

The concept of pruning columns that do not need to be read is similar to the RDBMS connectors. Instead of pushing down SQL, the Accumulo connector uses the Accumulo API to set what columns to fetch.

Using the Trino Accumulo Connector

To use Accumulo, create a catalog properties file (for example, *etc/catalog/accumulo.properties*) that references the Accumulo connector and configures the Accumulo access including the connection to ZooKeeper:

```
connector.name=accumulo
accumulo.instance=accumulo
accumulo.zookeepers=zookeeper.example.com:2181
accumulo.username=user
accumulo.password=password
```

Using our flights example from earlier, let's create a table in Accumulo with Trino, using the Trino CLI, or a RDBMS management tool connected to Trino via JDBC:

```
CREATE TABLE accumulo.ontime.flights (
    rowid VARCHAR,
    flightdate VARCHAR,
    flightnum, INTEGER,
    origin VARCHAR
    dest VARCHAR
);
```

When you create this table in Trino, the connector actually creates a table in Accumulo and the metadata about the table in ZooKeeper.

It is also possible to create a column family. A *column family* in Accumulo is an optimizer for applications that accesses columns together. By defining column families, Accumulo arranges how columns are stored on disk such that the frequently accessed columns, as part of a column family, are stored together. If you want to create a table using column families, you can specify this as a table property, specified in the WITH statement:

```
CREATE TABLE accumulo.ontime.flights (
    rowid VARCHAR,
    flightdate VARCHAR,
    flightnum, INTEGER,
    origin VARCHAR
    dest VARCHAR
)
WITH
    column_mapping = 'origin:location:origin,dest:location:dest'
);
```

By using column_mapping, you are able to define a column family location with column qualifiers origin and dest, which are the same as the Trino column names.

> When the column_mapping table property is not used, Trino auto-generates a column family and column qualifier to be the same name as the Trino column name. You can observe the Accumulo column family and column qualifier by running the DESCRIBE command on the table.

The Trino Accumulo connector supports INSERT statements:

```
INSERT INTO accumulo.ontime.flights VALUES
    (2232, '2019-10-19', 118, 'JFK', 'SFO');
```

This is a convenient way to insert data. However, it is currently low throughput when data is written to Accumulo from Trino. For better performance, you need to use the native Accumulo APIs. The Accumulo connector has utilities outside Trino for assisting with higher performance for inserting data. You can find more information about loading data by using the separate tool in the Trino documentation.

The table we created in the preceding example is an *internal table*. The Trino Accumulo connector supports both internal and external tables. The only difference between the types is that dropping an external table deletes only the metadata and not the data itself. External tables allow you to create Trino tables that already exist in Accumulo. Furthermore, if you need to change the schema, such as adding a column, you can simply drop the table and re-create it in Trino without losing the data. It's worth noting that Accumulo can support this schema evolution when each row does not need to have the same set of columns.

Using external tables requires a bit more work because the data is already stored in a particular way. For example, you must use the column_mapping table property when using external tables. You must set the external property to true when creating the table:

```
CREATE TABLE accumulo.ontime.flights (
    rowid VARCHAR,
    flightdate VARCHAR,
    flightnum, INTEGER,
    origin VARCHAR
    dest VARCHAR
)
WITH
    external = true,
    column_mapping = 'origin:location:origin,dest:location:dest'
);
```

Predicate Pushdown in Accumulo

In the Accumulo connector, Trino can take advantage of the secondary indexes built in Accumulo. To achieve this, the Accumulo connector requires a custom server-side iterator on each Accumulo tablet server. The iterator is distributed as a JAR file that you have to copy into *$ACCUMULO_HOME/lib/ext* on each tablet server. You can find the exact details of how to do this in the Trino documentation.

Indexes in Accumulo are used to look up the row IDs. These can be used to read the values from the actual table. Let's look at an example:

```
SELECT flightnum, origin
FROM flights
WHERE flightdate BETWEEN DATE '2019-10-01' AND '2019-11-05'
AND origin = 'BOS';
```

Without an index, Trino reads the entire data set from Accumulo and then filters it within Trino. The workers get splits that contain the Accumulo range to read. This range is the entire range of the tablet. Where there is an index, such as the example index in Table 7-3, the number of ranges to process can be significantly reduced.

Table 7-3. Example index on the flights table

2019-08-10	flightdate_flightdate:2232	[]
2019-10-19	flightdate_flightdate:2232	[]
2019-11-02	flightdate_flightdate:1234	[]
2019-11-02	flightdate_flightdate:5478	[]
2019-12-01	flightdate_flightdate:1111	[]
SFO	origin_origin:2232	[]
BOS	origin_origin:3498	[]
BOS	origin_origin:1234	[]
BOS	origin_origin:5678	[]
ATL	origin_origin:1111	[]
...	...	...

The coordinator uses the WHERE clause and the filters flightdate BETWEEN DATE '2019-10-01' AND '2019-11-05' AND origin = 'BOS' to scan the index to obtain the row IDs for the table. The row IDs are then packed into the split that the worker later uses to access the data in Accumulo. In our example, we have secondary indexes on flightdate and origin and we collected the row IDs {2232, 1234, 5478} and {3498, 1234, 5678}. We take the intersection from each index and know that we have to scan only row IDs {1234, 5678}. This range is then placed into the split for processing by the worker, which can access the individual values directly, as seen in the detailed view of the data in Table 7-4.

Table 7-4. Detailed view with the individual values for origin, dest, and others

rowid	column	value
2232	flightdate:flightdate	2019-10-19
2232	flightnum:flightnum	118
2232	origin:origin	JFK
2232	dest:dest	SFO
1234	flightdate:flightdate	2019-11-02
1234	flightnum:flightnum	2237

rowid	column	value
1234	origin:origin	BOS
1234	dest:dest	DTW
5678	flightdate:flightdate	2019-11-02
5678	flightnum:flightnum	133
5678	origin:origin	BOS
5678	dest:dest	SFO
3498	flightdate:flightdate	2019-11-10
3498	flightnum:flightnum	133
3498	origin:origin	BOS
3498	dest:dest	SFO
...	...	...

To take advantage of predicate pushdown, we need to have indexes on the columns we want to push down predicates for. Through the Trino connector, indexing on columns can be easily enabled with the index_columns table property:

```
CREATE TABLE accumulo.ontime.flights (
    rowid VARCHAR,
    flightdate VARCHAR,
    flightnum, INTEGER,
    origin VARCHAR
    dest VARCHAR
)
WITH
    index_columns = 'flightdate,origin'
);
```

In this section on Apache Accumulo, you learned about key-value storage and how Trino can be used to query it with standard SQL. Let's see another, much more widespread system that can benefit from Trino: Apache Cassandra.

Apache Cassandra Connector

Apache Cassandra (*https://cassandra.apache.org*) is a distributed, wide column store that supports massive amounts of data. Its fault-tolerant architecture and linear scalability have led to wide adoption of Cassandra.

The typical approach to work with the data in Cassandra is to use the custom query language created for Cassandra: Cassandra Query Language (CQL). While CQL on the surface looks quite a bit like SQL, it practically misses many of the useful features of SQL, such as joins. Overall, it is different enough to make using standard tools that rely on SQL impossible.

By using the Cassandra connector, however, you can allow SQL querying of your data in Cassandra. Minimal configuration is a simple catalog file like *etc/catalog/sitedata.properties* for a Cassandra cluster tracking all user interaction on a website, for example:

```
connector.name=cassandra
cassandra.contact-points=sitedata.example.com
```

With this simple configuration in place, users can query the data in Cassandra. Any keyspace in Cassandra (for example, `cart`) is exposed as a schema in Trino, and tables such as `users` now can be queried with normal SQL:

```
SELECT * FROM sitedata.cart.users;
```

The connector supports numerous configuration properties that allow you to adapt the catalog to your Cassandra cluster, enable authentication and TLS for the connection, and more.

Streaming System Connector Example: Kafka

Streaming systems and publish-subscribe (pub/sub) systems are designed for handling real-time data feeds. For example, Apache Kafka was created to be a high-throughput and low-latency platform at LinkedIn. Publishers write messages to Kafka for subscribers to consume. Such a system is generally useful for data pipelines between systems. Typically, the Trino Kafka connector is used to read data from Kafka, but you can also use the connector to publish data.

Using the connector, you can use SQL to query data on a Kafka topic and even join it with other data. The typical use case with Trino is ad hoc querying of the live Kafka topic streams to inspect and better understand the current status and data flowing through the system. Using Trino makes this much easier and accessible for data analysts and other users who typically don't have any specific Kafka knowledge but do know how to write SQL queries.

Another, less common use case for Trino with Kafka is the migration of data from Kafka. Using a `CREATE TABLE AS` or an `INSERT SELECT` statement, you can read data from the Kafka topic, transform the data using SQL, and then write it to HDFS, S3, or other storage.

Since Kafka is a streaming system, the exposed topics constantly change their content as new data comes in. This has to be taken into account when querying Kafka topics with Trino. Performing a migration of the data with Trino to HDFS or another database system with permanent storage allows you to preserve the information passing through your Kafka topics.

Once the data is permanently available in the target database or storage, Trino can be used to expose it to analytical tools such as Apache Superset; see "Queries, Visualizations, and More with Apache Superset" on page 241.

Using the Kafka connector works like any other connector. Create a catalog (for example, *etc/catalog/trafficstream.properties*) that uses the Kafka connector, configures any other required details, and points at your Kafka cluster:

```
connector.name=kafka
kafka.table-names=web.pages,web.users
kafka.nodes=trafficstream.example.com:9092
```

Now every topic from Kafka `web.pages` and `web.users` is available as a table in Trino. At any time, that table exposes the entire Kafka topic with all messages currently in the topic. Each message in the topic shows up as a row in the table in Trino. The data is now easily available with SQL queries on Trino, using catalog, schema, and table names:

```
SELECT * FROM trafficstream.web.pages;
SELECT * FROM trafficstream.web.users;
```

Essentially, you can inspect your Kafka topics as they are streamed live with simple SQL queries.

If you want to migrate the data to another system, such as an HDFS catalog, you can start with a simple `CREATE TABLE AS` (CTAS) query:

```
CREATE TABLE hdfs.web.pages
WITH (
    format = 'ORC',
    partitioned_by = ARRAY['view_date']
)
AS
SELECT *
FROM trafficstream.web.pages;
```

Once the table exists, you can insert more data into it by running insert queries regularly:

```
INSERT INTO hdfs.web.pages
SELECT *
FROM trafficstream.web.pages;
```

To avoid duplicate copying, you can keep track of some of the internal columns from Kafka that are exposed by the connector. Specifically, you can use `_partition_id`, `_partition_offset`, `_segment_start`, `_segment_end`, and `_segment_count`. The specific setup you use to run the query regularly depends on your Kafka configuration for removing messages as well as the tools used to run the queries, such as Apache Airflow, described in "Workflows with Apache Airflow" on page 243.

The mapping of Kafka topics, which are exposed as tables, and their contained message, can be defined with a JSON file for each topic located in *etc/kafka/schema.tablename.json*. For the preceding example, you can define the mapping in *etc/kafka/web.pages.json*.

Kafka messages can use different formats, and the Kafka connector includes decoders for the most common formats, including Raw, JSON, CSV, and Avro (*https://avro.apache.org*).

Detailed information for the configuration properties, mapping, and other internal columns is available in the Trino documentation; see "Documentation" on page 14.

Using Trino with Kafka opens new analysis and insights into the data streamed through Kafka and defines another valuable usage of Trino. Another stream processing system supported by Trino for similar usage is Amazon Kinesis.

Document Store Connector Example: Elasticsearch

Trino includes connectors for well-known document storage systems such as Elasticsearch or MongoDB. These systems support storage and retrieval of information in JSON-like documents. Elasticsearch is better suited for indexing and searching documents. MongoDB is a general-purpose document store.

Overview

The Trino connectors allow users to use SQL to access these systems and query data in them, even though no native SQL access exists.

Elasticsearch clusters are often used to store log data or other event streams for longer-term or even permanent storage. These data sets are often very large, and they can be a useful resource for better understanding the system emitting the log data in operation and in a wide variety of scenarios.

Elasticsearch and Trino are a powerful and performant combination, since both systems can scale horizontally. Trino scales by breaking up a query and running parts of it across many workers in the cluster.

Elasticsearch typically operates on its own cluster and scales horizontally as well. It can shard the index across many nodes and run any search operations in a distributed manner. Tuning the Elasticsearch cluster for performance is a separate topic that requires an understanding of the number of documents in the search index, the number of nodes in the cluster, the replica sets, the sharding configuration, and other details.

However, from a client perspective, and therefore also from the perspective of Trino, this is all transparent, and Elasticsearch simply exposes the cluster with a URL of the Elasticsearch server.

Configuration and Usage

Configuring Trino to access Elasticsearch is performed by creating a catalog file such as *etc/catalog/search.properties*:

```
connector.name=elasticsearch
elasticsearch.host=searchcluster.example.com
```

This configuration relies on default values for the port, the schema, and other details but is sufficient for querying the cluster. The connector supports numerous data types from Elasticsearch out of the box. It automatically analyzes each index, configures each as a table, exposes the table in the `default` schema, creates the necessary nested structures and row types, and exposes it all in Trino. Any document in the index is automatically unpacked into the table structure in Trino. For example, an index called `server` is automatically available as a table in the catalog's `default` schema, and you can query Trino for more information about the structure:

```
DESCRIBE search.default.server;
```

Users can start querying the index straightaway. The information schema, or the `DESCRIBE` command, can be used to understand the created tables and fields for each index/schema.

Fields in Elasticsearch schemas commonly contain multiple values as arrays. If the automatic detection does not perform as desired, you can add a field property definition of the index mapping. Furthermore, the `_source` hidden field contains the source document from Elasticsearch, and if desired, you can use the functions for JSON document parsing (see "JSON Functions" on page 195) as well as collection data types (see "Collection Data Types" on page 161). These can generally be helpful when working with the documents in an Elasticsearch cluster, which are predominately JSON documents.

In Elasticsearch, you can expose the data from one or more indexes as `alias`. This can also be filtered data. The Trino connector supports alias usage and exposes them just like any other index as a table.

Query Processing

Once you issue a query from Trino to Elasticsearch, Trino takes advantage of its cluster infrastructure in addition to the already clustered Elasticsearch to increase performance even more.

Trino queries Elasticsearch to understand all the Elasticsearch shards. It then uses this information when creating the query plan. It breaks the query into separate splits that are targeted at the specific shards, and then issues the separate queries to the shards all in parallel. Once the results come back, they are combined in Trino and returned to the user. This means that Trino combined with Elasticsearch can use SQL for querying and be more performant than Elasticsearch on its own.

Also note that this individual connection to specific shards also happens in typical Elasticsearch clusters where the cluster runs behind a load balancer and is just exposed via a DNS hostname.

Full-Text Search

A powerful feature of the connector for Elasticsearch is support for full-text search. It allows you to use Elasticsearch query strings within a SQL query issued from Trino.

For example, imagine an index full of blog posts on a website. The documents are stored in the `blogs` index. And maybe those posts consist of numerous fields such as `title`, `intro`, `post`, `summary`, and `authors`. With the full-text search, you can write a simple query that searches the whole content in all the fields for specific terms such as `trino`:

```
SELECT * FROM "blogs: +trino";
```

The query string syntax from Elasticsearch supports weighting different search terms and other features suitable for a full-text search.

Summary

The connector also supports the open source version of Elasticsearch from Amazon, OpenSearch. Users of the Amazon OpenSearch Service can take advantage of the support for AWS Identity and Access Management. Find out more details about this configuration as well as securing the connection to the Elasticsearch cluster with TLS and other tips from the Trino documentation (*https://trino.io/docs*).

Using Trino with Elasticsearch, you can analyze the rich data in your index with the powerful tools around SQL support. You can write queries manually or hook up rich analytical tools. This allows you to understand the data in the cluster better than previously possible.

Similar advantages are available when you connect MongoDB to Trino, taking advantage of the Trino MongoDB connector.

Query Federation in Trino

After reading about all the use cases for Trino in "Trino Use Cases" on page 7, and learning about all the data sources and available connectors in Trino, you are now ready to learn more about query federation in Trino. A *federated query* is a query that accesses data in more than one data source.

This query can be used to tie together the content and information from multiple RDBMS databases, such as an enterprise backend application database running on PostgreSQL with a web application database on MySQL. It could also be a data warehouse on PostgreSQL queried with data from the source also running in PostgreSQL or elsewhere.

The much more powerful examples, however, arise when you combine queries from a RDBMS with queries running against other non-relational systems. Combine the data from your data warehouse with information from your object storage, filled with data from your web application at massive scale. Or relate the data to content in your key-value store or your NoSQL database. Your object storage data lake, or even your modern data lakehouse, can suddenly be exposed with SQL, and the information can become the basis for better understanding your overall data.

Query federation can help you truly grasp the connections and dependencies between all your data in the different systems and therefore gain better insights about the bigger picture.

In the following example, you learn about the use case of joining data in distributed storage with data in a RDBMS. You can find information about the necessary setup in "Flight Data Set" on page 16.

With this data, you can ask questions such as "What is the average delay of airplanes by year?" by using a SQL query:

```
SELECT avg(depdelayminutes) AS delay, year
FROM flights_orc
GROUP BY year
ORDER BY year DESC;
```

Another question is "What are the best days of the week to fly out of Boston in the month of February?":

```
SELECT dayofweek, avg(depdelayminutes) AS delay
FROM flights_orc
WHERE month=2 AND origincityname LIKE '%Boston%'
GROUP BY dayofmonth
ORDER BY dayofweek;
```

Because the notion of multiple data sources and query federation is an integral part of Trino, we encourage you to set up an environment and explore the data. These queries serve as inspiration for you to create additional queries on your own.

We use the two example analytical queries on the airline data to demonstrate query federation in Trino. The setup we provide uses data stored in S3 and accessed by configuring Trino with the Hive connector. However, if you prefer, you can store the data in HDFS, Azure Storage, or Google Cloud Storage and use the Hive connector to query the data.

In this first example query, we want Trino to return the top 10 airline carriers with the most flights from the data in HDFS:

```
SELECT uniquecarrier, count(*) AS ct
FROM flights_orc
GROUP BY uniquecarrier
ORDER BY count(*) DESC
LIMIT 10;
 uniquecarrier |    ct
---------------+----------
   WN          | 24096231
   DL          | 21598986
   AA          | 18942178
   US          | 16735486
   UA          | 16377453
   NW          | 10585760
   CO          |  8888536
   OO          |  7270911
   MQ          |  6877396
   EV          |  5391487
(10 rows)
```

While the preceding query provides the results for the top 10 airline carriers with the most flights, it requires you to understand the values of uniquecarrier. It would be better if a more descriptive column provided the full airline carrier name instead of the abbreviations. However, the airline data source we are querying from does not contain such information. Perhaps if another data source with the information does exist, we can combine the data source to return more comprehensible results.

Let's look at another example. Here, we want Trino to return the top 10 airports that had the most departures:

```
SELECT origin, count(*) AS ct
FROM flights_orc
GROUP BY origin
ORDER BY count(*) DESC
LIMIT 10;
 origin |   ct
--------+---------
  ATL   | 8867847
  ORD   | 8756942
  DFW   | 7601863
  LAX   | 5575119
  DEN   | 4936651
  PHX   | 4725124
```

```
    IAH   | 4118279
    DTW   | 3862377
    SFO   | 3825008
    LAS   | 3640747
(10 rows)
```

As with the previous query, the results require some domain expertise. For example, you need to understand that the origin column contains airport codes. The code is meaningless to people with less expertise analyzing the results.

Let's enhance our results by combining them with additional data in a relational database. We use PostgreSQL in our examples, but similar steps are applicable for any relational database.

As with the airline data, our GitHub repository includes the setup for creating and loading tables in a relational database as well as configuring the Trino connector to access it. We've chosen to configure Trino to query from a PostgreSQL database that contains additional airline data. The table carrier in PostgreSQL provides a mapping of the airline code to the more descriptive airline name. You can use this additional data with our first example query.

Let's take a look at the table carrier in PostgreSQL:

```
SELECT * FROM carrier LIMIT 10;
 code |                description
------+------------------------------------------------
 02Q  | Titan Airways
 04Q  | Tradewind Aviation
 05Q  | Comlux Aviation, AG
 06Q  | Master Top Linhas Aereas Ltd.
 07Q  | Flair Airlines Ltd.
 09Q  | Swift Air, LLC
 0BQ  | DCA
 0CQ  | ACM AIR CHARTER GmbH
 0GQ  | Inter Island Airways, d/b/a Inter Island Air
 0HQ  | Polar Airlines de Mexico d/b/a Nova Air
(10 rows)
```

This table contains code column code along with a description column. Using this information, we can use our first example query for the flights_orc table and modify it to join with the data in the PostgreSQL carrier table:

```
SELECT f.uniquecarrier, c.description, count(*) AS ct
FROM datalake.ontime.flights_orc f,
    postgresql.airline.carrier c
WHERE c.code = f.uniquecarrier
GROUP BY f.uniquecarrier, c.description
ORDER BY count(*) DESC
LIMIT 10;
 uniquecarrier |        description        |    ct
---------------+---------------------------+----------
```

```
WN           | Southwest Airlines Co.   | 24096231
DL           | Delta Air Lines Inc.     | 21598986
AA           | American Airlines Inc.   | 18942178
US           | US Airways Inc.          | 16735486
UA           | United Air Lines Inc.    | 16377453
NW           | Northwest Airlines Inc.  | 10585760
CO           | Continental Air Lines Inc. | 8888536
OO           | SkyWest Airlines Inc.    | 7270911
MQ           | Envoy Air                | 6877396
EV           | ExpressJet Airlines Inc. | 5391487
(10 rows)
```

Voilà! Now that we have written a single SQL query to federate data from S3 and PostgreSQL, we're able to provide more valuable results of the data to extract meaning. Instead of having to know or separately look up the airline codes, the descriptive airline name is in the results.

In the query, you have to use fully qualified names when referencing the tables. When utilizing the USE command to set the default catalog and schema, a nonqualified table name is linked to that catalog and schema. However, anytime you need to query outside for the catalog and schema, the table name must be qualified. Otherwise, Trino tries to find it within the default catalog and schema, and returns an error. If you are referring to a table within the default catalog and schema, it is not required to fully qualify the table name. However, it's recommended as best practice whenever referring to data sources outside the default scope.

Next, let's look at the table `airport` in PostgreSQL. This table is used as part of federating our second example query:

```
SELECT code, name, city
FROM airport
LIMIT 10;
 code |          name          |         city
------+------------------------+----------------------
 01A  | Afognak Lake Airport   | Afognak Lake, AK
 03A  | Bear Creek Mining Strip | Granite Mountain, AK
 04A  | Lik Mining Camp        | Lik, AK
 05A  | Little Squaw Airport   | Little Squaw, AK
 06A  | Kizhuyak Bay           | Kizhuyak, AK
 07A  | Klawock Seaplane Base  | Klawock, AK
 08A  | Elizabeth Island Airport | Elizabeth Island, AK
 09A  | Augustin Island        | Homer, AK
 1B1  | Columbia County        | Hudson, NY
 1G4  | Grand Canyon West      | Peach Springs, AZ
(10 rows)
```

Looking at this data from PostgreSQL, you see that the code column can be used to join with our second query on the flight_orc table. This allows you to use the additional information in the airport table with the query to provide more details:

```
SELECT f.origin, c.name, c.city, count(*) AS ct
FROM hive.ontime.flights_orc f,
    postgresql.airline.airport c
WHERE c.code = f.origin
GROUP BY origin, c.name, c.city
ORDER BY count(*) DESC
LIMIT 10;
 origin |                   name                    |         city          |   ct
--------+-------------------------------------------+-----------------------+---------
 ATL    | Hartsfield-Jackson Atlanta International   | Atlanta, GA           | 8867847
 ORD    | Chicago OHare International                | Chicago, IL           | 8756942
 DFW    | Dallas/Fort Worth International            | Dallas/Fort Worth, TX | 7601863
 LAX    | Los Angeles International                  | Los Angeles, CA       | 5575119
 DEN    | Denver International                       | Denver, CO            | 4936651
 PHX    | Phoenix Sky Harbor International           | Phoenix, AZ           | 4725124
 IAH    | George Bush Intercontinental/Houston      | Houston, TX           | 4118279
 DTW    | Detroit Metro Wayne County                | Detroit, MI           | 3862377
 SFO    | San Francisco International                | San Francisco, CA     | 3825008
 LAS    | McCarran International                     | Las Vegas, NV         | 3640747
(10 rows)
```

Trino! As with our first example, we can provide more meaningful information by federating across two disparate data sources. Here, we are able to add the name of the airport instead of the user relying on airport codes that are hard to interpret.

With this quick example of query federation, you can see that the combination of different data sources and the central querying in one location, in Trino, can provide tremendous improvements to your query results. Our example enhanced only the appearance and readability of the results. However, in many cases, using richer, larger data sets, the federation of queries, and combination of data from different sources can result in a completely new understanding of the data.

Now that we've gone through some examples of query federation from an end-user perspective, let's discuss the architecture of how this works. We build on top of some of the concepts you learned about in Chapter 4 on the Trino architecture.

Trino is able to coordinate the hybrid execution of the query across the data sources involved in the query. In the earlier example, we were querying between distributed storage and PostgreSQL. For distributed storage via the Hive connector, Trino reads the data files directly, whether they are from HDFS, S3, Azure Blob Storage, etc. For a relational database connector such as the PostgreSQL connector, Trino relies on PostgreSQL to perform as part of the execution. Let's use our query from before but, to make it more interesting, we add a new predicate that refers to a column in the PostgreSQL airport table:

```
SELECT f.origin, c.name, c.city, count(*) AS ct
FROM datalake.ontime.flights_orc f,
  postgresql.airline.airport c
WHERE c.code = f.origin AND c.state = 'AK'
GROUP BY origin, c.name, c.city
```

```
ORDER BY count(*) DESC
LIMIT 10;
```

The logical query plan resembles something similar to Figure 7-5. You see the plan consists of scanning both the `flights_orc` and `airport` tables. Both inputs are fed into the join operator. But before the airport data is fed into the join, a filter is applied because we want to look at the results only for airports in Alaska. After the join, the aggregation and grouping operation is applied. And then, finally, the TopN operator performs the `ORDER BY` and `LIMIT` combined.

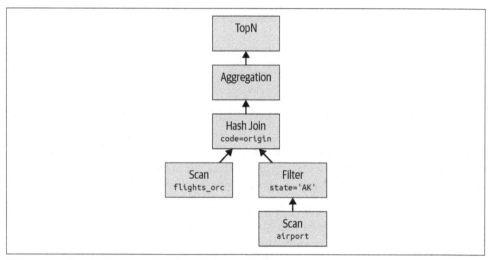

Figure 7-5. Logical query plan for a federated query

For Trino to retrieve the data from PostgreSQL, it sends a query via JDBC. For example, in the naive approach, the following query is sent to PostgreSQL:

```
SELECT * FROM airline.airport;
```

However, Trino is smarter than this, and the Trino optimizer tries to reduce the amount of data transferred between systems. In this example, Trino queries only the columns it needs from the PostgreSQL table, as well as pushes down the predicate into the SQL that is sent to PostgreSQL.

So now the query sent from Trino to PostgreSQL pushes more processing to PostgreSQL:

```
SELECT code, city, name FROM airline.airport WHERE state = 'AK';
```

As the JDBC connector to PostgreSQL returns data to Trino, Trino continues processing the data for the part that is executed in the Trino query engine.

Some simpler queries such as `SELECT * FROM public.airport` are entirely pushed down into the underlying data source, shown in Figure 7-6, such that the query execution happens outside Trino, and Trino acts as a pass-through.

Support for more complex SQL pushdown depends on the connector. For example, joins that involve only the RDBMS data can be pushed into PostgreSQL by the connector to eliminate data transfer to Trino. Numerous aggregate functions can also be pushed down by the PostgreSQL connector, while other connectors are not necessarily capable of this operation.

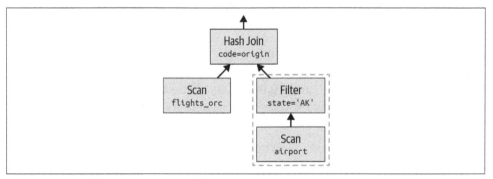

Figure 7-6. Pushdown in a query plan

Extract, Transform, Load and Federated Queries

Extract, transform, load (ETL) is a term used to describe the technique of copying data from data sources and landing it into another data source. Often there is a middle step of transforming the data from the source in preparation for the destination. This may include dropping columns, making calculations, filtering and cleaning up data, joining in data, performing pre-aggregations, and other ways to prepare and make it suitable for querying in the destination. In some use cases, the order of these operations is changed, and the process is then referred to as *extract, load, and transform (ELT)*. While there are some critical differences, Trino is suitable for both approaches.

Trino is not intended to be a full-fledged ETL tool comparable to a commercial solution. However, it can assist by avoiding the need for ETL. Because Trino can query from the data source, there may no longer be a need to move the data. Trino queries the data where it lives to alleviate the complexity of managing the ETL process.

You may still desire to do some type of ETL processes. Perhaps you want to query on pre-aggregated data, or you don't want to put more load on the underlying system. By using the `CREATE TABLE AS` or `INSERT SELECT` constructs, you can move data from one data source into another.

Trino can assist in these and other scenarios and work as a query processing and execution engine for ETL workloads orchestrated by other tools.

A large advantage of using Trino for ETL workloads and use cases is the support for other data sources beyond relational databases. The new support for fault-tolerant execution of queries elevates Trino to a first-class query engine for ETL use cases in combination with modern data lakehouse setups. Combined with the performance advantage Trino has over many other ETL solutions and the integration of modern data pipeline tools such as dbt, Apache Flink, and Apache Airflow, Trino is moving beyond the pure analytics use cases to become a major building block for modern lakehouse and data platform architectures.

Conclusion

You now have a really good understanding of connectors in Trino. It is time to put them to good use. Configure your catalogs and get ready to learn more about querying the data sources.

This brings us to our next topic, everything about SQL use in Trino. SQL knowledge is crucial to your successful use of Trino, and we cover all you need to know in Chapters 8 and 9.

Using SQL in Trino

After installing and running Trino, you first learned about the central feature of first-class SQL support in Trino in "SQL with Trino" on page 39. Go back and check out that content again if you need an overview or a reminder.

From Chapter 6 about connectors, you know that you can query a lot of data sources with SQL in Trino.

In this chapter, you get to dive deep into the details of SQL support of Trino, including a set of data definition language (DDL) statements for creating and manipulating database objects such as schemas, tables, columns, and views. You learn more about the supported data types and SQL statements. In Chapter 9, you learn about operators and functions for more advanced usage.

Overall, the goal of this chapter is not to serve as a reference guide for SQL but rather to demonstrate the SQL capabilities in Trino. For the latest and most complete information about SQL on Trino, you can refer to the official Trino documentation (*https://trino.io/docs*).

You can take advantage of all SQL support by using the Trino CLI, or any application using the JDBC driver, the Python client library, ODBC drivers, or any other client application, all discussed in Chapter 3.

Trino Statements

Before you dive into querying data in Trino, it's important to know what data is even available, where, and in what data types. *Trino statements* allow you to gather that type of information and more. Trino statements query the system tables and information for metadata about configured catalogs, schemas, and so on. These statements work in the same context as all SQL statements.

The FROM and FOR clauses in the statements need the input of a fully qualified table, catalog, or schema, unless a default is set with USE.

The LIKE clause, which can be used to restrict the result, uses pattern matching syntax like that of the SQL LIKE command.

Command sections in [ ] are optional. The following Trino statements are available:

SHOW CATALOGS [LIKE *pattern*]
: List the available catalogs.

SHOW SCHEMAS [FROM *catalog*] [LIKE *pattern*]
: List the schemas in a catalog.

SHOW TABLES [FROM *schema*] [LIKE *pattern*]
: List the tables in a schema.

SHOW FUNCTIONS [LIKE *pattern*]
: Display a list of available SQL functions.

SHOW COLUMNS FROM *table* or DESCRIBE *table*
: List the columns in a table along with their data type and other attributes.

USE *catalog.schema* or USE *schema*
> Update the session to use the specified catalog and schema as the default. If a catalog is not specified, the schema is resolved using the current catalog.

SHOW STATS FOR *table_name*
> Show statistics like data size and counts for the data in a specific table.

EXPLAIN query
> Generate the query plan and detail the individual steps for the specified SQL query.

Let's look at some examples that can come in handy in your own use:

```
SHOW SCHEMAS IN tpch LIKE '%3%';
 Schema
---------
 sf300
 sf3000
 sf30000
(3 rows)

DESCRIBE tpch.tiny.nation;
   Column   |     Type     | Extra | Comment
-----------+--------------+-------+--------
 nationkey | bigint       |       |
 name      | varchar(25)  |       |
 regionkey | bigint       |       |
 comment   | varchar(152) |       |
(4 rows)
```

The EXPLAIN statement is actually a bit more powerful than indicated in the previous list. Here is the full syntax:

```
EXPLAIN [ ( option [, ...] ) ] <query>
    options: FORMAT { TEXT | GRAPHVIZ | JSON}
             TYPE { LOGICAL | DISTRIBUTED | IO | VALIDATE }
```

You can use the EXPLAIN statement to display the query plan:

```
EXPLAIN
SELECT name FROM tpch.tiny.region;
                               Query Plan
---------------------------------------------------------------------------
 Fragment 0 [SOURCE]
     Output layout: [name]
     Output partitioning: SINGLE []
     Output[columnNames = [name]]
     │   Layout: [name:varchar(25)]
     │   Estimates: {rows: 5 (59B), cpu: 59, memory: 0B, network: 0B}
     └─ TableScan[table = tpch:tiny:region]
             Layout: [name:varchar(25)]
             Estimates: {rows: 5 (59B), cpu: 59, memory: 0B, network: 0B}
             name := tpch:name
```

Working with these plans is helpful for performance tuning and for better under-standing what Trino is going to do with your query. You can learn more about this in Chapters 4 and 12.

A very simple use case of EXPLAIN is to check whether the syntax of your query is even valid:

```
EXPLAIN (TYPE VALIDATE)
SELECT name FROM tpch.tiny.region;
 Valid
 ------
 true
(1 row)
```

Trino System Tables

The *Trino system tables* do not need to be configured with a catalog file. All schemas and tables are automatically available with the system catalog.

You can query the schemas and tables to find out more about the running instance of Trino by using the statements discussed in "Trino Statements" on page 142. The available information includes data about the runtime, nodes, catalog, and more. Inspecting the available information allows you to better understand and work with Trino at runtime.

 The Trino Web UI exposes information from the system tables in a web-based user interface. Find out more details in "Monitoring with the Trino Web UI" on page 251.

The system tables contain schemas:

```
SHOW SCHEMAS IN system;
       Schema
--------------------
 information_schema
 jdbc
 metadata
 runtime
(4 rows)
```

The most useful tables for the purpose of query tuning are system.runtime.queries and system.runtime.tasks:

```
DESCRIBE system.runtime.queries;
       Column        |            Type           | Extra | Comment
---------------------+---------------------------+-------+---------
 query_id            | varchar                   |       |
 state               | varchar                   |       |
 user                | varchar                   |       |
 source              | varchar                   |       |
 query               | varchar                   |       |
 resource_group_id   | array(varchar)            |       |
 queued_time_ms      | bigint                    |       |
 analysis_time_ms    | bigint                    |       |
 planning_time_ms    | bigint                    |       |
 created             | timestamp(3) with time zone |     |
 started             | timestamp(3) with time zone |     |
 last_heartbeat      | timestamp(3) with time zone |     |
 end                 | timestamp(3) with time zone |     |
 error_type          | varchar                   |       |
 error_code          | varchar                   |       |
(15 rows)

DESCRIBE system.runtime.tasks;
         Column         |            Type           | Extra | Comment
------------------------+---------------------------+-------+---------
 node_id                | varchar                   |       |
 task_id                | varchar                   |       |
 stage_id               | varchar                   |       |
 query_id               | varchar                   |       |
 state                  | varchar                   |       |
 splits                 | bigint                    |       |
 queued_splits          | bigint                    |       |
 running_splits         | bigint                    |       |
 completed_splits       | bigint                    |       |
 split_scheduled_time_ms | bigint                   |       |
 split_cpu_time_ms      | bigint                    |       |
 split_blocked_time_ms  | bigint                    |       |
 raw_input_bytes        | bigint                    |       |
 raw_input_rows         | bigint                    |       |
 processed_input_bytes  | bigint                    |       |
 processed_input_rows   | bigint                    |       |
 output_bytes           | bigint                    |       |
 output_rows            | bigint                    |       |
 physical_input_bytes   | bigint                    |       |
 physical_written_bytes | bigint                    |       |
 created                | timestamp(3) with time zone |     |
 start                  | timestamp(3) with time zone |     |
 last_heartbeat         | timestamp(3) with time zone |     |
 end                    | timestamp(3) with time zone |     |
(24 rows)
```

The preceding table descriptions show the underlying data explained in more detail in "Monitoring with the Trino Web UI" on page 251. The system.runtime.queries table provides information about current and past queries executed in Trino. The `system.runtime.tasks` table provides the lower-level details for the tasks in Trino. This is similar to the information output on the Query Details page of the Trino Web UI.

Following are a few useful examples for queries from the system tables.

List the nodes in the Trino cluster:

```
SELECT * FROM system.runtime.nodes;
```

Show all failed queries:

```
SELECT * FROM system.runtime.queries WHERE state='FAILED';
```

Show all running queries, including their `query_id`:

```
SELECT * FROM system.runtime.queries WHERE state='RUNNING';
```

The system tables also provide a mechanism to kill a running query with this `QUERY_ID`:

```
CALL system.runtime.kill_query(query_id => 'QUERY_ID', message => 'Killed');
```

In addition to all the information about Trino at runtime, the cluster, the worker nodes, and more, Trino connectors also have the ability to expose system data about the connected data source. For example, the Hive connector discussed in "Hive Connector for Distributed Storage Data Sources" on page 102 can be configured as a connector in a `datalake` catalog. It automatically exposes data about Hive in the system tables:

```
SHOW TABLES FROM datalake.system;
```

This information contains aspects such as used partitions.

Catalogs

A *Trino catalog* represents a data source configured with a catalog properties file using a connector, as discussed in Chapter 6. Catalogs contain one or more schemas, which provide a collection of tables.

For example, you can configure a catalog to access a relational database on PostgreSQL. Or you can configure a catalog to provide access to JMX information via the JMX connector. Other examples of catalogs include a catalog using the Iceberg connector to connect to an object storage data source using the Iceberg table format, or the Pinot connector configured to access the real-time distributed OLAP datastore. When you run an SQL statement in Trino, you are running it against one or more catalogs.

It is possible to have multiple catalogs using the same connector. For example, you can create two separate catalogs to expose two PostgreSQL databases running on the same server.

When addressing a table in Trino, the fully qualified table name is always rooted in a catalog. For example, a fully qualified table name of `datalake.test_data.test` refers to the `test` table in the `test_data` schema in the `datalake` catalog. That catalog could use any connector. The underlying system is therefore mostly abstracted for the user.

You can see a list of available catalogs in your Trino server by accessing the system data:

```
SHOW CATALOGS;
 Catalog
 ---------
 abyss
 datalake
 monitor
 salesdb
 stream
 system
(6 rows)
```

If you want to know what connector is used in a catalog, you have to query the system catalog:

```
SELECT *
FROM system.metadata.catalogs
WHERE catalog_name='brain';
 catalog_name | connector_id | connector_name
 -------------+--------------+----------------
 brain        | brain        | memory
(1 row)
```

Catalogs, schemas, and table information are not stored by Trino; Trino does not have its own permanent storage system. It is the responsibility of the connector to provide this information to Trino. Typically, this is done by querying the catalog from the underlying database, a metastore separate from the object storage, or by another configuration in the connector. The connector handles this and simply provides the information to Trino when requested.

Schemas

Within a catalog, Trino contains schemas. *Schemas* hold tables, views, and various other objects and are a way to organize tables. Together, the catalog and schema define a set of tables that can be queried.

When accessing a relational database such as PostgreSQL with Trino, a schema translates to the same concept in the target database. Other types of connectors may choose to organize tables into schemas in a way that makes sense for the underlying data source. The connector implementation determines how the schema is mapped in the catalog. For example, a database in Hive is exposed as a schema in Trino for the Hive connector.

Typically, schemas already exist when you configure a catalog. However, Trino also allows creation and other manipulation of schemas.

Let's look at the SQL statement to create a schema:

```
CREATE SCHEMA [ IF NOT EXISTS ] schema_name
[ WITH ( property_name = expression [, ...] ) ]
```

The WITH clause can be used to associate properties with the schema. For example, for the Hive connector, creating a schema actually creates a database in Hive. It is sometimes desirable to override the default location for the database as specified by hive.metastore.warehouse.dir:

```
CREATE SCHEMA datalake.web
WITH (location = 's3://example-org/web/')
```

Refer to the latest Trino documentation for the list of schema properties, or query the list of configured properties in Trino:

```
SELECT * FROM system.metadata.schema_properties;
-[ RECORD 1 ]-+-----------------------------
catalog_name  | datalake
property_name | location
default_value |
type          | varchar
description   | Base file system location URI
```

You can change the name of an existing schema:

```
ALTER SCHEMA name RENAME TO new_name
```

Deleting a schema is also supported:

```
DROP SCHEMA [ IF EXISTS ] schema_name
```

Specify IF EXISTS when you do not want the statement to error if the schema does not exist. Before you can successfully drop a schema, you need to drop the tables in it. Some database systems support a CASCADE keyword that indicates the DROP statement to drop everything within the object such as a schema. Trino does *not* support CASCADE at this stage.

Information Schema

The *information schema* is part of the SQL standard and supported in Trino as a set of views providing metadata about schemas, tables, columns, views, and other objects in a catalog. The views are contained within a schema named information_schema. Each Trino catalog has its own information_schema. Commands such as SHOW TABLES, SHOW SCHEMA, and others are shorthand for the same information you can retrieve from the information schema.

The information schema is essential for using third-party tools such as business intelligence tools. Many of these tools query the information schema so they know what objects exist.

The information schema has nine total views. These are the same in each connector. For some connectors that don't support certain features (for example, roles), queries to the information_schema in that connector may result in an unsupported error:

```
SHOW TABLES IN system.information_schema;
            Table
------------------------------
 applicable_roles
 columns
 enabled_roles
 role_authorization_descriptors
 roles
 schemata
 table_privileges
 tables
 views
(9 rows)
```

You can query the list of tables in the schema. Notice that the information schema tables are returned as well:

```
SELECT * FROM datalake.information_schema.tables;
 table_catalog |    table_schema    |    table_name    | table_type
---------------+--------------------+------------------+----------
 datalake      | web                | nation           | BASE TABLE
 datalake      | information_schema | enabled_roles    | BASE TABLE
 datalake      | information_schema | roles            | BASE TABLE
 datalake      | information_schema | columns          | BASE TABLE
 datalake      | information_schema | tables           | BASE TABLE
 datalake      | information_schema | views            | BASE TABLE
 datalake      | information_schema | applicable_roles | BASE TABLE
 datalake      | information_schema | table_privileges | BASE TABLE
 datalake      | information_schema | schemata         | BASE TABLE
(9 rows)
```

Additionally, you can view the columns for a particular table by leveraging the WHERE clause in these queries:

```
SELECT table_catalog, table_schema, table_name, column_name
FROM datalake.information_schema.columns
WHERE table_name = 'nation';
 table_catalog |    table_schema    |    table_name    |  column_name
---------------+--------------------+------------------+--------------
 datalake      | web                | nation           | regionkey
 datalake      | web                | nation           | comment
 datalake      | web                | nation           | nationkey
 datalake      | web                | nation           | name
 ...
```

Tables

Now that you understand catalogs and schemas, let's learn about table definitions in Trino. A *table* is a set of unordered rows, which are organized into named columns with specific data types. This is the same as in any relational database, in which the table consists of rows, columns, and data types for those columns. The mapping from source data to tables is defined by the catalog.

The connector implementation determines how a table is mapped into a schema. For example, exposing PostgreSQL tables in Trino is mostly straightforward because PostgreSQL natively supports SQL and the concept of tables. The only differences are often in terms of available and used data types. However, it requires more creativity to implement a connector to other systems, especially if they lack a strict table concept by design. For example, the Apache Kafka connector exposes Kafka topics as tables in Trino.

Tables are accessed in SQL queries by using a fully qualified name, such as *catalog-name.schema-name.table-name*.

Let's look at CREATE TABLE for creating a table in Trino:

```
CREATE TABLE [ IF NOT EXISTS ]
table_name (
  { column_name data_type [ COMMENT comment ]
  [ WITH ( property_name = expression [, ...] ) ]
  | LIKE existing_table_name [ { INCLUDING | EXCLUDING } PROPERTIES ] }
  [, ...]
)
[ COMMENT table_comment ]
[ WITH ( property_name = expression [, ...] ) ]
```

This general syntax should be familiar to you if you know SQL. In Trino, the optional WITH clause has an important use. Other systems such as Hive have extended the SQL language so that users can specify logic or data that otherwise cannot be expressed in standard SQL. Following this approach violates the underlying philosophy of Trino to stay as close to the SQL standard as possible. It also makes supporting many connectors unmanageable, and therefore has been replaced with having table and column properties use the WITH clause.

Once you have created the table, you can use the INSERT INTO statement from standard SQL.

For example, in the iris data set creation script, first a table is created; see "Iris Data Set" on page 15. Then values are inserted directly from the query:

```
CREATE TABLE iris (
  sepal_length_cm real,
  sepal_width_cm real,
  petal_length_cm real,
  petal_width_cm real,
  species varchar(10)
);
INSERT INTO iris (
  sepal_length_cm,
  sepal_width_cm,
  petal_length_cm,
  petal_width_cm,
  species )
VALUES
  ( ... )
```

If the data is available via a separate query, you can use SELECT with INSERT. Say, for example, you want to copy the data from a memory catalog to an existing table in PostgreSQL:

```
INSERT INTO postgresql.flowers.iris
SELECT * FROM brain.default.iris;
```

If the table does not exist in the target catalog yet, you can use the CREATE TABLE AS SELECT syntax. This is commonly called a CTAS query:

```
CREATE TABLE postgresql.flowers.iris AS
SELECT * FROM brain.default.iris;
```

The SELECT statement can include conditions and any other supported features for the statement.

Table and Column Properties

Let's learn how the WITH clause is used by creating a table using the Hive connector from "Hive Connector for Distributed Storage Data Sources" on page 102 (see Table 8-1).

Table 8-1. A selection of table properties supported by the Hive connector

Property name	Property description
external_location	The filesystem location for an external Hive table; e.g., on S3 or Azure Blob Storage
format	The file storage format for the underlying data such as ORC, AVRO, PARQUET, etc.

Using the properties from Table 8-1, let's create a table in Hive with Trino that is identical to the way the table is created in Hive.

Let's start with this Hive syntax:

```
CREATE EXTERNAL TABLE page_views(
   view_time INT,
   user_id BIGINT,
   page_url STRING,
   view_date DATE,
   country STRING)
 STORED AS ORC
 LOCATION 's3://example-org/web/page_views/';
```

Compare this to using SQL in Trino:

```
CREATE TABLE datalake.web.page_views(
   view_time timestamp,
   user_id BIGINT,
   page_url VARCHAR,
   view_date DATE,
   country VARCHAR
)
WITH (
   format = 'ORC',
   external_location = 's3://example-org/web/page_views'
);
```

As you can see, the Hive DDL has extended the SQL standard. Trino, however, uses properties for the same purpose and therefore adheres to the SQL standard.

You can query the system metadata of Trino to list the configured table properties:

```
SELECT * FROM system.metadata.table_properties;
```

To list the configured column properties, you can run the following query:

```
SELECT * FROM system.metadata.column_properties;
```

Copying an Existing Table

You can create a new table by using an existing table as a template. The LIKE clause creates a table with the same column definition as an existing table. Table and column properties are not copied by default. Since the properties are important in Trino, we suggest copying them as well by using INCLUDING PROPERTIES in the syntax. This feature is useful when using Trino to perform a transformation of the data:

```
CREATE TABLE datalake.web.page_view_bucketed(
  comment VARCHAR,
  LIKE datalake.web.page_views INCLUDING PROPERTIES
)
WITH (
  bucketed_by = ARRAY['user_id'],
  bucket_count = 50
)
```

Use the SHOW statement to inspect the newly created table definition:

```
SHOW CREATE TABLE datalake.web.page_view_bucketed;
                    Create Table
----------------------------------------------
 CREATE TABLE datalake.web.page_view_bucketed (
    comment varchar,
    view_time timestamp,
    user_id bigint,
    page_url varchar,
    view_date date,
    country varchar
 )
 WITH (
    bucket_count = 50,
    bucketed_by = ARRAY['user_id'],
    format = 'ORC',
    partitioned_by = ARRAY['view_date','country'],
    sorted_by = ARRAY[]
 )
(1 row)
```

You can compare this to the original table you copied:

```
SHOW CREATE TABLE datalake.web2.page_views;
                    Create Table
-------------------------------------------------
 CREATE TABLE datalake.web.page_views (
    view_time timestamp,
    user_id bigint,
    page_url varchar,
    view_date date,
    country varchar
 )
 WITH (
    format = 'ORC',
    partitioned_by = ARRAY['view_date','country']
 )
(1 row)
```

Creating a New Table from Query Results

The CREATE TABLE AS SELECT (CTAS) statement can be used to create a new table that contains the results of a SELECT query. The column definitions for the table are created dynamically by looking at the result column data from the query. The statement can be used for creating temporary tables or as part of a process to create transformed tables:

```
CREATE TABLE [ IF NOT EXISTS ] table_name [ ( column_alias, ... ) ]
[ COMMENT table_comment ]
[ WITH ( property_name = expression [, ...] ) ]
AS query
[ WITH [ NO ] DATA ]
```

By default, the new table is populated with the result data from the query.

CTAS can be used for transforming tables and data. Essentially, you are using Trino for ETL workloads within one catalog or even between different catalogs, and therefore data sources, as discussed in "Extract, Transform, Load and Federated Queries" on page 139. For example, you can load unpartitioned data in TEXTFILE format into a new partitioned table with data in ORC format:

```
CREATE TABLE datalake.web.page_views_orc_part
WITH (
    format = 'ORC',
    partitioned_by = ARRAY['view_date','country']
)
AS
SELECT *
FROM datalake.web.page_view_text
```

The next example shows creating a table from the resulting sessionization query over the page_views table:

```
CREATE TABLE datalake.web.user_sessions
AS
SELECT user_id,
       view_time,
       sum(session_boundary)
         OVER (
           PARTITION BY user_id
           ORDER BY view_time) AS session_id
FROM (SELECT user_id,
             view_time,
             CASE
                WHEN to_unixtime(view_time) -
                     lag(to_unixtime(view_time), 1)
                       OVER(
                           PARTITION BY user_id
                           ORDER BY view_time) >= 30
             THEN 1
             ELSE 0
             END AS session_boundary
      FROM page_views) T
ORDER BY user_id,
         session_id
```

Occasionally, you need to create a copy of a table definition only. You can do this by using CTAS and adding a WITH NO DATA clause at the end of the statement.

Modifying a Table

The ALTER TABLE statement can perform actions such as renaming a table, adding a column, dropping a column, or renaming a column in a table:

```
ALTER TABLE name RENAME TO new_name

ALTER TABLE name ADD COLUMN column_name data_type
  [ COMMENT comment ] [ WITH ( property_name = expression [, ...] ) ]

ALTER TABLE name DROP COLUMN column_name

ALTER TABLE name RENAME COLUMN column_name TO new_column_name
```

It is important to note that, depending on the connector and authorization model for the connector, these operations may not be allowed when using the default behavior. For example, the Hive connector restricts these operations by default.

Deleting a Table

Using the DROP TABLE statement, you can delete a table:

```
DROP TABLE [ IF EXISTS ] table_name
```

Depending on the connector implementation, this may or may not drop the underlying data. You should refer to the connector documentation for further explanation.

In some cases, you just want to remove the data in a table, while leaving the table itself intact so new data can be added. Trino supports TRUNCATE TABLE for this purpose:

```
TRUNCATE TABLE table_name
```

For connectors that don't support TRUNCATE, you have to resort to using DROP TABLE and then CREATE TABLE.

Table Limitations from Connectors

So far in this chapter, we've gone over the various SQL statements Trino supports. However, it does not mean that every data source in Trino supports all statements and syntax possibilities or provides the same semantics.

The connector implementation and the capabilities and semantics of the underlying data source have a large impact on the possibilities.

If you try a statement or operation that is not supported by a particular connector, Trino returns an error. For example, the system schema and tables are used to expose information about the Trino system. It does not support table creation, since that simply does not make sense for internal system data tables. If you attempt to create a table anyway, you receive an error:

```
CREATE TABLE system.runtime.foo(a int);
Query failed: This connector does not support creating tables
```

Similar errors are displayed if you insert data with a connector that does not support write operations, create a view or materialized view with a connector that does not support views, and so on. Check the SQL support section in the documentation for each connector to learn details about the statements the connector supports.

Views

Views are virtual tables based on the result set of an SQL query. They are well supported in many RDBMSs. When it comes to Trino, however, the situation is more complex.

Trino treats views from an underlying data source like tables. This allows you to use views for some very useful purposes:

- Exposing data from multiple tables in an easier consumable view
- Restricting data available with views that have limited columns and/or rows
- Providing processed, transformed data conveniently

This functionality relies on the support for creating and managing those views in the connected data source. Using views automatically requires the underlying data source to take full ownership of the data in the view, and therefore the processing to create the view and keep it up to date. As a result, using views can enable you to push the processing of a query to the RDBMS in a few steps:

1. Discover a performance problem on an SQL query on table data running in Trino.
2. Troubleshoot the system by looking at the EXPLAIN plan of the execution.
3. Realize that a specific subquery causes a bottleneck.
4. Create a view that preprocesses the subquery.
5. Use that view in your SQL query, replacing a table.
6. Enjoy the performance benefits.

Trino also supports the creation of views in Trino itself. A view in Trino is just the SQL statement that defines the view and a name for the view. To be able to create and use views in Trino, you need a catalog that uses the Hive connector or any other connector that configures a Hive metastore service or similar metadata storage system. This is necessary since Trino itself does not have any integrated metadata storage. The SQL query that defines the data available in the view can access any catalog or even multiple catalogs. The view is created and used with the catalog that includes the metastore, even if the query that defines the view accesses a different catalog.

When a user queries the view, the definition is loaded from the metastore, and the SQL query that defines the view is run as if the user submitted the actual query. This allows the user to create much simpler queries, while at the same time accessing potentially numerous catalogs, schemas, tables, and specific columns, and hiding all the complexity of the query.

Materialized views are an even more powerful feature, as supported by the Iceberg connector. A *materialized view* is a view with cached data. Upon first creation, the SQL statement that defines the materialized views has to be run so that the data is fetched and stored in separate a table. Subsequent queries can then access the cached data directly, and are therefore potentially much faster to query. A side effect of any changes to the underlying data is that the materialized view has to be refreshed regularly.

Another special case is Hive views. These are views from a legacy Hive system that are written in the Hive query language. These Hive views are also stored in the Hive metastore. At a glance, the Hive query language looks very similar to SQL. It is incompatible, however, and differs enough so that Hive views cannot be directly parsed and executed as an SQL statement. However, Trino users are able to use these views with the Hive connector and the help of the built-in translation library Coral.

Overall, you can see that views can significantly improve the ease of accessing complex data and are a well-supported feature in Trino.

Session Information and Configuration

When using Trino, all configuration is maintained in a user-specific context called a *session*. This session contains key-value pairs that signify the configuration of numerous aspects used for the current user's interaction with Trino.

You can use SQL commands to interact with that information. For starters, you can just view the current configuration, and even use LIKE patterns to narrow the options you are interested in:

```
SHOW SESSION LIKE 'query%';
```

This query returns information about a number of properties, such as query_max_cpu_time, query_max_execution_time, query_max_planning_time, including the current value, the default value, the data type (`integer`, `boolean`, or `varchar`), and a brief description of the property.

The list of properties is long and includes many configuration options for Trino behavior, such as memory and CPU limits for queries, query planning algorithms, and cost-based optimizer usage.

As a user, you can change these properties, which affects the performance for the current user session. You can set specific options for specific queries or workloads or test them for global rollout into the main file-based Trino configuration in `con fig.properties` used by the cluster.

For example, you can activate the experimental algorithm to use colocated joins for query planning:

```
SET SESSION colocated_join = true;
SET SESSION
```

You can confirm that the setting worked:

```
SHOW SESSION LIKE 'colocated_join';
      Name      | Value | Default ...
----------------+-------+---------
 colocated_join | true  | false   ...
```

To undo the setting and get back to the default value, you can reset the session property:

```
RESET SESSION  colocated_join;
RESET SESSION
```

In addition to the global session properties, a number of catalog configuration properties can be modified for a specific user session. For example, the PostgreSQL connector supports the property `unsupported-type-handling`. It defaults to `IGNORE`, and data from columns with unsupported data types is therefore omitted.

This property is also available as a catalog session property named `unsuppor ted_type_handling`. Note that catalog session properties use a similar name that replaces dashes with underscores when compared to the catalog configuration property. You can use this property to change processing of columns for the specific `crm` catalog and session, and convert data to `VARCHAR` with the following query:

```
SET SESSION crm.unsupported_type_handling='CONVERT_TO_VARCHAR';
```

Now the data is no longer ignored but is available as a string in Trino queries, and you can use the various string, date, JSON, and other formatting-related properties to modify the data and even cast it into the desired Trino data type.

Data Types

Trino supports most of the data types described by the SQL standard, which are also supported by many relational databases. In this section, we discuss data type support in Trino.

Not all Trino connectors support all Trino data types. And Trino may not support all the types from the underlying data source. The way the data types are translated to and from the underlying data source and into Trino depends on the connector implementation. The underlying data sources may not support the same type, or the same type may be named differently. For example, the MySQL connector maps the Trino REAL type to a MySQL FLOAT.

In some cases, data types need to be converted. Some connectors convert an unsupported type into a Trino VARCHAR—basically, a string representation of the source data—or ignore reading the column entirely. Specific details are available in the type mapping section for each connector documentation and the source code.

Back to the long list of well-supported data types. Tables 8-2 through 8-6 describe the data types in Trino and provide example data where applicable.

Table 8-2. Boolean data type

Type	Description	Example
BOOLEAN	Boolean value of true or false	True

Table 8-3. Integer data type

Type	Description	Example
TINYINT	8-bit signed integer, minimum value of -2^7, maximum value of 2^{7-1}	42
SMALLINT	16-bit signed integer, minimum value of -2^{15}, maximum value of 2^{15-1}	42
INTEGER, INT	32-bit signed integer, minimum value of -2^{31}, maximum value of 2^{31-1}	42
BIGINT	64-bit signed integer, minimum value of -2^{63}, maximum value of 2^{63-1}	42

Table 8-4. Floating-point data types

Type	Description	Example
REAL	32-bit floating-point, follows the IEEE Standard 754 for Binary Floating-Point Arithmetic	2.71828
DOUBLE	64-bit floating-point, follows the IEEE Standard 754 for Binary Floating-Point Arithmetic	2.71828

Table 8-5. Fixed-precision data types

Type	Description	Example
DECIMAL	Fixed-precision decimal number	123456.7890

Table 8-6. String data types

Type	Description	Example
VARCHAR or VARCHAR(*n*)	Variable-length string of characters. There is an optional maximum length when defined as VARCHAR(*n*), where *n* is a positive integer representing the maximum number of characters.	"Hello World"
CHAR CHAR(*n*)	A fixed-length string of characters. There is an optional length when defined as CHAR(*n*), where *n* is a positive integer defining the length of the character. CHAR is equivalent to CHAR(1).	"Hello World "
VARBINARY	A variable length binary byte string.	VARBINARY

Unlike VARCHAR, CHAR always allocates *n* characters. Here are some characteristics and errors you should be aware of:

- If you are casting a character string with fewer than *n* characters, trailing spaces are added.

- If you are casting a character string with more than *n* characters, it is truncated without error.

- If you insert a VARCHAR or CHAR longer than defined in the column into a table, an error occurs.

- If you insert a CHAR that is shorter than as defined in the column into a table, the value is space padded to match the defined length.

- If you insert a VARCHAR that is shorter than as defined in the column into a table, the exact length of the string is stored. Leading and trailing spaces are included when comparing CHAR values.

The following examples highlight these behaviors:

```
SELECT length(cast('hello world' AS char(100)));
 _col0
 -----
   100
(1 row)

SELECT cast('hello world' AS char(15)) || '~';
      _col0
 ----------------
 hello world    ~
(1 row)

SELECT cast('hello world' AS char(5));
 _col0
 -------
 hello
(1 row)
```

```
SELECT length(cast('hello world' AS varchar(15)));
 _col0
 -------
     11
(1 row)

SELECT cast('hello world' AS varchar(15)) || '~';
     _col0
 --------------
 hello world~
(1 row)

SELECT cast('hello world' as char(15)) = cast('hello world' as char(14));
 _col0
 -------
 true
(1 row)

SELECT cast('hello world' as varchar(15)) = cast('hello world' as varchar(14));
 _col0
 -------
 true
(1 row)

USE brain.default;
CREATE TABLE varchars(col varchar(5));
CREATE TABLE

INSERT INTO varchars values('1234');
INSERT: 1 row

INSERT INTO varchars values('123456');
Query failed: Cannot truncate non-space characters when casting
from varchar(6) to varchar(5) on INSERT
```

Collection Data Types

As data becomes increasingly vast and complex, it is sometimes stored in more complex data types such as arrays and maps. Many RDBMS systems, and specifically also some NoSQL systems, support complex data types natively. Trino supports some of these collection data types, listed in Table 8-7. It also provides support for the UNNEST operation detailed in "Unnesting Complex Data Types" on page 194.

Table 8-7. Collection data types

Collection data type	Example
ARRAY	ARRAY['apples', 'oranges', 'pears']
MAP	MAP(ARRAY['a', 'b', 'c'], ARRAY[1, 2, 3])
ROW	ROW(1, 2, 3)

Temporal Data Types

Table 8-8 describes *temporal data types*, data types related to dates and time.

Table 8-8. Temporal data types

Type	Description	Example
DATE	A calendar date representing the year, month, and day.	DATE '1983-10-19'
TIME(P)	A time of day representing hour, minute, second, and P digits of precision for the fractional part of the seconds. A value of P=3 is equivalent to milliseconds, with up to picoseconds (P=12) supported. The type TIME is equivalent to TIME(3).	TIME '02:56:15.123'
TIME WITH TIMEZONE	A time of day representing hour, minute, second, and millisecond, including a time zone.	
TIMESTAMP(P)	A date and time with P digits of precision for the fractional part of the seconds. The type TIMESTAMP is equivalent to TIMESTAMP(3).	
TIMESTAMP WITH TIMEZONE	A date and time with a time zone.	
INTERVAL YEAR TO MONTH	An interval span of years and months.	INTERVAL '1-2' YEAR TO MONTH
INTERVAL DAY TO SECOND	An interval span of days, hours, minutes, seconds, and milliseconds.	INTERVAL '5' DAY to SECOND

In Trino, `TIMESTAMP` is represented as a Java `Instant` type representing the amount of time before or after the Java epoch. This should be transparent to the end user as values are parsed and displayed in a different format.

For types that do not include time-zone information, the values are parsed and displayed according to the Trino session time zone. For types that include the time-zone information, the values are parsed and displayed using the time zone.

String literals can be parsed by Trino into a `TIMESTAMP`, `TIMESTAMP WITH TIME ZONE`, `TIME`, `TIME WITH TIMEZONE`, or `DATE`. Tables 8-9 through 8-11 describe the formats accepted for parsing. If you want to use ISO 8601, you can use the `from _iso8601_timestamp` or `from_iso8601_date` functions.

> The precision support for time values below seconds is impacted by the data source, the connector, and the JVM running Trino. The default precision of three digits, equivalent to milliseconds, is widely supported. Higher precision such as nanoseconds or picoseconds is supported by the Trino engine, but for example, if the underlying file format in object storage, or the relational database used by the connector, does not support picosecond precision, Trino cannot use full precision in queries.

Table 8-9. Supported string literals for parsing to timestamp data types

TIMESTAMP	TIMESTAMP WITH TIMEZONE
yyyy-M-d	yyyy-M-d ZZZ
yyyy-M-d H:m	yyyy-M-d H:m ZZZ
yyyy-M-d H:m:s	yyyy-M-d H:m:s ZZZ
yyyy-M-d H:m:s.SSS	yyyy-M-d H:m:s.SSS ZZZ

Table 8-10. Supported string literals for parsing to time data types

TIME	TIMESTAMP WITH TIMEZONE
H:m	H:m ZZZ
H:m:s	H:m:s ZZZ
H:m:s.SSS	H:m:s.SSS ZZZ

Table 8-11. Supported string literals for parsing to date data type

DATE
YYYY-MM-DD

When printing the output for TIMESTAMP, TIMESTAMP WITH TIMEZONE, TIME, TIME WITH TIMEZONE, or DATE, Trino uses the output formats in Table 8-12. If you want to output in strict ISO 8601 format, you can use the to_iso8601 function.

Table 8-12. Temporal output formats

Data type	Format
TIMESTAMP	yyyy-MM-dd HH:mm:ss.SSS ZZZ
TIMESTAMP WITH TIMEZONE	yyyy-MM-dd HH:mm:ss.SSS ZZZ
TIME	yyyy-MM-dd HH:mm:ss.SSS ZZZ
TIME WITH TIMEZONE	yyyy-MM-dd HH:mm:ss.SSS ZZZ
DATE	YYYY-MM-DD

Time zones

The time zone adds important additional temporal information. Trino supports TIME WITH TIMEZONE, but it is often best to use time zones with a DATE or TIMESTAMP. This enables accounting of daylight saving time with the DATE format. Time zones must be expressed as the numeric UTC offset value:

- +08:00
- -10:00

Let's look at some examples:

```
SELECT TIME '02:56:15' AS utc;
   utc
 ---------
 02:56:15
(1 row)

SELECT TIME '02:56:15' AT TIME ZONE '+08:00' AS perth_time;
   perth_time
 ---------------
 17:56:15+08:00

SELECT TIME '02:56:15' AT TIME ZONE '-08:00' AS sf_time;
    sf_time
 ---------------
 01:56:15-08:00
(1 row)

SELECT TIMESTAMP '1983-10-19 07:30:05.123456';
           _col0
 ---------------------------
 1983-10-19 07:30:05.123456
(1 row)

SELECT TIMESTAMP '1983-10-19 17:30:05.123456' AT TIME ZONE '-08:00';
           _col0
 ---------------------------
 1983-10-19 06:30:05.123456 -08:00
(1 row)
```

Intervals

The data type INTERVAL can be either YEAR TO MONTH or DAY TO SECOND, as shown in Tables 8-13 and 8-14.

Table 8-13. Years-to-months intervals

YEAR TO MONTH
INTERVAL '<years>-<months>' YEAR TO MONTH
INTERVAL '<years>' YEAR TO MONTH
INTERVAL '<years>' YEAR
INTERVAL '<months>' MONTH

Table 8-14. Days-to-seconds intervals

DAY TO SECOND
INTERVAL '<days> <time>' DAY TO SECOND
INTERVAL '<days>' DAY TO SECOND
INTERVAL '<days>' DAY
INTERVAL '<hours>' HOUR
INTERVAL '<minutes>' MINUTE
INTERVAL '<seconds>' SECOND

The following examples highlight some behaviors we've described:

```
SELECT INTERVAL '1-2' YEAR TO MONTH;
 _col0
 ------
 1-2
(1 row)

SELECT INTERVAL '4' MONTH;
 _col0
 -------
 0-4
(1 row)

SELECT INTERVAL '4-1' DAY TO SECOND;
Query xyz failed: '4-1' is not a valid interval literal

SELECT INTERVAL '4' DAY TO SECOND;
     _col0
 ---------------
 4 00:00:00.000
(1 row)

SELECT INTERVAL '4 01:03:05.44' DAY TO SECOND;
     _col0
 ---------------
 4 01:03:05.440
(1 row)

SELECT INTERVAL '05.44' SECOND;
     _col0
 ---------------
 0 00:00:05.440
(1 row)
```

Type Casting

Sometimes it is necessary to explicitly change a value or literal to a different data type. This is called *type casting* and is performed by the CAST function:

```
CAST(value AS type)
```

Now let's say you need to compare the column `view_date` with the data type DATE to the date 2019-01-01, which is a literal string:

```
SELECT *
FROM datalake.web.page_views
WHERE view_date > '2019-01-01';
Query failed: line 1:42: '>' cannot be applied to date, varchar(10)
```

This query fails because Trino does not have a greater than (>) comparison operator that knows how to compare a date and a string literal. However, it has a comparison function that knows how to compare two dates. Therefore, we need to use the CAST function to coerce one of the types. In this example, it makes the most sense to convert the string to a date:

```
SELECT *
FROM datalake.web.page_views
WHERE view_date > CAST('2019-01-01' as DATE);
        view_time        | user_id | page_url | view_data  | country
-------------------------+---------+----------+------------+---------
 2019-01-26 20:40:15.477 |       2 | http://  | 2019-01-26 | US
 2019-01-26 20:41:01.243 |       3 | http://  | 2019-01-26 | US
...
```

Trino provides another conversion function, `try_cast`. It attempts to perform the type coercion, but unlike CAST, which returns an error if the cast fails, `try_cast` returns a `null` value. This can be useful when an error is not necessary:

```
try_cast(value AS type)
```

Let's take, for example, coercing a character literal to a number type:

```
SELECT cast('1' AS integer);
 _col0
-------
     1
(1 row)

SELECT cast('a' as integer);
Query failed: Cannot cast 'a' to INT

SELECT try_cast('a' as integer);
 _col0
------
 NULL
(1 row)
```

SELECT Statement Basics

The SELECT statement is critical, as it allows you to return data from one or multiple tables in a table format, at minimum collapsing down to one row or potentially just one value.

SELECT queries with Trino have the additional complexity to include tables from different catalogs and schemas—completely different data sources. You learned about this in "Query Federation in Trino" on page 133.

Now you are going to dive into the details and learn about all the power available. Let's start with a syntax overview:

```
[ WITH with_query [, ...] ]
SELECT [ ALL | DISTINCT ] select_expr [, ...]
[ FROM from_item [, ...] ]
[ WHERE condition ]
[ GROUP BY [ ALL | DISTINCT ] grouping_element [, ...] ]
[ HAVING condition]
[ { UNION | INTERSECT | EXCEPT } [ ALL | DISTINCT ] select ]
[ ORDER BY expression [ ASC | DESC ] [, ...] ]
[ LIMIT [ count | ALL ] ]
```

select_expr represents the data returned by the query in the form of a table column, a derived table column, a constant, or a general expression in zero, one, or more rows. A general expression can include functions, operators, columns, and constants. You can run a query with just a SELECT select_expr, for testing, but its usefulness beyond that is limited:

```
SELECT 1, 1+1, upper('lower');
 _col0 | _col1 | _col2
-------+-------+------
     1 |     2 | LOWER
(1 row)
```

SELECT select_expr [, ...] FROM from_item is the most basic form of the query. It allows you to retrieve all data from an underlying table or only a selection of columns. It also allows you to calculate expressions on the underlying data.

Say we have two tables, also known as relations, nation and customer. The examples are taken from the TPC-H, discussed in "Trino TPC-H and TPC-DS Connectors" on page 100. For brevity, the example tables were truncated to just a few rows and columns each. We use this data throughout the chapter over multiple examples of select queries.

You can return select columns and data from the `nation` table in the `sf1` schema:

```
SELECT nationkey, name, regionkey
FROM tpch.sf1.nation;
 nationkey |     name     | regionkey
-----------+--------------+-----------
         0 | ALGERIA      |         0
         1 | ARGENTINA    |         1
         2 | BRAZIL       |         1
         3 | CANADA       |         1
         4 | EGYPT        |         4
         5 | ETHIOPIA     |         0
...
```

And now some sample data from the `customer` table:

```
SELECT custkey, nationkey, phone, acctbal, mktsegment
FROM tpch.tiny.customer;
 custkey | nationkey |      phone      | acctbal | mktsegment
---------+-----------+----------------+---------+-----------
     751 |         0 | 10-658-550-2257 | 2130.98 | FURNITURE
     752 |         8 | 18-924-993-6038 | 8363.66 | MACHINERY
     753 |        17 | 27-817-126-3646 | 8114.44 | HOUSEHOLD
     754 |         0 | 10-646-595-5871 | -566.86 | BUILDING
     755 |        16 | 26-395-247-2207 | 7631.94 | HOUSEHOLD
...
```

Beyond just returning select data, we can transform data with functions and return the result:

```
SELECT acctbal, round(acctbal) FROM tpch.sf1.customer;
 acctbal | _col1
---------+--------
 7470.96 | 7471.0
 8462.17 | 8462.0
 2757.45 | 2757.0
 -588.38 | -588.0
 9091.82 | 9092.0
...
```

WHERE Clause

The WHERE clause is used as a filter in SELECT queries. It consists of a condition that evaluates to TRUE, FALSE, or UNKNOWN. During query execution, the condition is evaluated for each row. If the evaluation does not equal TRUE, the row is skipped and omitted from the result set. Otherwise, the row is emitted and sent back as part of the results to the user or for further processing.

The WHERE clause condition consists of one or more Boolean expressions connected by conjunctive ANDs and disjunctive ORs:

```
SELECT custkey, acctbal
FROM tpch.sf1.customer WHERE acctbal < 0;
 custkey | acctbal
---------+---------
   75016 | -735.89
   75027 | -399.78
   75028 | -222.92
   75034 | -679.38
   75037 | -660.07
...

SELECT custkey, acctbal FROM tpch.sf1.customer
WHERE acctbal > 0 AND acctbal < 500;
 custkey | acctbal
---------+---------
   75011 |  165.71
   75012 |   41.65
   75021 |   176.2
   75022 |  348.24
   75026 |   78.64
...
```

The WHERE clause condition is important because it is used for several query optimizations. In "Query Planning" on page 57, you can learn more about query planning
and optimizations. When querying multiple tables, you can connect them via conditions in the WHERE clause. Trino uses this information to determine efficient query
execution plans.

GROUP BY and HAVING Clauses

The GROUP BY and HAVING clauses are commonly used in analytical queries. GROUP BY
is used to combine rows of the same value into a single row:

```
SELECT mktsegment
FROM tpch.sf1.customer
GROUP BY mktsegment;
 mktsegment
-----------
 MACHINERY
 AUTOMOBILE
 HOUSEHOLD
 BUILDING
 FURNITURE
(5 rows)
```

For analytical queries in Trino, GROUP BY is often combined with aggregation functions. These functions are computed from the data in the rows that make up a single
group. The following query calculates the total account balance of all customers,
breaking it down by market segment:

```
SELECT mktsegment, round(sum(acctbal) / 1000000, 3) AS acctbal_millions
FROM tpch.sf1.customer
GROUP BY mktsegment;
 mktsegment | acctbal_millions
------------+------------------
 MACHINERY  |          134.439
 AUTOMOBILE |          133.867
 BUILDING   |          135.889
 FURNITURE  |          134.259
 HOUSEHOLD  |          135.873
```

Aggregation functions can also be used, even if the GROUP BY clause is not used. In this case, the entire relation serves as input to the aggregation function, so we can calculate the overall account balance:

```
SELECT round(sum(acctbal) / 1000000, 3) AS acctbal_millions
FROM tpch.sf1.customer;
 acctbal_millions
------------------
          674.327
```

The HAVING clause is similar to the WHERE clause. It is evaluated for each row, and rows are emitted only if the condition evaluates to TRUE. The HAVING clause is evaluated after GROUP BY and operated on the grouped rows. The WHERE clause is evaluated before GROUP BY and evaluated on the individual rows.

Here is the full query:

```
SELECT mktsegment,
       round(sum(acctbal), 1) AS acctbal_per_mktsegment
FROM tpch.tiny.customer
GROUP BY mktsegment;
 mktsegment | acctbal_per_mktsegment
------------+------------------------
 BUILDING   |              1444587.8
 HOUSEHOLD  |              1279340.7
 AUTOMOBILE |              1395695.7
 FURNITURE  |              1265282.8
 MACHINERY  |              1296958.6
(5 rows)
```

And here are the filtered results using the condition on grouped data:

```
SELECT mktsegment,
       round(sum(acctbal), 1) AS acctbal_per_mktsegment
FROM tpch.tiny.customer
GROUP BY mktsegment
HAVING round(sum(acctbal), 1) > 1300000;
 mktsegment | acctbal_per_mktsegment
------------+------------------------
 AUTOMOBILE |              1395695.7
 BUILDING   |              1444587.8
(2 rows)
```

ORDER BY and LIMIT Clauses

The `ORDER BY` clause contains expressions that are used to order the results. The clause, which can contain multiple expressions, is evaluated from left to right. Multiple expressions are typically used to break ties when the left expression evaluates to the same value for more than one row. The expressions can indicate the sort order to be ascending (e.g., A–Z, 1–100) or descending (e.g., Z–A, 100–1).

The `LIMIT` clause is used to return only the specified number of rows. Together with the `ORDER BY` clause, `LIMIT` can be used to find the first *N* results of an ordered set:

```
SELECT mktsegment,
       round(sum(acctbal), 2) AS acctbal_per_mktsegment
FROM tpch.sf1.customer
GROUP BY mktsegment
HAVING sum(acctbal) > 0
ORDER BY acctbal_per_mktsegment DESC
LIMIT 3;
 mktsegment | acctbal_per_mktsegment
------------+-----------------------
 BUILDING   |         1.3588862194E8
 HOUSEHOLD  |         1.3587334117E8
 MACHINERY  |         1.3443886167E8
(3 rows)
```

Often Trino is able to optimize executing `ORDER BY` and `LIMIT` as a combined step rather than separately.

`LIMIT` can be used without the `ORDER BY` clause, but most often they are used together. The reason is that the SQL standard, and therefore also Trino, does not guarantee any order of the results. This means that using `LIMIT` without an `ORDER BY` clause can return different nondeterministic results with each run of the same query. This becomes more apparent in a distributed system such as Trino.

JOIN Statements

SQL allows you to combine data from different tables by using `JOIN` statements. Trino supports the SQL standard joins such as `INNER JOIN`, `LEFT OUTER JOIN`, `RIGHT OUTER JOIN`, `FULL OUTER JOIN`, and `CROSS JOIN`. A full exploration of `JOIN` statements is beyond the scope of this book but is covered in many others.

Let's focus on a few examples and explore specific details relevant to Trino:

```
SELECT custkey, mktsegment, nation.name AS nation
FROM tpch.tiny.nation JOIN tpch.tiny.customer
ON nation.nationkey = customer.nationkey;
 custkey | mktsegment |     nation
---------+------------+----------------
     745 | FURNITURE  | CHINA
```

```
 746 | MACHINERY  | SAUDI ARABIA
 747 | FURNITURE  | INDIA
 748 | AUTOMOBILE | UNITED KINGDOM
 749 | MACHINERY  | UNITED STATES
...
```

Trino also has an implicit cross join: a list of tables is separated by commas, and the join is defined with conditions in the WHERE clause:

```
SELECT custkey, mktsegment, nation.name AS nation
FROM tpch.tiny.nation, tpch.tiny.customer
WHERE nation.nationkey = customer.nationkey;
 custkey | mktsegment |     nation
---------+------------+----------------
    1210 | AUTOMOBILE | MOZAMBIQUE
    1211 | HOUSEHOLD  | CHINA
    1212 | HOUSEHOLD  | RUSSIA
    1213 | HOUSEHOLD  | GERMANY
    1214 | BUILDING   | EGYPT
...
```

Joins can be one of the most expensive operations of query processing. When multiple joins are in a query, the joins can be processed by different permutations. The Q09 query from the TPC-H benchmark is a good example of such a complex query:

```
SELECT
  nation,
  o_year,
  sum(amount) AS sum_profit
FROM (
      SELECT
        N.name AS nation,
        extract(YEAR FROM o.orderdate) AS o_year,
        l.extendedprice * (1 - l.discount) - ps.supplycost * l.quantity
            AS amount
      FROM
        part AS p,
        supplier AS s,
        lineitem AS l,
        partsupp AS ps,
        orders AS o,
        nation AS n
      WHERE
        s.suppkey = l.suppkey
        AND ps.suppkey = l.suppkey
        AND ps.partkey = l.partkey
        AND p.partkey = l.partkey
        AND o.orderkey = l.orderkey
        AND s.nationkey = n.nationkey
        AND p.name LIKE '%green%'
    ) AS profit
GROUP BY
  nation,
```

```
    o_year
ORDER BY
  nation,
  o_year DESC;
```

UNION, INTERSECT, and EXCEPT Clauses

UNION, INTERSECT, and EXCEPT are known as *set operations* in SQL. They are used to combine the data from multiple SQL statements into a single result.

While you can use joins and conditions to get the same semantics, it is often easier to use set operations. Trino executes them more efficiently than equivalent SQL.

As you learn the semantics of the set operations, it's usually easier to start with basic integers. You can start with UNION, which combines all values and removes duplicates:

```
SELECT * FROM (VALUES 1, 2)
UNION
SELECT * FROM (VALUES 2, 3);
 _col0
 ------
     2
     3
     1
(3 rows)
```

UNION ALL leaves any duplicates in place:

```
SELECT * FROM (VALUES 1, 2)
UNION ALL
SELECT * FROM (VALUES 2, 3);
 _col0
 -----
     1
     2
     2
     3
(4 rows)
```

INTERSECT returns all elements found in both queries as a result:

```
SELECT * FROM (VALUES 1, 2)
INTERSECT
SELECT * FROM (VALUES 2, 3);
 _col0
 ------
     2
(1 row)
```

EXCEPT returns elements from the first query after removing all elements found in the second query:

```
SELECT * FROM (VALUES 1, 2)
EXCEPT
SELECT * FROM (VALUES 2, 3);
 _col0
 ------
     1
(1 row)
```

Each set operator supports use of an optional qualifier, ALL or DISTINCT. The DIS
TINCT keyword is the default and need not be specified. The ALL keyword is used as a
way to preserve duplicates.

Grouping Operations

You learned about the basic GROUP BY and aggregations. Trino also supports advanced
grouping operations from the SQL standard. Using GROUPING SETS, CUBE, and
ROLLUP, users can perform aggregations on multiple sets in a single query.

Grouping sets allows you to group multiple lists of columns in the same query. For
example, let's say we want to group on (state, city, street), (state, city),
and (state). Without grouping sets, you have to run each group in its own separate
query and then combine the results. With grouping sets, Trino computes the grouping for each set. The resulting schema is the union of the columns across the sets. For
columns that are not part of a group, a null value is added.

ROLLUP and CUBE can be expressed using GROUPING SETS and are shorthand. ROLLUP
is used to generate group sets based on a hierarchy. For example ROLLUP(a, b, c)
generates grouping sets (a, b, c), (a, b), (a), (). The CUBE operation generates
all possible combinations of the grouping. For example. CUBE (a, b, c) generates
group sets (a, b, c), (a, b), (a, c), (b, c), (a), (b), (c), ().

For example, say you want to compute the total of account balances per market
segment and compute the total account balances for all market segments:

```
SELECT mktsegment,
  round(sum(acctbal), 2) AS total_acctbal,
  GROUPING(mktsegment) AS id
FROM tpch.tiny.customer
GROUP BY ROLLUP (mktsegment)
ORDER BY id, total_acctbal;
 mktsegment | total_acctbal | id
------------+---------------+----
 FURNITURE  |     1265282.8 |  0
 HOUSEHOLD  |    1279340.66 |  0
 MACHINERY  |    1296958.61 |  0
 AUTOMOBILE |    1395695.72 |  0
 BUILDING   |     1444587.8 |  0
 NULL       |    6681865.59 |  1
(6 rows)
```

With ROLLUP, you can compute aggregations on different groups. In this example, the first five rows represent the total of account balances per market segment. The last row represents the total of all account balances. Because there is no group for mktsegment, that is left as NULL. The GROUPING function is used to identify which rows belong to which groups.

Without ROLLUP, you have to run this as two separate queries and combine them. In this example, we can use UNION, which helps you to understand conceptually what ROLLUP is doing:

```
SELECT mktsegment,
       round(sum(acctbal), 2) AS total_acctbal,
       0 AS id
FROM tpch.tiny.customer
GROUP BY mktsegment
UNION
SELECT NULL, round(sum(acctbal), 2), 1
FROM tpch.tiny.customer
ORDER BY id, total_acctbal;
mktsegment | total_acctbal | id
-----------+---------------+----
 FURNITURE  |     1265282.8 |  0
 HOUSEHOLD  |    1279340.66 |  0
 MACHINERY  |    1296958.61 |  0
 AUTOMOBILE |    1395695.72 |  0
 BUILDING   |     1444587.8 |  0
 NULL       |    6681865.59 |  1
(6 rows)
```

WITH Clause

The WITH clause is used to define an inline view within a single query. This is often used to make a query more readable because the query may need to include the same nested query multiple times.

In this query, let's find the market segments whose total account balances are greater than the average of the market segments:

```
SELECT mktsegment,
       total_per_mktsegment,
       average
FROM
  (
    SELECT mktsegment,
       round(sum(acctbal)) AS total_per_mktsegment
    FROM tpch.tiny.customer
    GROUP BY 1
  ),
  (
    SELECT round(avg(total_per_mktsegment)) AS average
```

```
FROM
  (
    SELECT mktsegment,
       sum(acctbal) AS total_per_mktsegment
    FROM tpch.tiny.customer
    GROUP BY 1
  )
)
WHERE total_per_mktsegment > average;
 mktsegment | total_per_mktsegment |  average
------------+----------------------+----------
 BUILDING   |            1444588.0 | 1336373.0
 AUTOMOBILE |            1395696.0 | 1336373.0
(2 rows)
```

As you can see, this query is a bit complex. Using the WITH clause, we can simplify it as follows:

```
WITH
total AS (
  SELECT mktsegment,
     round(sum(acctbal)) AS total_per_mktsegment
  FROM tpch.tiny.customer
  GROUP BY 1
),
average AS (
  SELECT round(avg(total_per_mktsegment)) AS average
  FROM total
)
SELECT mktsegment,
  total_per_mktsegment,
  average
FROM total,
  average
WHERE total_per_mktsegment > average;
 mktsegment | total_per_mktsegment |  average
------------+----------------------+----------
 AUTOMOBILE |            1395696.0 | 1336373.0
 BUILDING   |            1444588.0 | 1336373.0
(2 rows)
```

In this example, the second inline view is referring to the first. You can see that the WITH inline view is executed twice. Currently, Trino does not materialize the results to share across multiple executions. In fact, it would have to be a cost-based decision on the complexity of the query, as it could be more efficient to execute a query multiple times than to store and retrieve the results.

Subqueries

Trino supports many common uses of subqueries. A *subquery* is an expression that serves as input into a higher-level expression. In SQL, subqueries can be placed into three categories:

- Scalar subqueries
- ANY/SOME
- ALL

Each category has two types, uncorrelated and correlated. A *correlated subquery* is one that references other columns from outside the subquery.

Scalar Subquery

A *scalar subquery* is one that returns a single value—one row and one column:

```
SELECT regionkey, name
FROM tpch.tiny.nation
WHERE regionkey =
  (SELECT regionkey FROM tpch.tiny.region WHERE name = 'AMERICA');
 regionkey |     name
-----------+---------------
         1 | ARGENTINA
         1 | BRAZIL
         1 | CANADA
         1 | PERU
         1 | UNITED STATES
(5 rows)
```

In this scalar example, the result from the subquery is 1. The WHERE condition essentially becomes regionkey = 1 and is evaluated for each row. Logically, the subquery is evaluated for every row in the nation table, for example, one hundred times for one hundred rows. However Trino is smart enough to evaluate the subquery only once and to use the static value all other times.

EXISTS Subquery

An EXISTS subquery evaluates to true if there are any rows. These queries are commonly used as correlated subqueries. While an uncorrelated subquery is possible for EXISTS, it is not as practical because anything that returns a single row evaluates to true:

```
SELECT
  EXISTS(
    SELECT t.*
    FROM tpch.tiny.region AS r
```

```
        WHERE r.name = 'ASIA'
        AND t.name = 'CHINA'),
    t.name
FROM tpch.tiny.nation AS t;
```

Another common form of EXISTS subqueries is NOT EXISTS. However, this is simply applying the negation to the result of the EXISTS subquery.

Quantified Subquery

ANY subqueries take the form expression operator quantifier (subquery). Valid operator values are <, >, <=, >=, =, or <>. The token SOME may be used in place of ANY. The most familiar form of this type of query is *expression* IN *subquery*, which is equivalent to *expression* = ANY *subquery*.

```
SELECT name
FROM nation
WHERE regionkey = ANY (SELECT regionkey FROM region)
```

This query is equivalent to the following, where IN is the shorthand form:

```
SELECT name
FROM nation
WHERE regionkey IN (SELECT regionkey FROM region)
```

The subquery must return exactly one column. Today, Trino does not support row expression subqueries comparing more than one column. Semantically, for a given row of the outer query, the subquery is evaluated and the expression is compared to each result row of the subquery. If at least one of these comparisons evaluates to TRUE, the result of the ANY subquery condition is TRUE. The result is FALSE if none of the comparisons evaluates to TRUE. This is repeated for each row of the outer query.

You should be aware of some nuances. If the expression is NULL, the result of the IN expression is NULL. Additionally, if no comparisons evaluate to TRUE, but there is a NULL value in the subquery, the IN expression evaluates to NULL. In most cases, this remains unnoticed because a result of FALSE or NULL filters out the row. However, if this IN expression is to serve as input to a surrounding expression that is sensitive to NULL values (e.g., surrounded with NOT), then it would matter.

ALL subqueries work similarly to ANY. For a given row of the outer query, the subquery is evaluated and the expression is compared to each result row of the subquery. If all of the comparisons evaluate to TRUE, the result of ALL is TRUE. If there is at least one FALSE evaluation, the result of ALL is FALSE.

As with ANY, some nuances are not obvious at first. When the subquery is empty and returns no rows, ALL evaluates to TRUE. If none of the comparisons returns FALSE and at least one comparison returns NULL, the result of ALL is NULL. The most familiar form of ALL is <> ALL, which is equivalent to NOT IN.

Deleting Data from a Table

The DELETE statement can delete rows of data from a table. The statement provides an optional WHERE clause to restrict which rows are deleted. Without a WHERE clause, all the data is deleted from the table:

```
DELETE FROM table_name [ WHERE condition ]
```

Various connectors have limited or no support for deletion. For example, deletion is not supported by the Kafka connector. The Hive connector supports deletion only if a WHERE clause specifies a partition key that can be used to delete entire partitions:

```
DELETE FROM datalake.web.page_views
WHERE view_date = DATE '2019-01-14' AND country = 'US'
```

Conclusion

Exciting what you can do with SQL in Trino, isn't it? With the knowledge from this chapter, you can already craft very complex queries and achieve some pretty complex analysis of any data exposed to Trino.

Of course, there is more. So read on in Chapter 9 to learn about functions, operators, and other features for querying your data with Trino.

Advanced SQL

While you can certainly achieve a lot with the power of SQL statements, as covered in Chapter 8, you are really only scratching the surface of what you can do with more complex processing with queries in Trino. In this chapter, you are going to cover more advanced features such as functions, operators, and other features.

Functions and Operators Introduction

So far, you've learned about the basics, including catalogs, schemas, tables, data types, and various SQL statements. This knowledge is useful when querying data from one or more tables in one or more catalogs in Trino. In the examples, we focused mostly on writing queries by using data from the different attributes, or columns, in a table.

SQL functions and operators exist to enable more complex and comprehensive SQL queries. In this chapter, we focus on the functions and operators supported by Trino and provide examples of their use.

Functions and operators in SQL are internally equivalent. Functions generally use the syntax form *function_name(function_arg1, ...)* and operators use a different syntax, similar to operators in programming languages and mathematics. Operators are a syntactic abbreviation and improvement for commonly used functions. An example of an equivalent operator and function are the || operator and the `concat()` function. Both are used to concatenate strings.

Operators in SQL and in Trino come in two general types:

Binary operators
> A binary operator takes the input of two operands to produce a single value result. The operator itself defines what the operand data types must be and what the result data type is. A binary operator is written in the format *operand* `operator operand`.

Unary operators
> A unary operator takes the input of a single operator and produces a single value result. As with binary operators, the operator requires what the operand data type must be and what the result data type must be. A unary operator is written in the format `operator operand`.

With both binary and unary operators, the operand input may be the result of an operator itself creating a tree of operators. For example, in 2 × 2 × 2, the result of the first operator 2 × 2 is input to the second multiplier operator.

In the following sections of this chapter, you learn details about numerous functions and operators supported by Trino.

Scalar Functions and Operators

A *scalar function* in SQL is invoked within an SQL statement. Abstractly, it takes one or more single-value input parameters, performs an operation based on the input, and then produces a single-value result. As a concrete example, consider the SQL function in `power(x, p)`. This power function returns *x* raised to the power of *p*:

```
SELECT power(2, 3);
 _col0
-------
   8.0
(1 row)
```

Of course, you could simply use the multiplication operators to achieve the same goal. Using our example, 2 × 2 × 2 also produces the value 8. But using functions allows the logic to be encapsulated, making it easier to reuse in SQL. Moreover, we achieve other benefits such as reducing room for mistakes and optimizing execution of the function.

Scalar functions can be used anywhere in an SQL statement where an expression can be used, provided it is semantically correct. For example, you can write an SQL query `SELECT * FROM page_views WHERE power(2, 3)`. This passes the syntactic checks but fails during semantic analysis because the return type of the `power` function is a double value and not the required Boolean. Writing the SQL query as `SELECT * FROM` `page_views WHERE power(2, 3) = 8` works, even though it may not be a useful query.

Trino contains a set of built-in functions and operators that can be used immediately. In this section, you learn about common uses and highlights of some interesting ones. We do not fully enumerate every function and operator, since this chapter is not meant to be a reference. After learning the basics here, you can refer to the Trino documentation to learn more.

 Trino also supports user-defined functions (UDFs), which allow you to write your own function implementations in Java and deploy them in Trino to execute within SQL queries. This is, however, beyond the scope of this book.

Boolean Operators

Boolean operators are binary operators and used in SQL to compare the values of two operands producing a Boolean result of TRUE, FALSE, or NULL. These are most commonly used on conditional clauses such as WHERE, HAVING, or ON, and are listed in Table 9-1. They can be used anywhere in a query that an expression can be used.

Table 9-1. Boolean operators

Operator	Description
<	Less than
<=	Less than or equal
>	Greater than
>=	Greater than or equal
=	Equal
<>	Not equal
!=	Not equal

 The syntax != is not part of the SQL standard but is commonly used in various programming languages. It is implemented in other popular databases and therefore also provided in Trino for convenience.

Here are some example usages of Boolean operators:

What are the best days of the week to fly out of Boston in the month of February?

```
SELECT dayofweek, avg(depdelayminutes) AS delay
FROM flights_orc
WHERE month = 2 AND origincityname LIKE '%Boston%'
GROUP BY dayofweek
ORDER BY dayofweek;
```

```
 dayofweek |        delay
-----------+--------------------
         1 | 10.613156692553677
         2 |  9.97405624214174
         3 |  9.548045977011494
         4 | 11.822725778003647
         5 | 15.875475113122173
         6 | 11.184173669467787
         7 | 10.788121285791464
(7 rows)
```

What is the average delay per carrier per year between the years 2010 and 2014?

```
SELECT avg(arrdelayminutes) AS avg_arrival_delay, carrier
FROM flights_orc
WHERE year > 2010 AND year < 2014
GROUP BY carrier, year;
```

```
 avg_arrival_delay  | carrier
--------------------+---------
 11.755326255888736 | 9E
 12.557365851045104 | AA
  13.39056266711295 | AA
 13.302276406082575 | AA
 6.4657695873247745 | AS
  7.048865559750841 | AS
  6.907012760530203 | AS
 17.008730526574663 | B6
  13.28933909176506 | B6
 16.242635221309246 | B6
 ...
```

Logical Operators

Three more operators used in SQL and in Trino are the *logical operators* AND, OR, and NOT. The operators AND and OR are referred to as *binary operators* since they take two parameters as input. NOT is a unary operator that takes a single parameter as input.

These logical operators return a single Boolean variable of TRUE, FALSE, or NULL (UNKNOWN), based on Boolean type input data. Typically, these operators are used together to form a conditional clause, just like the Boolean operators.

The concept of these three operators is similar to programming languages but with different semantics because of the way the NULL value affects the semantics. For example, NULL AND NULL does not equate to TRUE but rather to NULL. If you think of NULL as the absence of a value, this becomes easier to comprehend. Table 9-2 displays how the operators handle the three values.

Table 9-2. Logical operator results for AND and OR

x	y	x AND y	x OR y
TRUE	TRUE	TRUE	TRUE
TRUE	FALSE	FALSE	TRUE
TRUE	NULL	NULL	TRUE
FALSE	TRUE	FALSE	TRUE
FALSE	FALSE	FALSE	FALSE
FALSE	NULL	FALSE	NULL
NULL	TRUE	NULL	TRUE
NULL	FALSE	FALSE	NULL
NULL	NULL	NULL	NULL

When it comes to the NOT operator, just keep in mind that NOT NULL evaluates to NULL, not TRUE or FALSE.

Range Selection with the BETWEEN Statement

The *BETWEEN statement* can be considered a special case of a binary operator and defines a range. It's really two comparisons connected by an AND. The data types of the selected field and the two range values have to be identical. NOT BETWEEN is simply the negation. The following two queries are equivalent, as you can see from the result:

```
SELECT count(*) FROM flights_orc WHERE year BETWEEN 2010 AND 2012;
  _col0
----------
 18632160
(1 row)

SELECT count(*) FROM flights_orc WHERE year >= 2010 AND year <= 2012;
  _col0
----------
 18632160
(1 row)
```

Value Detection with IS (NOT) NULL

The IS NULL statement allows you to detect if a value exists. It can be considered a special type of unary operator. IS NOT NULL is the negation. You may want to count some rows but not want to count rows without values. Perhaps the data is incomplete or does not make sense.

For example, to calculate the average delay of airplanes by year, you have to ensure that you are counting only flights that actually happened. This is reflected by the fact that airtime has a value, which this query takes into account:

```
SELECT avg(DepDelayMinutes) AS delay, year
FROM flights_orc
WHERE airtime IS NOT NULL and year >= 2015
GROUP BY year
ORDER BY year desc;
       delay         | year
---------------------+------
 12.041834908176538  | 2019
 13.178923805354275  | 2018
 12.373612267166829  | 2017
  10.51195619395339  | 2016
 11.047527214544516  | 2015
(5 rows)
```

Mathematical Functions and Operators

Mathematical functions and operators open up a wide range of use cases and are critically important for many of them. Table 9-3 lists mathematical operators, and Table 9-4 lists mathematical functions.

Table 9-3. Mathematical operators

Operator	Description	Example
+	Addition	SELECT 1 + 1
-	Subtraction	SELECT 2 - 1
*	Multiplication	SELECT 2 * 3
/	Division	SELECT 9 / 2
%	Modulus	SELECT 6 % 5

Table 9-4. Commonly used mathematical functions

Function	Return type	Description	Example
abs(x)	Same as input	Absolute value of x	SELECT abs(-1)
cbrt(x)	double	Cube root of x	SELECT cbrt(9)
ceiling(x)	Same as input	Round x up to nearest integer	SELECT ceiling(4.2)
degrees(x)	double	Convert the angle x from radians to degrees	SELECT degrees(1.047)
exp(x)	double	Euler's number raised to the power of x	SELECT exp(1)
floor(x)	Same as input	Round x down to the nearest integer	SELECT floor(4.2)
ln(x)	double	Natural logarithm of x	SELECT ln(exp(1))
log(b, x)	double	Base b logarithm of x	SELECT log(2, 64)
log2(x)	double	Base 2 logarithm of x	SELECT log2(64)
log10(x)	double	Base 10 logarithm of x	SELECT log10(140)
mod(n, m)	Same as input	Modulus. Equivalent to n % m	SELECT mod(3, 2)
power(x, p)	double	X raised to the power of p	SELECT pow(2, 6)
radians(x)	double	Convert the angle x from degrees to radians	SELECT radians(60)
round(x)	Same as input	Round x to the nearest integer	SELECT round(pi())
round(x, d)	Same as input	Round x to d decimal places	SELECT round(pi(), 2)
sqrt(x)	double	Square root of x	SELECT sqrt(64)
truncate(x)	double	Round x to integer by truncating the digits after the decimal point	SELECT truncate(e())

Trigonometric Functions

Trino provides a set of *trigonometric functions* that take the argument type radians. The return data type is double for all functions.

If you wish to convert between radians and degrees, Trino provides conversion functions degrees(x) and radians(x). Table 9-5 lists the trigonometric functions.

Table 9-5. Trigonometric functions

Function	Description
cos(x)	Cosine of x
acos(x)	Arc cosine of x
cosh(x)	Hyperbolic cosine of x
sin(x)	Sine of x
asin(x)	Arc sine of x
tan(x)	Tangent of x
atan(x)	Arc tangent of x
atan2(y, x)	Arc tangent of y / x
tanh(x)	Hyperbolic tangent of x

Constant and Random Functions

Trino provides functions that return *mathematical constants* and conceptual values as well as random values, as shown in Table 9-6.

Table 9-6. Miscellaneous mathematical constants and functions

Function	Return type	Description	Example
e()	double	Euler's number	2.718281828459045
pi()	double	Pi	3.141592653589793
infinity()	double	Trino constant used to represent infinity	Infinity
nan()	double	Trino constant used to represent not a number	NaN
random()	double	Random double >= 0.0 and < 1.0	SELECT random()
random(n)	Same as input	Random double >= 0.0 and < *n*	SELECT random(100)

String Functions and Operators

String manipulation is another common use case, and Trino includes rich support for it. The || operator is used to concatenate strings:

```
SELECT 'Emily' || ' Grace';
    _col0
-------------
 Emily Grace
(1 row)
```

Trino provides several useful string functions, shown in Table 9-7.

Table 9-7. String functions

Function	Return type	Description	Example
chr(*n*)	varchar	Unicode code point *n* as a character string.	SELECT chr(65)
codepoint(*string*)	integer	Unicode code point of character.	SELECT codepoint('A')
concat(*string1*, ..., *stringN*)	varchar	Equivalent to the || operator.	SELECT concat('Emily', ' ', 'Grace');
length(*string*)	bigint	Length of string.	SELECT length('saippuakivikauppias')
lower(*string*)	varchar	Convert string to lowercase.	SELECT lower('UPPER');
lpad(*string, size, padstring*)	varchar	Left pad the string with *size* number of characters. Truncates the string if the *size* is less than the actual length of the string.	SELECT lpad('A', 4, ' ')
ltrim(*string*)	varchar	Trim the leading whitespace.	SELECT ltrim(lpad('A', 4, ' '))
replace(*string, search, replace*)	varchar	Replace instances of *search* in string with *replace*.	SELECT replace('555.555.5555', '.', '-')
reverse(*string*)	varchar	Reverse the character string.	SELECT reverse('saippuakivikauppias')

Function	Return type	Description	Example
rpad(*string, size, padstring*)	varchar	Right pad the string with *size* number of character. Truncates the string if *size* is less than the actual length of the string.	SELECT rpad('A', 4, '#')
rtrim(*string*)	varchar	Trim the trailing whitespace.	SELECT rtrim(rpad('A', 4, ' '))
split(*string, delimiter*)	array(varchar)	Splits string on delimiter and returns an array.	SELECT split('2017,2018,2019', ',')
strpos(*string, substring*)	bigint	Starting position at first instance of the substring in the string. Index starts at 1; 0 is returned if the substring is not found.	SELECT strpos('trino.io', '.io');
substr(*string, start, length*)	varchar	Substring from *start* position of length. Index starts at 1. Negative index is backward from end.	SELECT substr('trino.io', 1, 5)
trim(*string*)	varchar	Remove leading and trailing whitespace. Same as applying both rtrim and ltrim.	SELECT trim(' A ')
upper(*string*)	varchar	Converts string to uppercase.	SELECT upper('lower')
word_stem(*word, lang*)	varchar	Returns the stem of the word using the specified language.	SELECT word_stem('trino', 'it')

Strings and Maps

Two string functions return maps that are interesting, given Trino's ability to further process map data:

```
split_to_map(string, entryDelimiter, keyValueDelimiter) → map<varchar, varchar>
```

This function splits the `string` argument by using the `entryDelimiter`, which splits the string into key-value pairs and then uses the `keyValueDelimiter` to split each pair into a key and value. The result is a map.

A useful example usage of this function is parsing of URL parameters:

```
SELECT split_to_map('userid=1234&reftype=email&device=mobile', '&', '=');
                     _col0
-------------------------------------------
 {device=mobile, userid=1234, reftype=email}
(1 row)
```

When there are multiple occurrences of the same key, the `split_to_map` function returns an error.

The similar function `split_to_multimap` can be used when there are multiple occurrences of the same key. In the preceding example, say there is a duplicate device:

```
SELECT
split_to_multimap(
  'userid=1234&reftype=email&device=mobile&device=desktop',
  '&',
  '=');
```

Unicode

Trino provides a set of *Unicode functions*, shown in Table 9-8. These functions work on valid UTF-8 encoded Unicode points. Functions consider each code point separately, even if multiple code points are used to represent a single character.

Table 9-8. Unicode-related functions

Function	Return type	Description
chr(*n*)	varchar	Returns the Unicode code point *n* as a single character string
codepoint(*string*)	integer	Returns the Unicode code point of the only character of *string*
normalize(*string*)	varchar	Transforms *string* with NFC normalization form
normalize(*string, form*)	varchar	Transforms *string* with the specified normalization form

The form argument must be one of the keywords in Table 9-9.

Table 9-9. Normalization forms

Form	Description
NFD	Canonical decomposition
NFC	Canonical decomposition, followed by canonical composition
NFKD	Compatibility decomposition
NFKC	Compatibility decomposition, followed by canonical composition

The Unicode standard (*http://unicode.org/reports/tr15/#Norm_Forms*) describes these forms in detail.

> This SQL-standard function has special syntax and requires specifying form as a keyword, not as a string.

to_utf8(*string*) → varbinary
    The function encodes the string into an UTF-8 varbinary representation.

from_utf8(*binary*) → varchar
    The function decodes the UTF-8 encoded string from binary. Any invalid UTF-8 sequences are replaced with the Unicode replacement character U+FFFD.

from_utf8(*binary, replace*) → varchar
    This function decodes a UTF-8 encoded string from binary. Any invalid UTF-8 sequences are replaced with *replace*.

Let's use the chr function to return the Unicode code point as a string:

```
SELECT chr(241);
 _col0
-------
 ñ
(1 row)
```

In this example, we are using the function codepoint to return the Unicode code point of the string:

```
SELECT codepoint(u&'\00F1');
 _col0
-------
   241
(1 row)
```

Now we are demonstrating how the Spanish eñe character can be represented multiple ways in Unicode. It can be represented as either a single code point or by composing multiple code points. When compared to each other directly, they are not treated as equivalent. This is where the normalization function can be used to normalize them to a common form to be compared and treated as equivalent:

```
SELECT u&'\00F1',
u&'\006E\0303',
u&'\00F1' = u&'\006E\0303',
normalize(u&'\00F1') = normalize(u&'\006E\0303');

 _col0 | _col1 | _col2 | _col3
-------+-------+-------+-------
 ñ     | ñ     | false | true
(1 row)
```

In some instances, code points can be composed as a single code point. For example, the Roman number IX can be written with two code points for I and X. Or you can use a single code point for it. To compare the two for equivalence, you need to use the normalization function:

```
SELECT u&'\2168', 'IX', u&'\2168' = 'IX', normalize(u&'\2168', NFKC) = 'IX';
 _col0 | _col1 | _col2 | _col3
-------+-------+-------+-------
 IX    | IX    | false | true
(1 row)
```

Regular Expressions

Trino supports pattern matching by providing both the SQL LIKE operator and regular expression (regex) functions. LIKE returns a Boolean and uses the syntax *search* LIKE *pattern*.

LIKE is simple to use for basic patterns but may not be expressive enough for all situations. LIKE patterns support two symbols: _ denotes matching any single character, and % denotes matching zero or more characters.

For example, let's say you want to find flights originating from the Dallas area. You can write the following query:

```
SELECT origincityname, count(*)
FROM flights_orc
WHERE origincityname LIKE '%Dallas%'
GROUP BY origincityname;

    origincityname     | _col1
-----------------------+---------
 Dallas/Fort Worth, TX | 7601863
 Dallas, TX            | 1297795
(2 rows)
```

Anything more complex requires using regular expression functions, which provide powerful pattern matching using the Java pattern syntax. The functions listed in Table 9-10 are used for more complex matching, replacing matching strings, extracting matching strings, and splitting strings based on the matched location.

Table 9-10. Regular expression functions

Function	Description
regexp_extract_all(*string, pattern,* [*group*]) → array(varchar)	Returns an array of substrings matched by the pattern in *string*. A variant of the function takes a group argument for the capturing group.
regexp_extract(*string, pattern* [*group*]) → varchar	Returns the substring matched by the pattern in *string*. A variant of the function takes a group argument for the capturing group.
regexp_like(*string, pattern*) → boolean	Returns a Boolean whether or not the pattern is contained within the string. This differs from LIKE, as LIKE tries to match the entire string with the pattern.
regexp_replace(*string, pattern,* [*replacement*]) → varchar	Returns a string for which the substrings matched by *pattern* are replaced with *replacement*. There is a variant of the function without *replacement*. In this case, the strings are simply removed. Capturing groups can be used in the replacement string.
regexp_replace(*string, pattern, function*) → varchar	Similar to regexp_replace(*string, pattern,* [*replacement*]) except that it takes a lambda expression.
regexp_split(*string, pattern*) → array(varchar)	Returns an array of strings split by the pattern. The pattern is like a delimiter. Similar to split(*string, delimiter*) with a more expressive delimiter as a pattern.

Table 9-11 shows common selected pattern examples you can use. The full range of supported patterns is extensively documented in the Java documentation about regular expressions.

Table 9-11. Regular expression examples

Pattern	Description	Examples
.	Any character	A
a	The single character a	regexp_like('abc', 'a') → true
[a-zA-Z]	Range of characters	regexp_like('abc', '[a-zA-Z]'), regexp_like('123', '[a-zA-Z]')
1	The single digit 1	regexp_like('123', '1')
\d	Any digit	regexp_like('123', '\d')
^	Match to beginning of line	regexp_like('abc', '^ab^'), regexp_like('abc', '^bc^')
$	Match to end of line	regexp_like('abc', 'bc$'), regexp_like('abc', 'ab$')
?	One or zero	regexp_like('abc', 'd?')
+	One or more	regexp_like('abc', 'd+')
*	Zero or more	regexp_like('abc', 'd*')

In this example, we want to extract the character b from the string. This results in an array in which each entry is a match:

```
SELECT regexp_extract_all('abbbbcccb', 'b');
   _col0
--------------
 [b, b, b, b, b]
(1 row)
```

Let's extract the character b again. However, we wish to extract a sequence of them. The result is an array with only two entries this time, since one of the entries contains the contiguous sequence:

```
SELECT regexp_extract_all('abbbbcccb', 'b+');
 _col0
--------
 [bbbb, b]
(1 row)
```

In this example, we leverage the capturing groups in the replacement. We are searching for a sequence of bc and then swap the order:

```
SELECT regexp_replace('abc', '(b)(c)', '$2$1');
 _col0
-------
 acb
(1 row)
```

Unnesting Complex Data Types

The UNNEST operation allows you to expand the complex collection data types, discussed in "Collection Data Types" on page 161, into a relation. This is extremely powerful for using big data and nested structural data types. By unnesting the data into a relation, you can more easily access the values that are wrapped inside the structure for querying.

As an example, let's say you have stored some access control policies and wish to query them. First, we have a user that can be associated with one or more roles. And a role can be associated with one or more sets of permissions. And perhaps this logic is defined by a schema that looks like this:

```
SELECT * FROM permissions;
  user  |                              roles
--------+--------------------------------------------------
  matt  | [[WebService_ReadWrite, Storage_ReadWrite],
           [Billing_Read]]
 martin | [[WebService_ReadWrite, Storage_ReadWrite],
           [Billing_ReadWrite, Audit_Read]]
(2 rows)
```

We can expand each role and associate it to the user by using UNNEST:

```
SELECT user, t.roles
FROM permissions,
UNNEST(permissions.roles) AS t(roles);
  user  |                  roles
--------+-----------------------------------------
 martin | [WebService_ReadWrite, Storage_ReadWrite]
 martin | [Billing_ReadWrite, Audit_Read]
 matt   | [WebService_ReadWrite, Storage_ReadWrite]
 matt   | [Billing_Read]
(4 rows)
```

Now let's say we want to filter the data and find only the users with the Audit_Read permission. We can expand it further:

```
SELECT user, permission
FROM permissions,
UNNEST(permissions.roles) AS t1(roles),
UNNEST(t1.roles) AS t2(permission);
  user  |      permission
--------+----------------------
 martin | WebService_ReadWrite
 martin | Storage_ReadWrite
 martin | Billing_ReadWrite
 martin | Audit_Read
 matt   | WebService_ReadWrite
 matt   | Storage_ReadWrite
```

```
   matt  | Billing_Read
 (7 rows)
```

And finally, let's add our filter:

```
SELECT user, permission
FROM permissions,
UNNEST(permissions.roles) AS t1(roles),
UNNEST(t1.roles) AS t2(permission)
WHERE permission = 'Audit_Read';
  user  | permission
--------+-----------
 martin | Audit_Read
 (1 row)
```

JSON Functions

JavaScript Object Notation (JSON) is a human readable and flexible data format. In modern applications and systems, JSON data is ubiquitous and has a variety of applications. It is commonly used in web applications for transferring data between the browser and server. A lot of data that requires analysis originates from web traffic and is therefore commonly produced and stored using the JSON format. Dedicated document stores as well as many relational database systems now support JSON data.

As Trino is an SQL-on-Anything engine, it may retrieve data from data sources in JSON format. For example, the Kafka, Elasticsearch, and MongoDB connectors return JSON or can expose the source JSON data. Trino also can use JSON files in HDFS or cloud object storage. Rather than force the connectors to transform data from JSON format into a strict relational data structure with columns and rows, Trino can operate on the JSON data. This allows the user to perform the actions they would like with the original data.

The functions in Table 9-12 show only a small subset of the available functions to work with JSON data. Trino includes rich support for the JSON path language, functions to create JSON objects, functions to cast to and from JSON, and the `json_query` function to extract a JSON object from a larger JSON object. Check out the Trino documentation for a full reference of the rich support for the JSON format.

Table 9-12. Example JSON-related functions

Function	Description	Example
is_json_scalar(*json*)	Returns Boolean if the value is a scalar	SELECT is_json_scalar('_abc_')
json_array_contains(*json, value*)	Returns Boolean true if the value is contained in the JSON array	SELECT json_array_contains([*1, 2, 3*], 1)
json_array_length(*json*)	Returns the length of the array in bigint	SELECT json_array_length([*1, 2, 3*])

Date and Time Functions and Operators

In "Temporal Data Types" on page 162, we discussed temporal data types in Trino. You learned about the varying types that exist, input and output formatting and representations, time zones and their nuances, and intervals. While that covered storing and representing the temporal types, it's often common and important to operate on the data using functions and operators.

Trino supports + and - operators for temporal types. These operators can be used when adding or subtracting a date time with an interval type, or with two interval types. However, it doesn't have any meaning to add two timestamps. Additionally, YEAR TO MONTH and DAY TO SECOND interval types cannot be combined.

You can add one hour to the time 12:00 to get the value 13:00:

```
SELECT TIME '12:00' + INTERVAL '1' HOUR;
    _col0
--------------
 13:00:00.000
(1 row)
```

Next, you can add 1 year and 15 months, and get the result of 2 years and 3 months:

```
SELECT INTERVAL '1' YEAR + INTERVAL '15' MONTH;
 _col0
-------
 2-3
(1 row)
```

Another useful operator AT TIME ZONE allows you to calculate the time in different time zones:

```
SELECT TIME '02:56:15' AT TIME ZONE '-08:00';
         _col0
--------------------
  1:56:15.000 -08:00
(1 row)
```

You can parse a literal string to a timestamp value as long as you use the correct format:

```
SELECT TIMESTAMP '1983-10-19 07:30:05.123';
         _col0
------------------------
 1983-10-19 07:30:05.123
```

In many cases, it is more convenient to parse a date or timestamp from a string by using the ISO 8601 format and one of the functions in Table 9-13.

Table 9-13. ISO 8061 parsing functions

Function	Return type	Description
from_iso8601_timestamp(*string*)	timestamp with time zone	Parses the ISO 8601 formatted string and returns a timestamp with time zone
from_iso8601_date(*string*)	date	Parses the ISO 8601 formatted string and returns a date

ISO 8061 is a well-documented standard for formatting the time string. When specifying a string to one of the preceding functions, it must use one of the following formats:

- YYYY
- YYYY-MM
- YYYY-MM-DD
- HH
- HH:MM
- HH:MM:SS
- HH:MM:SS.SSS

In addition, you can combine the date and time by using the T delimiter. Let's look at a few examples.

Here, we are parsing the iso8601 date and time into an SQL timestamp:

```
SELECT from_iso8601_timestamp('2019-03-17T21:05:19Z');
            _col0
----------------------------
 2019-03-17 21:05:19.000 UTC
(1 row)
```

Next, we specify a time zone other than the default UTC:

```
SELECT from_iso8601_timestamp('2019-03-17T21:05:19-05:00');
              _col0
--------------------------------
 2019-03-17 21:05:19.000 -05:00
(1 row)
```

The standard also allows you to specify the weeks into the year. In this example, week 10 of 2019 equates to March 4, 2019:

```
SELECT from_iso8601_timestamp('2019-W10');
            _col0
----------------------------
 2019-03-04 00:00:00.000 America/Vancouver
(1 row)
```

In this example, we do not specify time and parse the `iso8601` string to an SQL `date` type:

```
SELECT from_iso8601_date('2019-03-17');
  _col0
------------
 2019-03-17
(1 row)
```

Trino provides a rich set of date- and time-related functions. These are crucial for any application involving time, where you may often want to convert, compare, or extract time elements. Table 9-14 shows a selection of available functions. Check out the Trino documentation (*https://trino.io/docs/current/functions.html*) for further useful functions and other tips and tricks.

Table 9-14. Miscellaneous temporal functions and values

Function	Return type	Description
current_timezone()	varchar	Returns the current time zone
current_date	date	Returns the current date
current_time	time with time zone	Returns the current time and time zone
current_timestamp or now()	timestamp with time zone	Returns the current date, time and time zone
localtime	time	Returns the time only, based on the local time zone
localtimestamp	timestamp	Returns the date and time, based on the local time zone
from_unixtime(unixtime)	timestamp	Converts a Unix time and produces the date and time
to_unixtime(timestamp)	double	Converts a date and time to a Unix time value
to_milliseconds(interval)	bigint	Converts interval to milliseconds

Histograms

Trino provides the `width_bucket` function that can be used to create *histograms* with consistent widths:

```
width_bucket(x, bound1, bound2, n) -> bigint
```

The expression *x* is the numeric expression for which to create the histogram. The consistent-width histogram contains *n* buckets and is bounded between the values for *bound1* and *bound2*. The function returns the bucket number for each value of expression *x*.

Let's take our flight data set and compute a histogram over a 10-year period from 2010 to 2020:

```
SELECT count(*) count, year, width_bucket(year, 2010, 2020, 4) bucket
FROM flights_orc
WHERE year >= 2010
GROUP BY year;
```

```
 count  | year | bucket
--------+------+--------
7129270 | 2010 |      0
7140596 | 2011 |      1
7141922 | 2012 |      1
7455458 | 2013 |      1
7009726 | 2014 |      2
6450285 | 2015 |      2
6450117 | 2016 |      3
6085281 | 2017 |      3
6096762 | 2018 |      3
6369482 | 2019 |      4
(10 rows)
```

Note that in addition to the expected buckets 1, 2, 3, and 4, we have buckets 0 and 5. These buckets are used for the values outside the minimum and maximum bounds of the histogram—values for years 2010 and 2019, in this case.

Aggregate Functions

In SQL, *aggregate functions* operate and compute a value or a set of values. Unlike scalar functions that produce a single value for each input value, aggregate functions produce a single value for a set of input values. Trino supports the common general aggregate functions you find in most other database systems, as you can see in Table 9-15.

Aggregate functions can take an optional ORDER BY clause after the argument. Semantically, this means that the input set is ordered before performing the aggregation. For most aggregations, the order doesn't matter.

Table 9-15. Aggregate functions

Function	Return type	Description
count(*)	bigint	Counts the number of values returned
count(x)	bigint	Counts the number of non-null values
sum(x)	Same as input	Computes the sum of the input values
min(x)	Same as input	Returns the minimum value of all the input values
max(x)	Same as input	Returns the maximum of all the input values
avg(x)	double	Returns the arithmetic mean of the input values

Map Aggregate Functions

Trino supports several useful map-related functions, detailed in Table 9-16. For some of these functions, the optional ORDER BY clause is needed, depending on the desired results. We demonstrate this use with an example from our iris data set (see "Iris Data Set" on page 15).

Table 9-16. Map aggregate functions

Function	Return type	Description
histogram(*x*)	map(*K, bigint*)	Creates a histogram from the *x* item. Returns a map where the key is *x* and the value is the number of times *x* appears.
map_agg(*key, value*)	map(*K, V*)	Creates a map from a column of keys and values. Duplicates chosen at random. Use multimap_agg to retain all the values.
map_union(*x(K, V)*)	map(*K, V*)	Performs the unions of multiple maps into a single map. If the same key is found in multiple maps, the value chosen has no guarantee. Does not merge the two values.
multimap_agg(*key, value*)	map(*K, array(V)*)	Creates a map from the column and keys, similar to map_agg.

Let's create a histogram of `petal_length_cm`. Because the data is precise, you can use the `floor` function to create wider buckets for the histogram:

```
SELECT histogram(floor(petal_length_cm))
FROM brain.default.iris;
                    _col0
-----------------------------------------
 {1.0=50, 4.0=43, 5.0=35, 3.0=11, 6.0=11}
(1 row)
```

You may recognize that a histogram output is similar to what you see when doing a `GROUP BY` and `COUNT`. We can use the result as input to the `map_agg` function to create the histogram with the same results:

```
SELECT floor(petal_length_cm) k, count(*) v
FROM brain.default.iris
GROUP BY 1
ORDER BY 2 DESC;
  k  | v
-----+----
 1.0 | 50
 4.0 | 43
 5.0 | 35
 3.0 | 11
 6.0 | 11
(5 rows)

SELECT map_agg(k, v) FROM (
  SELECT floor(petal_length_cm) k,
    count(*) v
  FROM iris
  GROUP BY 1
);
                  _col0
```

```
-------------------------------------------
 {4.0=43, 1.0=50, 5.0=35, 3.0=11, 6.0=11}
(1 row)

SELECT multimap_agg(species, petal_length_cm)
FROM brain.default.iris;
-----------------------------------------------------
 {versicolor=[4.7, 4.5, 4.9..], ,
  virginica=[6.0, 5.1, 5.9, ..],
  setosa=[1.4, 1.4, 1…] ..
(1 row)
```

The `map_union` function is useful for combining maps. Say you have multiple maps. We'll use the histogram function in this example to create them:

```
SELECT histogram(floor(petal_length_cm)) x
FROM brain.default.iris
GROUP BY species;
            x
------------------------
 {4.0=6, 5.0=33, 6.0=11}
 {4.0=37, 5.0=2, 3.0=11}
 {1.0=50}
(3 rows)
```

We can use `map_union` to combine them. However, notice how keys 4.0 and 5.0 exist in different maps. In these cases, Trino arbitrarily picks one set of values. It does not perform any type of merging. While adding them is correct in this case, it does not always make sense. For example, the values could be strings, which make it less clear how to combine them:

```
SELECT map_union(m)
FROM (
  SELECT histogram(floor(petal_length_cm)) m
  FROM brain.default.iris
  GROUP BY species
  );
                _col0
-------------------------------------------
 {4.0=6, 1.0=50, 5.0=33, 6.0=11, 3.0=11}
(1 row)
```

Approximate Aggregate Functions

When working with large amounts of data and aggregations, data processing can be resource intensive, requiring more hardware to scale Trino out to provide interactivity. Sometimes scaling out becomes prohibitively expensive.

To help in this scenario, Trino provides a set of aggregation functions that return the approximation rather than the exact result. These *approximation aggregation functions* use much less memory and computational power at the expense of not providing the exact result.

In many cases when dealing with big data, this is acceptable since the data itself is often not completely exact. There may be a missing day of data, for example. But when considering aggregations over a year, the missing data doesn't matter for certain types of analysis.

Remember, Trino is not designed or meant to be used for OLTP-style queries. It is not suitable to produce reports for a company's ledger with absolute accuracy. However, for OLAP use cases—analytics requiring you to understand trends only but not to have completely accurate results—Trino can be acceptable and satisfy the requirements.

Trino provides two main approximation functions: `approx_distinct` and `approx_percentile`.

Trino implements `approx_distinct` by using the HyperLogLog algorithm. Counting distinct rows is a very common query that you likely need to satisfy a data analysis requirement. For example, you may want to count the number of distinct user IDs or IP addresses in your logs to know how many users visited your website on a given day, month, or year. Because users may have visited your website multiple times, simply counting the number of entries in your log does not work. You need to find the distinct number of users, requiring you to count each user's representation only once. Doing so requires you to keep a structure in memory so you know not to double-count membership. For large amounts of data, this becomes impractical and certainly slow. HyperLogLog provides an alternative approach. The actual algorithm is not discussed in this book.

To implement the approximate distinct result, Trino provides a HyperLogLog (HLL) data type that you can also use. Because Trino provides HyperLogLog as a data type, this means it can be stored as a table. This becomes incredibly valuable because you can store computations to merge them back later. Say your data is partitioned by day. Each day, you can create a HyperLogLog structure for the users that day and store it. Then when you want to compute the approximate distinct result, you can merge the HLLs to get the cardinality for `approx-distinct`.

Window Functions

Trino supports the use of standard *window functions* from SQL, which allow you to define a set of records to use as input for a function. For example, let's look at the sepal length of our iris flowers (see "Iris Data Set" on page 15). Without the window function, you can get the average sepal length for all species:

```
SELECT avg(sepal_length_cm)
FROM brain.default.iris;
5.8433332
```

Alternatively, you can calculate the average for a specific species:

```
SELECT avg(sepal_length_cm)
FROM brain.default.iris
WHERE species = 'setosa';
5.006
```

However, what if you want a list of all measurements and each compared to the overall average? The OVER() window function allows you to do just that:

```
SELECT species, sepal_length_cm,
  avg(sepal_length_cm) OVER() AS avgsepal
FROM brain.default.iris;
  species    | sepal_length_cm | avgsepal
------------+-----------------+----------
 setosa     |             5.1 | 5.8433332
 setosa     |             4.9 | 5.8433332
 ...
 versicolor |             7.0 | 5.8433332
 versicolor |             6.4 | 5.8433332
 versicolor |             6.9 | 5.8433332
 ...
```

The window function basically says to calculate the average overall values in the same table. You can also create multiple windows with the PARTITION BY statement:

```
SELECT species, sepal_length_cm,
  avg(sepal_length_cm) OVER(PARTITION BY species) AS avgsepal
FROM brain.default.iris;
  species    | sepal_length_cm | avgsepal
------------+-----------------+----------
 setosa     |             5.1 |    5.006
 setosa     |             4.9 |    5.006
 setosa     |             4.7 |    5.006
 ...
 virginica  |             6.3 |    6.588
 virginica  |             5.8 |    6.588
 virginica  |             7.1 |    6.588
 ...
```

Now the average length is specific to the species. With the help of DISTINCT and by omitting the individual length, you can get a list of the averages per species:

```
SELECT DISTINCT species,
  avg(sepal_length_cm) OVER(PARTITION BY species) AS avgsepal
FROM brain.default.iris;
  species    | avgsepal
------------+----------
 setosa     |    5.006
 virginica  |    6.588
```

```
versicolor |   5.936
(3 rows)
```

The window functions in Trino support all aggregate functions as well as numerous window-specific functions:

```
SELECT DISTINCT species,
    min(sepal_length_cm) OVER(PARTITION BY species) AS minsepal,
    avg(sepal_length_cm) OVER(PARTITION BY species) AS avgsepal,
    max(sepal_length_cm) OVER(PARTITION BY species) AS maxsepal
FROM brain.default.iris;
  species    | minsepal | avgsepal | maxsepal
-------------+----------+----------+----------
 virginica   |    4.9   |  6.588   |    7.9
 setosa      |    4.3   |  5.006   |    5.8
 versicolor  |    4.9   |  5.936   |    7.0
(3 rows)
```

Check out the Trino documentation (*https://trino.io/docs*) for more details.

Lambda Expressions

An advanced concept for working with array elements is the use of *lambda expressions* in SQL statements. If you have a programming background, you might be familiar with them in terms of syntax, or you may know these expressions by other names such as *lambda functions*, *anonymous functions*, or *closures*.

A number of array functions, such as `zip_with`, support the use of lambda expressions. The expression simply defines a transformation from an input value to an output value separated by `->`:

```
x -> x + 1
(x, y) -> x + y
x -> IF(x > 0, x, -x)
```

Other functions commonly used with lambda expressions are `transform`, `filter`, `reduce`, `array_sort`, `none_match`, `any_match`, and `all_match`.

Take a look at this example:

```
SELECT zip_with(ARRAY[1, 2, 6, 2, 5],
                ARRAY[3, 4, 2, 5, 7],
                (x, y) -> x + y);

[4, 6, 8, 7, 12]
```

As you can see, the lambda expression is simple yet powerful. It adds the *n*th elements from the two arrays, creating a new array with the sums. Basically, an iteration over both arrays takes place, and the function is called in each iteration, all without needing to write any code for looping through the array data structure.

Geospatial Functions

The SQL support of Trino expands beyond standard SQL and includes a significant set of functionality in the realm of geospatial analysis. As with other SQL support, Trino aligns closely with relevant standard and common usage across other tools.

In the case of *geospatial functions*, Trino uses the ST_ prefix supporting the SQL/MM specifications and the Open Geospatial Consortium's (OGC) OpenGIS Specifications. Because of the large scope of the geospatial support, you get only a glimpse in this section.

Trino supports numerous constructors to create geospatial objects, for example:

- ST_GeometryFromText(varchar) -> Geometry
- ST_GeomFromBinary(varbinary) -> Geometry
- ST_LineFromText(varchar) -> LineString
- ST_LineString(array(Point)) -> LineString
- ST_Point(double, double) -> Point
- ST_Polygon(varchar) -> Polygon

These objects can then be used in the many, many functions to compare locations and other aspects:

- ST_Contains(Geometry, Geometry) -> boolean
- ST_Touches(Geometry, Geometry) -> boolean
- ST_Within(Geometry, Geometry) -> boolean
- ST_Length(Geometry) -> double
- ST_Distance(Geometry, Geometry) -> double
- ST_Area(SphericalGeography) -> double

The geospatial support in Trino is detailed in the Trino documentation (*https://trino.io/docs*). We strongly suggest you check it out if you are using Trino to deal with geospatial data.

Prepared Statements

Prepared statements are a useful approach to be able to run the same SQL statement with different input parameter values. This allows reuse, simplifies repeated usage for users, and creates cleaner, more maintainable code. Prepared statements are queries that are saved in the Trino session for the user.

Use and creation of prepared statements are separated into two steps. The PREPARE statement is used to create the statement and make it available for repeated use in the session:

```
PREPARE example
FROM SELECT count(*) FROM datalake.ontime.flights_orc;
```

The EXECUTE command can be used to run the query once or multiple times:

```
EXECUTE example;
  _col0
-----------
 166628027
(1 row)
```

Prepared statements can support parameter values to be passed at execution time:

```
PREPARE delay_query FROM
SELECT dayofweek,
       avg(depdelayminutes) AS delay
FROM flights_orc
WHERE month = ?
AND origincityname LIKE ?
GROUP BY dayofweek
ORDER BY dayofweek;
```

Using the query with parameters requires you to pass them along for execution in the correct order after the USING keyword:

```
EXECUTE delay_query USING 2, '%Boston%';
 dayofweek |         delay
-----------+--------------------
         1 | 10.613156692553677
         2 |  9.97405624214174
         3 |  9.548045977011494
         4 | 11.822725778003647
         5 | 15.875475113122173
         6 | 11.184173669467787
         7 | 10.788121285791464
(7 rows)
```

Difference Between PREPARE Statement in RDBMSs and Trino

Using `PREPARE` in other relational database systems has a purpose more than just convenience of executing similar queries with different parameter values. Many systems may actually parse and plan the SQL during the `PREPARE` statement. Then, during the `EXECUTE` command, the values are passed to the system and bound to the execution plan operators. For transaction systems, this is often an important optimization since it has to parse and plan the query only once for many executions, even with different values. This is the original purpose behind prepared statements.

Another common example of this is `INSERT` queries, where you want to insert a lot of new values as quickly as possible. `PREPARE` eliminates the overhead of planning for each insert.

Currently, Trino does not implement this optimization, and the query and parse are planned for each `EXECUTE`. Given the nature of Trino's main use case, it's not as important an optimization to be concerned about. Prepared statements were originally introduced into Trino for the JDBC and ODBC drivers, since tools may rely on the functionality.

The `DESCRIBE` command can be useful for understanding prepared statements with the `DESCRIBE INPUT` and `DESCRIBE OUTPUT` commands. These commands are used internally by the JDBC and ODBC drivers for metadata information and error-handling purposes:

```
DESCRIBE INPUT delay_query;
 Position | Type
----------+---------
        0 | integer
        1 | varchar
(2 rows)

DESCRIBE OUTPUT delay_query;
 Column Name | Catalog | Schema |    Table    |  Type   | Type Size | Aliased
-------------+---------+--------+-------------+---------+-----------+--------
 dayofweek   | hive    | ontime | flights_orc | integer |         4 | false
 delay       |         |        |             | double  |         8 | true
(2 rows)
```

When you exit the Trino session, the prepared statements are automatically deallocated. You can manually remove the prepared statement with `DEALLOCATE PREPARE`:

```
DEALLOCATE PREPARE delay_query;
```

Conclusion

Congratulations, you made it! This chapter is pretty deep in terms of documenting SQL support and processing in Trino. This is a central feature of Trino and, as such, very important. And you did not even learn all the details. Make sure you refer to the official documentation (described in "Documentation" on page 14) for the latest and greatest information, including a full list of all functions and operators and lots more detail about all of them.

Understanding the depth of SQL support hopefully gets you into the idea of running Trino in production to bring the benefits to your users. In the next part of the book, you learn more about what is involved in terms of security, monitoring, and more. And you get to find examples of applications to use with Trino and some information about real-world use in other organizations and companies.

With the knowledge from the last two chapters about the SQL support in Trino, you can now go back to Chapter 4 and learn more about query planning and optimizations. Or you can advance to the next part of this book to learn more about Trino use in production, integrations with Trino, and other uses.

Trino in Real-World Uses

So far you've gotten an introduction to Trino, learned how to install it for production use, learned how to hook up data sources with different connectors, and seen how powerful the SQL support is.

In this third part, you learn other aspects of using Trino in production, such as security and monitoring, and you get to explore applications that can be used together with Trino to provide tremendous value for your users.

Last but not least, you learn about other organizations and their use of Trino.

Security

Deploying Trino at scale, discussed in Chapter 5, is an important step toward production usage. In this chapter, you learn more about securing Trino itself as well as the underlying data.

In a typical Trino cluster deployment and use, you can consider securing several aspects:

- Transport from the user client to the Trino coordinator
- Transport within the Trino cluster, between coordinator and workers
- Transport between the Trino cluster and each data source, configured per catalog
- Access to specific data within each data source

In Figure 10-1, you can see how the different network connections of Trino need to be secured. The connection to your client—for example, the Trino CLI or an application using the JDBC driver—needs to be secured. The traffic within the cluster needs to be secured. And the connections with all the different data sources need to be secured.

Let's explore these needs in more detail in the following sections, starting with authenticating to Trino as a user.

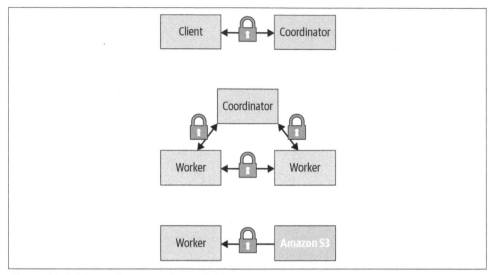

Figure 10-1. Network connections of Trino usage to secure

Authentication

Authentication is the process of proving an identity to a system. Authentication is essential to any secure system. A variety of authentication methods are supported by computer systems, including Kerberos, password with Lightweight Directory Access Protocol (LDAP), certificate authentication, and others. It is up to each system to support the particular authentication method. In Trino, clients commonly authenticate to the Trino cluster via one of these methods:

- Password—see details that follow
- Certificates—see "Certificate Authentication" on page 232
- Kerberos—see "Kerberos" on page 235

By default, no authentication is configured in Trino. Anyone who can access the coordinator can connect and therefore issue queries and perform other operations. In this chapter, you will learn details about LDAP and password authentication mechanisms, since they are the most commonly used.

However, authentication is just one piece. Once the principal is authenticated, they are assigned the privileges that determine what the user is able to do. What you can do is referred to as *authorization* and is governed by the `SystemAccessControl` and `ConnectorAccessControl`. We describe this in more detail in "Authorization" on page 216. For now, let's assume that once authenticated, the user can perform any action. By default, this is true for accessing anything at the system level, such as querying the system catalog.

A general requirement for any authentication system usage is that the traffic from the clients to the coordinator can be trusted. In practice this means that TLS must be configured, so the coordinator needs to be accessed via HTTPS (see "Encryption" on page 221 and specifically "Encrypting Trino Client-to-Coordinator Communication" on page 224).

In addition, the coordinator and workers have to authenticate with each other. This is achieved by configuring a shared secret that is configured to the same value on all nodes in the cluster in *config.properties*:

```
internal-communication.shared-secret=aLongRandomString
```

The value for the shared secret should be a long random string. One way to create a value is by using `openssl`:

```
openssl rand 512 | base64
```

You can also use TLS in the cluster; see "Encrypting Communication Within the Trino Cluster" on page 229.

Password and LDAP Authentication

Password authentication is an authentication method you probably use every day. By providing a username and password to the system, you are proving who you say you are by providing something you know. Trino supports this basic form of authentication by using its password authenticator. The *password authenticator* receives the username and password credentials from the client, validates them, and creates a principal. The password authenticator is designed to support custom password authenticators deployed as a plug-in in Trino.

Currently, password authentication supported by Trino uses the LDAP authenticator, and therefore an LDAP service.

 Password file authentication is a less commonly used, simple, and supported authentication mechanism. Rather than using a powerful LDAP system, the users are managed in a file on the coordinator. This is useful for testing purposes or simple deployments.

LDAP stands for *Lightweight Directory Access Protocol*, an industry-standard application protocol for accessing and managing information in a directory server. The data model in the directory server is a hierarchical data structure that stores identity information. We won't elaborate on too many more details about what LDAP is or how it works. If you are interested in learning more, plenty of information is available in books or on the web (*https://ldap.com*).

When using the LDAP authenticator, a user passes a username and password to the Trino coordinator. This can be done from the CLI, JDBC driver, or any other client that supports passing the username and password. The coordinator then validates these credentials with an external LDAP service and creates the principal from the username. You can see a visualization of this flow in Figure 10-2. To enable LDAP authentication with Trino, you need to add to the *config.properties* file on the Trino coordinator:

```
http-server.authentication.type=PASSWORD
```

By setting the authentication type to PASSWORD, we are telling the Trino coordinator to use the password authenticator to authenticate.

In addition, you need to configure the LDAP service with the additional file *password-authenticator.properties* in the *etc* directory:

```
password-authenticator.name=ldap
ldap.url=ldaps://ldap-server:636
ldap.user-bind-pattern=${USER}@example.com
```

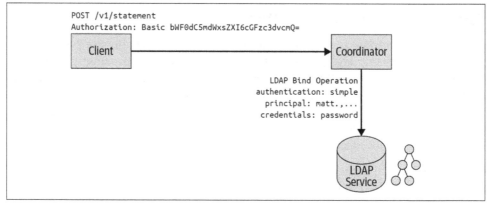

Figure 10-2. LDAP authentication to Trino using an external LDAP service

The `password-authenticator.name` specifies to use the LDAP plug-in for the password authenticator. The following lines configure the LDAP server URL and the pattern to locate the user record. The preceding bind pattern is an example usage with Active Directory. Other LDAP servers or configurations define a user ID (UID):

```
ldap.user-bind-pattern=uid=${USER},OU=people,DC=example,DC=com
```

In LDAP, several operation types interact with the LDAP directory, such as add, delete, modify, search, and bind. *Bind* is the operation used to authenticate clients to the directory server and is what Trino uses for supporting LDAP authentication. In order to bind, you need to supply identification and proof of identity such as a password. LDAP allows for different types of authentication, but user identity, also known as the *distinguished name*, and password is the main supported method by Trino for LDAP authentication.

A secondary method, which was recently added, is to authenticate and authorize with a LDAP service user. Check the Trino documentation for configuration tips.

Trino requires using *secure LDAP*, which is referred to as *LDAPS*. Therefore, you need to make sure you have TLS enabled on your LDAP server. In addition, ensure that the URL for the `ldap-url` property uses `ldaps://` and not `ldap://`. This communication occurs over TLS. This works transparently if both certificates are globally trusted certificates. Otherwise you need to import the LDAP server TLS certificate to the truststore used by the Trino coordinator. Or if the LDAP server is using a certificate signed by a certificate authority (CA), you need to make sure that the CA chain is in the truststore.

To securely use the LDAP authenticator, you also need to configure HTTPS access to the Trino coordinator. This ensures that the password sent from the client is not in clear text over an unsecure network. We discuss this setup in "Encryption" on page 221.

Once the LDAP configuration is in place, you can test it with the Trino CLI:

```
trino --user matt --password
```

Specifying `--password` causes the CLI to prompt you to enter the password.

When the username and password are passed to the Trino coordinator from the client, the CLI in our example, Trino replaces this username in the bind pattern and sends this as a security principal, and the password as the security credentials, as part of the bind request for LDAP. In our example, the principal used to match the distinguished name in the directory structure is `uid=matt,OU=people,DC=exam ple,DC=com`. Each entry in the LDAP directory may consist of multiple attributes. One such attribute is `userPassword`, which the bind operation uses to match the password sent.

Trino can further restrict access based on group memberships. You learn more about the importance of groups in the following authorization sections. By using groups, you can assign privileges to a group, so the users in that group inherit all the privileges of that group rather than having to manage privileges individually. Say, for example, you want to allow only people in the `engineering` group to authenticate with Trino. In our example, we want users `matt` and `maria` to be able to authenticate to Trino, but not user `jane`.

To further restrict users based on group membership, Trino allows you to specify additional properties in the *password-authenticator.properties* file:

```
ldap.user-base-dn=OU=people,DC=example,DC=com

ldap.group-auth-pattern=(&(objectClass=inetOrgPerson)(uid=${USER})(memberof=
CN=developers,OU=groups,DC=example,DC=com))
```

In our example, the preceding filter restricts users from the base distinguished name and allows only users who belong to the developers group in LDAP. If user jane tries to authenticate, the bind operation succeeds since jane is a valid user, but the user is filtered out of the results because she does not belong to the developers group.

Other Authentication Types

Besides the popular password authentication type, backed by a password file or a LDAP system, Trino can also be configured to use other authentication types, in addition or alternatively.

The legacy Kerberos authentication, often used with HDFS deployments, is described in "Kerberos" on page 235. Refer to the Trino documentation for information on the more modern usage of OAuth 2.0 authentication of JSON Web Token (JWT) authentication. Certificate authentication, detailed in "Certificate Authentication" on page 232, is commonly used for services or automated systems that access Trino to process queries. Support for authentication types is implemented in separate plug-ins, and commercial vendors like Starburst offer support for additional authentication types like the common identity provider (IdP) Okta.

Authorization

In the previous section, you learned about authentication, or proving to Trino who you are. However, in an environment with many users and sensitive data, you do not want to provide access to the data to every user who can authenticate.

To restrict access, you need to configure *authorization* of what a user can do. Let's first examine the SQL model in Trino in terms of what access controls exist. Then you learn how to control access to Trino at the system and connector level.

System Access Control

System access control enforces authorization at the global Trino level and allows you to configure access for catalogs and rules for the principals used. Lower-level rights and restrictions within a catalog have to be configured with connector access control; see "Connector Access Control" on page 219.

As you learned in the authentication section, security principals are the entity used to authenticate to Trino. The principal may be an individual user or a service account.

Trino also separates the principal for authentication from the user who is running queries. For example, multiple users may share a principal for authenticating, but run queries as themselves. By default, Trino allows any principal who can authenticate to run queries as anyone else:

```
$ trino --krb5-principal alice@example.com --user bob
```

This is generally not what you would want to run in a real environment, since it potentially elevates the access granted to one user, bob, beyond his authorization. Changing this default behavior requires additional configuration. Trino supports a set of built-in system access control configurations.

By default, Trino allows any authenticated user to do anything. This is the least secure and not recommended when deploying in a production environment. While it is the default, you can set it explicitly by creating *access-control.properties* within the *etc* directory:

```
access-control.name=allow-all
```

Read-only authorization is slightly more secure in that it allows only any operation that is reading data or metadata. This includes SELECT queries, but not CREATE, INSERT, or DELETE queries:

```
access-control.name=read-only
```

 Using this method to set access control to read-only is a very fast, simple, and effective way to reduce risk from Trino usage to the underlying data. At the same time, read access is completely suitable to analysis usage, and you can easily create a dedicated Trino cluster with read-only access to allow anybody in your company access to a large amount of data for analysis, troubleshooting, or simply exploration or learning more about Trino.

To configure system access control beyond simple allow-all or read-only, you can use a file-based approach. This allows you to specify access control rules for catalog access by users and what users a principal can identify as. These rules are specified in a file that you maintain.

When using file-based system access control, all access to catalogs is denied unless there is a matching rule for a user that explicitly gives them permission. You can enable this in the *access-control.properties* file in the *etc* configuration directory:

```
access-control.name=file
security.config-file=etc/rules.json
```

The security.config-file property specifies the location of the file containing the rules. It must be a JSON file using the format detailed in the following code. Best practice is to keep it in the same directory as all other configuration files:

```
{
  "catalogs": [
    {
      "user": "admin",
      "catalog": "system",
      "allow": true
    },
    {
      "catalog": "hive",
      "allow": true
    },
    {
      "user": "alice",
      "catalog": "postgresql",
      "allow": true
    }
    {
      "catalog": "system",
      "allow": false
    }
  ]
}
```

Rules are examined in order, and the first rule that matches is used. In this example, the admin user is allowed access to the system catalog, whereas all other users are denied because of the last rule. We mentioned earlier that all catalog access is denied by default unless there is a matching rule. The exception is that all users have access to the system catalog by default.

The example file also grants access to the hive catalog for all users, but only the user alice is granted access to the postgresql catalog.

 System access controls are very useful for restricting access. However, they can be used to configure access only at the catalog level. More fine-grained access cannot be configured with it.

As we mentioned earlier, authenticated principals can run queries as any user by default. This is generally not desirable, as it allows users to potentially access data as someone else. If the connector has implemented a connector access control, it means that a user can authenticate with a principal and pretend to be another user to access data they should not have access to. Therefore, it is important to enforce an appropriate matching between the principal and the user running the queries.

Let's say we want to set the username to that of the LDAP principal:

```
{
  "catalogs": [
    {
      "allow": "all"
    }
  ],
  "principals": [
    {
      "principal": "(.*)",
      "principal_to_user": "$1",
      "allow": "all"
    }
  ]
}
```

This can be further extended to enforce the user to use exactly their Kerberos principal name. In addition, we can match the username to a group principal that may be shared:

```
"principals": [
  {
    "principal": "([^/]+)/?.*@example.com",
    "principal_to_user": "$1",
    "allow": "all"
  },
  {
    "principal": "group@example.com",
    "user": "alice|bob",
    "allow": "all"
  }
]
```

Therefore, if you want a different behavior, you must override the rule; in this case, the users bob and alice can use the principal group@example.com as well as their own principals, bob@example.com and alice@example.com.

Connector Access Control

Recall the set of objects Trino exposes in order to query data. A *catalog* is the configured instance of a connector to access a specific data source. A catalog may consist of a set of namespaces called *schemas*. And, finally, the schemas contain a collection of tables with columns using specific data types and rows of data. With connector access control, Trino allows you to configure fine-grained rights within a catalog.

Trino supports the SQL standard GRANT to grant privileges on tables and views to a user or role, and also to grant user membership to a role. Today, Trino supports a subset of privileges defined by the SQL standard. In Trino, you can grant the following privileges to a table or view:

SELECT
Equivalent to read access

INSERT
Equivalent to create access, or write access for new rows

UPDATE
Equivalent to update access, or write access for existing rows

DELETE
Equivalent to delete access, or removal of rows

 As of this writing, only the Hive connector supports roles and grants. Because this depends on the connector implementation, each connector needs to implement the ConnectorAccessControl to support this SQL standard functionality.

Let's look at an example:

```
GRANT SELECT on datalake.ontime.flights TO matt;
```

The user running this query is granting to user matt the SELECT privilege on table flights that is in the ontime schema of the hive catalog.

Optionally, you can specify the WITH GRANT OPTION that allows the grantee matt to grant the same privileges to others. You can also specify more than one privilege by separating commas or by specifying ALL PRIVILEGES to grant SELECT, INSERT, UPDATE, and DELETE to the object:

```
GRANT SELECT, DELETE on datalake.ontime.flights TO matt WITH GRANT OPTION;
```

 To grant privileges, you must possess the same privileges as the GRANT OPTION. Or you must be an owner of the table or view, or member of the role that owns the table or view. You can assign ownership in Trino by setting the authorization for a specific role or user:

```
ALTER SCHEMA ontime SET AUTHORIZATION matt;
```

A *role* consists of a collection of privileges that can be assigned to a user or another role. This makes administering privileges for many users easier. By using roles, you avoid the need to assign privileges directly to users. Instead, you assign the privileges to a role, and then users are assigned to that role and inherit those privileges. Users can also be assigned multiple roles. Using roles to manage privileges is generally the best practice.

Let's reuse our example of the `flights` table and use roles:

```
CREATE ROLE admin;
GRANT SELECT, DELETE on datalake.ontime.flights TO admin;
GRANT admin TO USER matt, martin;
```

Now let's say you wish to remove privileges from a user. Instead of having to remove all the privileges on an object granted to a user, you can simply remove the role assignment from the user:

```
REVOKE admin FROM USER matt;
```

In addition to removing users from a role, you can also remove privileges from a role so that all users with the role no longer have that privilege:

```
REVOKE DELETE ON datalake.ontime.flights FROM admin;
```

In this example, we revoked the DELETE privileges on the `flights` table from the admin role. However, the admin role and its members still have the SELECT privilege.

Users may belong to multiple roles, and those roles may have distinct or an intersection of privileges. When a user runs a query, Trino examines the privileges that the user has either assigned directly or through the roles. If you wish to use only the privileges of a single role you belong to, you can use the SET ROLE command. For example, say you belong to both an admin role and the developer role, but you want to be using only the privileges assigned to the developer role:

```
SET ROLE developer;
```

You can also set the role to ALL so that Trino examines your privileges for every role you belong to. Or you can set it to NONE.

Encryption

Encryption is a process of transforming data from a readable form to an unreadable form, which is then used in transport or for storage, also called *at rest*. At the receiver end, only authorized users are able to transform data back to a readable form. This prevents any malicious attacker who intercepts the data from being able to read it. Trino uses standard cryptographic techniques to encrypt data in motion and at rest, and you can see a comparison between the plain text and the encrypted version in Table 10-1.

Table 10-1. Comparison of equivalent text in plain and encrypted format

Plain text	Encrypted text
SSN: 123-45-6789	5oMgKBe38tSsOpl/Rg7IITExIWtCITEzIfSVydAHF8Gux1cpnCg=

Encrypted data in motion includes the following data transfers and is displayed in Figure 10-3:

- Between the client, such as a JDBC client or the Trino CLI, and the Trino coordinator (at the top of the figure)
- Within the Trino cluster, between the coordinator and workers (center)
- From the data sources (for example, Amazon S3 object storage) configured in the catalogs, to the workers and the coordinator in the cluster (bottom)

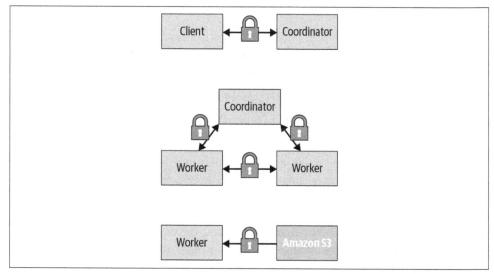

Figure 10-3. Encryption options for data in transit

Encryption of data at rest includes the following locations and is displayed in Figure 10-4:

- Data sources, so outside the Trino cluster (right)
- Storage on the workers and/or coordinator used for the spilling to disk functionality, so inside the Trino cluster (left)

Figure 10-4. Encryption options for data at rest

Each of these can be configured in Trino independently. S3 is used as an example for a connected data source.

These different encryption usages can be combined. For example, you can configure Trino to encrypt client-to-coordinator communication and intercluster communication, but leave data at rest unencrypted and therefore not secured. Or you may choose to configure Trino only for encrypted client-to-coordinator communication.

While each combination is possible to configure, some combinations do not make much sense. For example, configuring only intercluster communication but leaving client-to-coordinator communication unencrypted does not make sense because it leaves any data accessed by queries from a Trino client open to attacks.

As you've learned, external and internal communication in Trino happens exclusively over HTTP. To secure communication between the client and coordinator and intercluster communication, Trino can be configured to use TLS on top of HTTP, referred to as *HTTPS*. TLS is a cryptographic protocol for encrypting data over a network, and HTTPS uses TLS to secure HTTP.

 TLS is the successor to Secure Sockets Layer (SSL), and sometimes the terms are used interchangeably. SSL is an older protocol with known vulnerabilities and is considered insecure. Because of the prominence and name recognition of SSL, when someone refers to SSL, they often are referring to TLS.

You are probably familiar with HTTPS from visiting websites because most sites use HTTPS now. For example, if you are logged into your online bank account, HTTPS is used to encrypt data between the web server and your web browser. On modern web browsers, you typically see the padlock icon in the address line, indicating the data transfer is secured and the server you are connected to is identical to the one identified in the certificate.

How Does HTTPS Work?

While this chapter is not intended to give a deep dive on the technical details of TLS, you should understand the basic concepts in order to understand how HTTPS works with Trino. We have discussed how Trino uses TLS/HTTPS to encrypt the data in motion. Any malicious user eavesdropping on the network and intercepting data being processed in Trino won't be able to view the original unencrypted data.

The process of setting up this secured communication occurs when a user connects to a web page from their browser, and the server where the web page is hosted sends a TLS certificate to start the TLS handshake process. The TLS certificate relies on public-key (asymmetric) cryptography and is used during the handshake process to establish a secret key used for symmetric encryption during the session. During the handshake, both sides agree on the encryption algorithms to use and verify that the TLS certificate is authentic and the server is who they say they are. They generate session secret keys to be used for encrypting data after the handshake. Once the handshake is completed, data remains encrypted between the two, and the secure communication channel, displayed in Figure 10-5, is established for the duration of the session.

Figure 10-5. Secured communication between a client web browser and web server using TLS

Encrypting Trino Client-to-Coordinator Communication

It's important to secure the traffic between the client and Trino for two reasons. First, if you are using LDAP authentication, the password is in clear text. And with Kerberos authentication, the SPNEGO token (*https://en.wikipedia.org/wiki/SPNEGO*) can be intercepted as well. Trino therefore requires usage of TLS/HTTPS when any authentication is configured. Additionally, any data returned from queries is in plain text.

Understanding the lower-level details of the TLS handshake for encryption algorithms is not crucial to understanding how Trino encrypts network traffic. But it is important to understand more about certificates, since you need to use, and potentially create and configure, certificates for use by Trino. Figure 10-5 depicts communications between a client web browser and web server secured over HTTPS. This is exactly how HTTPS communication is used between the Trino coordinator and a Trino client such as the Trino Web UI, the Trino CLI, or the JDBC driver, displayed in Figure 10-6.

A TLS certificate relies on public-key (asymmetric) cryptography using key pairs:

- A public key, which is available to anyone
- A private key, which is kept private by the owner

Anyone can use the public key to encrypt messages that can be decrypted only by those who have the private key. Therefore, any message encrypted with the public key should be secret, as long as only the owner of the key pair does not share or have its private key stolen. A TLS certificate contains information such as the domain the certificate was issued for, the person or company it was issued to, the public key, and several other items. This information is then hashed and encrypted using a private key. The process of signing the certificate creates the signature to include in the certificate.

Figure 10-6. Secured communication over HTTP between Trino clients and the Trino coordinator

These certificates are often signed by a trusted CA such as DigiCert or GlobalSign. These authorities verify that the person requesting a certificate to be issued is who they say they are and that they own the domain as stated in the certificate. The certificate is signed by the authority's private key, for which their public keys are made widely available and typically installed by default on most operating systems and web browsers but also in runtime environments such as the JVM.

The process of signing the certificate is important during the TLS handshake to verify authenticity. The client uses the public key of the pair to decrypt the signature and compare to the content in the certificate to make sure it was not tampered with.

Now that you understand the basics of TLS, let's look at how we can encrypt data between the Trino clients and coordinator. To enable HTTPS on the Trino coordinator, you need to set additional properties in the *config.properties* file (see Table 10-2).

Table 10-2. Configuration properties for HTTPS communication

Property	Description
http-server.https.enabled	Set this to true to enable HTTPS for Trino. Defaults to false.
http-server.http.enabled	Set this to false to disable HTTP for Trino. Defaults to true.
http-server.https.port	Specify the HTTPS port to use. 8443 is a common default port for HTTPS for Java application servers.
http-server.https.keystore.path	Specify the path to the Java keystore file that stores the private key and certificate used by Trino for TLS. Alternatively, you can use a standard certificate file in the PEM format.
http-server.https.keystore.key	Specify the Java keystore password Trino needs to access the keystore.

Even though you are configuring Trino to use HTTPS, by default HTTP is still enabled as well. Enabling HTTPS does not disable HTTP. If you wish to disable HTTP access, this needs to be configured. However, you may want to keep HTTP enabled until you have completed configuring the secured Trino environment. Testing how or if something works over HTTP may be a good way to debug an issue if you run into complications during configurations.

Take, for example, the following minimal configuration to add to your *config.properties*:

```
http-server.https.enabled=true
http-server.https.port=8443
http-server.https.keystore.path=etc/mytrinocluster.pem
```

Remember to restart the Trino coordinator after you update the properties file. The preceding setup relies on using a globally trusted certificate obtained from a CA in PEM format. With this certificate in place, TLS works seamlessly. Client applications do not need to configure any certificate on their end, because the certificate is globally trusted, including the operating system, web browser, and runtime on the client.

Alternatively you can use a Java keystore file and password:

```
http-server.https.enabled=true
http-server.https.port=8443
http-server.https.keystore.path=/etc/trino/trino_keystore.jks
http-server.https.keystore.key=slickpassword
```

Java Keystores and Truststores

While configuring encryption, you can work with standard PEM files or Java keystores. A *keystore* is a repository used to store cryptographic keys, X.509 certificate chains, and trusted certificates. In Trino, the keystore can be used as either a keystore or truststore. There is no difference in the implementation or tools using these stores. The major difference is what is stored in the keystore and truststore and how each is used. A keystore is used when you need to prove your identity, while the truststore is used when you need to confirm another identity.

For Trino, the Trino coordinator needs a keystore that contains the private key and signed certificate. When the Trino client connects, Trino presents this certificate to the client as part of the TLS handshake.

The Trino client, such as the CLI, uses a truststore that contains the certificates needed to verify the authenticity of the certificate presented by the server. If the Trino coordinator certificate is signed by a CA, then the truststore contains the root and intermediate certificates. If you are not using a CA, the truststore contains the same Trino TLS certificate. Self-signed certificates simply mean that the certificate is signed by the private key of the public key in the certificate. These are far less secure, as an attack can spoof a self-signed certificate as part of a man-in-the-middle attack. You must be sure of the security of the network and machine the client is connecting to when using self-signed certificates.

What Is an X.509 Certificate?

X.509 is the standard that defines the format of a public-key certificate such as the ones we want to generate to secure Trino. The certificate includes the domain name it is issued for, the person or organization it is issued to, the issue date and expiration, the public key, and the signature. The certificate is signed by a CA, or is self-signed. You can learn more from the official standard (*https://www.itu.int/rec/T-REC-X.509*).

Creating Java Keystores and Java Truststores

The Java `keytool`, a command-line tool for creating and managing keystores and truststores, is available as part of any Java Development Kit (JDK) installation. Let's go over a simple example for creating a Java keystore and truststore. For simplicity, we use self-signed certificates.

 We strongly recommend obtaining a globally trusted certificate from a vendor and using it on a load balancer in front of Trino or directly with Trino. This avoids all certificate management and creation discussed in this section. No certificate management on the client is needed, because the certificate is globally trusted, including the operating system, web browser, and runtime environments like the JVM.

Let's first create the keystore to be used by the Trino coordinator. The following `keytool` command creates a public/private key pair and wraps the public key in a certificate that is self-signed:

```
$ keytool -genkeypair \
    -alias trino_server \
    -dname CN=*.example.com \
    -validity 10000 -keyalg RSA -keysize 2048 \
    -keystore keystore.jks \
    -keypass password \
    -storepass password
```

The generated *keystore.jks* file needs to be used on the server and specified in the `http-server.https.keystore.path` property. Similar usage applies for the `store pass` password in the `http-server.https.keystore.key` property.

In this example, you are using a *wildcard certificate*. We specify the common name (CN) to be `*.example.com`. This certificate can be shared by all the nodes on the Trino cluster, assuming they use the same domain; this certificate works with `coordinator.example.com`, `worker1.example.com`, `worker2.example.com`, and so on. The disadvantage of this approach is that any node under the *example.com* domain can use the certificate.

You can limit the subdomains by using a subject alternative name (`SubjectAltName`), where you list the subdomains. This allows you to create a single certificate to be shared by a limited, specific list of hosts. An alternative approach is to create a certificate for each node, requiring you to explicitly define the full domain for each. This adds an administrative burden and makes it challenging when scaling a Trino cluster, as the new nodes require certificates bound to the full domain.

When connecting a client to the coordinator, the coordinator sends its certificate to the client to verify its authenticity. A truststore is used to verify the authenticity by containing the coordinator certificate if self-signed, or a certificate chain if signed by a CA. (Later we discuss how to use a certificate chain of a CA.) Because the keystore also contains the certificate, you could simply copy the keystore to the client machine and use that as the truststore. However, that is not secure, as the keystore also contains the private key that we want to keep secret. To create a custom truststore, you need to export the certificate from the keystore and import it into a truststore.

First, on the coordinator where your keystore was created, you export the certificate:

```
$ keytool --exportcert \
    -alias trino_server \
    -file trino_server.cer \
    -keystore keystore.jks \
    -storepass password
```

This command creates a *trino_server.cer* certificate file. As a next step, you use that file to create the truststore:

```
$ keytool --importcert \
    -alias trino_server \
    -file trino_server.cer \
    -keystore truststore.jks \
    -storepass password
```

Since the certificate is self-signed, this `keytool` command prompts you to confirm that you want to trust this certificate. Simply type **yes**, and the *truststore.jks* is created. Now you can safely distribute this truststore to any machine from which you use a client to connect the coordinator.

Now that we have the coordinator enabled with HTTPS using a keystore and we've created a truststore for the clients, we can securely connect to Trino such that the communication between the client and coordinator is encrypted. Here is an example using the Trino CLI:

```
$ trino --server https://trino-coordinator.example.com:8443 \
      --truststore-path ~/truststore.jks \
      --truststore-password password
```

Encrypting Communication Within the Trino Cluster

Next let's look at how to secure the communication between the workers, and the workers and the coordinator, all within the Trino cluster, by using HTTP over TLS again as shown in Figure 10-7.

While the client-to-coordinator communication may be over an untrusted network, the Trino cluster is generally deployed on a more secure network, making secured intercluster communication more optional. However, if you're concerned about a malicious attacker being able to get onto the network of the cluster, communication can be encrypted.

Trino is capable of automatically creating and managing the certificates on the coordinator and all workers to enable TLS for internal communication.

Figure 10-7. Secured communication over HTTPS between nodes in the Trino cluster

The same method of performing the TLS handshake to establish trust between the client and server, and create an encrypted channel, works for the intercluster communication. Communication in the cluster is bidirectional, meaning a node may act as a client sending the HTTPS request to another node, or a node can act as a server when it receives the request and presents the certificate to the client for verification. All of this is managed automatically after you configure a shared secret as required for any authentication (as described in "Authentication" on page 212) and require TLS/HTTPS for internal communication on all nodes:

```
internal-communication.shared-secret=aLongRandomString
internal-communication.https.required=true
http-server.https.enabled=true
```

```
http-server.https.port=8443
discovery.uri=https://coordinator.example.com:8443
```

Remember to restart the coordinator and workers after you update the properties files. Now you have entirely secured the internal and external communication and secured it against eavesdroppers on the network trying to intercept data from Trino.

 Once you have everything working, it's important to disable HTTP by setting `http-server.http.enabled=false` in *config.properties*; otherwise, a user can still connect to the cluster using HTTP.

Certificate Authority Versus Self-Signed Certificates

When you try out Trino for the first time and work to get it configured securely, it's easiest to use a self-signed certificate. In practice, however, it may not be allowed in your organization as they are much less secure and susceptible to attacks in certain situations. Therefore, you may use a certificate that was digitally signed by a CA.

Once you have created the keystore, you need to create a certificate signing request (CSR) to send to the CA to get the keystore signed. The CA verifies you are who you say you are and issues you a certificate signed by them. The certificate is then imported into your keystore. This CA-signed certificate is presented to the client instead of the original self-signed one.

An interesting aspect is related to the use of the Java truststore. Java provides a default truststore that may contain the CA already. In this case, the certificate presented to the client can be verified by the default truststore. Using the Java default truststore can be cumbersome because it may not contain the CA. Or perhaps your organization has its own internal CA for issuing organizational certifications to employees and services. So if you're using a CA, it is still recommended that you create your own truststore for Trino to use.

However, you can import the CA certificate chain instead of the actual certificates being used for Trino. A *certificate chain* is a list of two or more TLS certificates, where each certificate in the chain is signed by the next one in the chain. At the top of the chain is the root certificate, and this is always self-signed by the CA itself. It is used to sign the downstream certificates known as *intermediate certificates*. When you are issued a certificate for Trino, it is signed by an intermediate certificate, which is the first one in the chain. The advantage to this is that, if there are multiple certificates for multiple Trino clusters or if certificates are reissued, you don't need to reimport them into your truststore each time. This reduces the need for the CA to reissue an intermediate or root certificate.

The scenario in **Figure 10-8** shows the use of a certificate issued by a CA. The truststore contains only the intermediate and root certificates of the CA. The TLS certificate from the Trino coordinator is verified using this certificate chain in the client truststore.

Figure 10-8. Trino using a certificate issued by a CA

Let's say you had your Trino certificate signed by a CA. For the client to trust it, we need to create a truststore containing the intermediate and root certificates. As in the earlier example in which we imported the Trino self-signed certificate, you perform the same import of the CA certificate chain:

```
$ keytool --importcert \
    -alias trino_server \
    -file root-ca.cer \
    -keystore truststore.jks \
    -storepass password
```

After the root CA certificate is imported, you continue to import all necessary intermediate certificates from the chain:

```
$ keytool --importcert \
    -alias trino_server \
    -file intermediate-ca.cer \
    -keystore truststore.jks \
    -storepass password
```

Note that there may be more than a single intermediate certificate and that we're using a single one here for simplicity.

Certificate Authentication

Now that you've learned about TLS, certificates, and the related usage of the Java keytool, you can look at using these tools for authenticating clients connecting to Trino with TLS. This certificate authentication is displayed in Figure 10-9.

As part of the TLS handshake, the server provides the client a certificate so that the client can authenticate the server. *Mutual TLS* means that the client, as a part of the handshake, provides a certificate to the server to be authenticated. The server verifies the certificate in the same way you have seen the client verify the certificate. The server requires a truststore that contains the CA chain, or the self-signed certificate for verification.

Figure 10-9. Certificate authentication for Trino clients

To configure the Trino coordinator for mutual TLS authentication, you need to add some properties to the *config.properties* file on the coordinator. Let's look at a complete configuration:

```
http-server.http.enabled=false
http-server.https.enabled=true
http-server.https.port=8443

http-server.https.keystore.path=/etc/trino/trino_keystore.jks
http-server.https.keystore.key=slickpassword

http-server.https.truststore.path=/etc/trino/trino_truststore.jks
http-server.https.truststore.key=slickpassword
internal-communication.shared-secret=aLongRandomString
internal-communication.https.required=true

http-server.authentication.type=CERTIFICATE
```

The property `http-server.authentication.type` indicates the type of authentication to use. In this case, Trino is using `CERTIFICATE` authentication. This causes the Trino coordinator to use the full TLS handshake for mutual authentication. In particular, the server-side coordinator sends a certificate request message as part of the full TLS handshake to the client to provide the signed certificate for verification. In addition, you need to configure the truststore on the coordinator in order to verify the certificate presented by the client.

Let's use our command to connect with the CLI to Trino:

```
$ trino --server https://trino-coordinator.example.com:8443 \
     --truststore-path ~/truststore.jks \
     --truststore-password password \
     --user matt
trino> SELECT * FROM system.runtime.nodes;
Error running command: Authentication failed: Unauthorized
```

This authentication failed because the client does not use the keystore that has the certificate to provide the client certificate to the coordinator for mutual authentication.

You need to modify your command to include a keystore. Note that this keystore is different from the keystore on the cluster. This keystore specifically contains the key pair for the client. Let's first create our keystore on the client side:

```
$ keytool -genkeypair \
    -alias trino_server \
    -dname CN=matt \
    -validity 10000 -keyalg RSA -keysize 2048 \
    -keystore client-keystore.jks \
    -keypass password
    -storepass password
```

In this example, you see that we set the CN to user `matt`. In this case, it's more than likely that this is a self-signed certificate or that an organization has its own internal CA. Let's specify the client keystore in the CLI command:

```
$ trino --server https://trino-coordinator.example.com:8443 \
     --truststore-path ~/truststore.jks \
     --truststore-password password \
     --keystore-path ~/client-keystore.jks \
     --keystore-password password \
     --user matt

trino> SELECT * FROM system.runtime.nodes;
Query failed: Access Denied:
Authenticated user AuthenticatedUser[username=CN=matt,principal=CN=matt]
cannot become user matt
```

Now that we have authenticated, authorization is failing. Recall that authentication proves who you are, and authorization controls what you can do.

In the case of certificate authentication, Trino extracts the subject distinguished name from the X.509 certificate. This value is used as the principal to compare to the username. The username defaults to the operating system username unless it is specified explicitly using the `--user` option in the CLI. In this case, the user `matt` is compared to the distinguished common name in the certificate `CN=matt`. One workaround is to simply pass the option to the CLI as `--user CN=matt`. Alternatively, you can leverage the built-in file-based system access control you learned about earlier for some customization.

First, you need to create a file in the Trino installation directory *etc/access-control.properties*, on the Trino coordinator:

```
access-control.name=file
security.config-file=/etc/trino/rules.json
```

Next, we need to create the *rules.json* file on the coordinator as the path location specified in the *access-control.properties* file and define the mapping from principal to user to include CN=:

```
{
  "catalogs": [
    {
      "allow": true
    }
  ],
  "principals": [
    {
      "principal": "CN=(.*)",
      "principal_to_user": "$1",
      "allow": true
    }
  ]
}
```

We are matching a principal regex with a capturing group. We then use that capturing group to map the principal to the user. In our example, the regex matches `CN=matt`, where `matt` is part of the capturing group to map to the user. Once you create these files and restart the coordinator, both the certificate authentication and authorization of that subject principal to the user work:

```
SELECT * FROM system.runtime.nodes;
-[ RECORD 1 ]+-------------------------------------------------------------
node_id      | i-0779df73d79748087
http_uri     | https://coordinator.example.com:8443
node_version | 312
coordinator  | true
state        | active
-[ RECORD 2 ]+-------------------------------------------------------------
node_id      | i-0d3fba6fcba08ddfe
http_uri     | https://worker-1.example.com:8443
```

```
node_version | 312
coordinator  | false
state        | active
```

Kerberos

The network authentication protocol *Kerberos* (*http://web.mit.edu/kerberos*) is widely used. Support for Kerberos in Trino is especially critical for Trino users who are using the Hive connector (see "Hive Connector for Distributed Storage Data Sources" on page 102), since Kerberos is a commonly used authentication mechanism with HDFS and Hive.

> The Kerberos (*http://web.mit.edu/kerberos*) documentation can be a useful resource for learning about the protocol and the related concepts and terms. In this section, we assume that you are sufficiently familiar with these aspects or that you have read some of the documentation and other resources available.

Trino supports clients to authenticate to the coordinator by using the Kerberos authentication mechanism. The Hive connector can authenticate with a Hadoop cluster that uses Kerberos authentication.

Similar to LDAP, Kerberos is an authentication protocol, and a principal can be authenticated using a username and password or a *keytab* file.

Prerequisites

Kerberos needs to be configured on the Trino coordinator, which needs to be able to connect to the Kerberos key distribution center (KDC). The *KDC* is responsible for authenticating principals and issues session keys that can be used with Kerberos-enabled services. KDCs typically use TCP/IP port 88.

Using MIT Kerberos, you need to have a [realms] section in the */etc/krb5.conf* configuration file.

Kerberos Client Authentication

To enable Kerberos authentication with Trino, you need to add details to the *config.properties* file on the Trino coordinator. You need to change the authentication type, configure the location of the *keytab* file, and specify the username of the Kerberos service account to use:

```
http-server.authentication.type=KERBEROS
http.server.authentication.krb5.service-name=trino
http.server.authentication.krb5.keytab=/etc/trino/trino.keytab
```

No changes to the worker configuration are required. The worker nodes continue to connect to the coordinator over unauthenticated HTTP, or with the internal communication described in "Encrypting Communication Within the Trino Cluster" on page 229.

To connect to this kerberized Trino cluster, a user needs to set up their *keytab* file, their principal, and their *krb5.conf* configuration file on the client and then use the relevant parameters for the Trino CLI or the properties for a JDBC connection. You can find all the details including a small wrapper script in the Trino documentation.

Data Source Access and Configuration for Security

Another aspect of securing the data available to Trino users is visible in Figure 10-10. Each catalog configured in Trino includes the connection string as well as the user credentials used to connect to the data source. Different connectors and target data source systems allow different access configurations.

A user first authenticates to the coordinator. The Trino connector issues requests to the data sources, which typically require authentication as well.

Figure 10-10. Data source security configuration impacting data for users

Authentication from the connectors to the data sources depend on the connector implementation. In many connector implementations, Trino authenticates as a service user. Therefore, for any user who runs a query using such a connector, the query is executed in the underlying system as that service user.

For example, if the user credentials to the target data source do not include the rights to perform any write operations, you effectively restrict all Trino users to read-only operations and queries. Similarly, if the user does not have access rights to a specific schema, database, or even table, Trino usage has the same restrictions.

To provide a more fine-grained access control, you can create several service users with different permissions. You can then have multiple catalog configurations with the same connector to the same data source, but using different service users.

Similar to using different service users, you can also create catalogs with different connections strings. For example, the PostgreSQL connection string includes a database name, which means you can create different catalogs to separate access to these databases running on the same PostgreSQL server. The MS SQL Server connections string allows an optional configuration of a database.

Details such as connection strings, user credentials, and other aspects are discussed in Chapter 6.

Beyond the schema and database level, you can even push access rights and data content configuration all the way down to the database itself. For example, if you want to limit access to certain columns or certain rows in a table, you can limit access to the source tables and instead create views with the desired content. These are then available in Trino like traditional tables and therefore implement your security. The extreme case of this scenario is the creation of a separate database or data warehouse using ETL tools, including even Trino itself. These target databases with the desired data can then be configured for access in Trino with separate catalogs as well.

If you end up having multiple catalogs defined on your Trino deployment using some of the preceding logic, and you want to allow access to these catalogs to specific users, you can take advantage of the system access control discussed in "System Access Control" on page 216.

A relatively new feature available in some connectors from Trino, as well as some commercially available connectors, is end-user impersonation. This allows the end-user credentials in the Trino CLI or other tools to be passed through all the way to the data source. The access rights in Trino then reflect the configured access rights in the database.

One example of data source security configuration is the use of Kerberos with HDFS and therefore with the Hive connector; see "Hive Connector for Distributed Storage Data Sources" on page 102. Let's look at the details now.

Kerberos Authentication with the Hive Connector

You've learned about Kerberos configuration and data source security in general earlier; now let's now look at the combination of Kerberos, HDFS/Hive, and the Hive connector.

By default, no authentication is enabled for Hive connector use. However, the connector does support Kerberos authentication. All you need to do is configure the connector to work with two services on the Hadoop cluster:

- The Hive Metastore Service
- The Hadoop Distributed File System (HDFS)

If your *krb5.conf* location is different from */etc/krb5.conf*, you must set it explicitly using the `java.security.krb5.conf` JVM property in the *jvm.config* file:

```
-Djava.security.krb5.conf=/example/path/krb5.conf
```

Hive Metastore Service Authentication

In a kerberized Hadoop cluster, Trino connects to the Hive Metastore Service by using Simple Authentication and Security Layer (SASL) and authenticates by using Kerberos. You can enable Kerberos authentication for the metastore service in your catalog properties file:

```
hive.metastore.authentication.type=KERBEROS
hive.metastore.service.principal=hive/hive-metastore-host.example.com@EXAMPLE.COM
hive.metastore.client.principal=trino@EXAMPLE.COM
hive.metastore.client.keytab=/etc/trino/hive.keytab
```

This setting activates the use of Kerberos for the authentication to HMS. It also configures the Kerberos principal and *keytab* file location that Trino uses when connecting to the metastore service. The *keytab* file must be distributed to every node in the cluster.

`hive.metastore.service.principal` can use the _HOST placeholder in the value. When connecting to the HMS, the Hive connector substitutes this with the hostname of the metastore server it is connecting to. This is useful if the metastore runs on multiple hosts. Similarly, `hive.metastore.client.principal` can have the _HOST placeholder in its value. When connecting to the HMS, the Hive connector substitutes this with the hostname of the worker node Trino is running on. This is useful if each worker node has its own Kerberos principal.

Trino connects as the Kerberos principal specified by the property `hive.meta store.client.principal` and authenticates this principal by using the *keytab* specified by the `hive.metastore.client.keytab` property. It verifies that the identity of the metastore matches `hive.metastore.service.principal`.

The principal specified by `hive.metastore.client.principal` must have sufficient privileges to remove files and directories within the *hive/warehouse* directory. Without this access, only the metadata is removed, and the data itself continues to consume disk space. This is because the HMS is responsible for deleting internal table data. When the metastore is configured to use Kerberos authentication, all HDFS operations performed by the metastore are impersonated. Errors deleting data are silently ignored.

HDFS Authentication

Enabling Kerberos authentication to HDFS is similar to metastore authentication, with the following properties in your connectors properties file. When the authentication type is KERBEROS, Trino accesses HDFS as the principal specified by the `hive.hdfs.trino.principal` property. Trino authenticates this principal by using the *keytab* specified by the `hive.hdfs.trino.keytab` property:

```
hive.hdfs.authentication.type=KERBEROS
hive.hdfs.trino.principal=hdfs@EXAMPLE.COM
hive.hdfs.trino.keytab=/etc/trino/hdfs.keytab
```

Cluster Separation

Another large-scale security option is the complete separation of the data sources and configured catalogs by using them on separate Trino clusters. This separation can make sense in various scenarios:

- Isolating read-only operations from ETL and other write operation use cases
- Hosting clusters on completely different infrastructure because of regulatory requirements for the data; for example, web traffic data as compared to heavily regulated data such as medical or financial or personal data

This separation of clusters can allow you to optimize the cluster configuration for the different use cases and data or to locate the clusters closer to the data. Both situations can achieve considerable performance as well as cost advantages, while at the same time satisfying security needs.

Conclusion

Now you can feel safe about your data and the access Trino provides to it. You know about the many options you have to secure Trino access and the exposed data. This is a critical part of running Trino and has to be augmented by other activities such as monitoring, discussed in Chapter 12.

But first you need to learn about numerous tools to use with Trino to achieve some amazingly powerful results. Check it out in our next chapter, Chapter 11.

Integrating Trino with Other Tools

As you learned in Chapter 1, Trino unlocks a wide array of uses. By now you've learned a lot about running a Trino cluster, connecting with JDBC, and writing queries running against one or multiple catalogs.

It is time now to look at some applications that are successfully used with Trino in numerous organizations. The following sections cover various scenarios representing a small subset of the possibilities.

Queries, Visualizations, and More with Apache Superset

Apache Superset (*https://superset.apache.org*) can be described as a modern, enterprise-ready business intelligence web application. But this short, concise description really does not do justice to Superset.

Superset runs as a web application in your infrastructure and therefore does not require your business analysts and other users to install or manage their tools on their workstations. It supports Trino as a data source and so can be used as a frontend for your users accessing Trino and all the configured data sources.

Once connected to Superset, users can start writing their queries in the included rich SQL query editor called *SQL Lab*. SQL Lab allows you to write queries in multiple tabs, browse the metadata of the database for assistance, run the queries, and receive the results in the user interface in a table. Even long-running queries are supported. SQL Lab also has numerous UI features that help you write the queries or reduce that effort to a button click or two. For users, SQL Lab alone is already valuable and powerful. However, it is only the first step of benefiting from Superset. SQL Lab allows you a smooth transition to the real power of Superset: visualizing your data.

The visualizations supported by Superset are rich. You can get a first glance by looking at the visualizations gallery (*https://superset.apache.org/gallery.html*). You can create all the typical visualizations including data point plots, line charts, bar charts, or pie charts. Superset, however, is much more powerful and supports 3D visualizations, map-based data analysis, and more.

Once you have created the necessary queries and visualizations, you can assemble them into a dashboard and share them with the rest of your organization. This allows business analysts and other specialists to create useful aggregations of data and visualizations and expose them to other users conveniently.

Using Trino with Superset is simple. Superset includes Trino support via the Trino Python Client and the SQLAlchemy standard library. Once both systems are up and running, you just need to configure Trino as a database in Superset.

After Trino and Superset are connected, it can be useful to slowly expose it to your users. The simplicity of Superset allows users to create powerful but also computationally heavy queries with large data sets that can have a significant impact on the sizing and configuration of your Trino cluster. Scaling usage step-by-step in terms of users and use cases allows you to keep track of the cluster utilization and ensure that you scale the cluster based on the new demands.

Performance Improvements with RubiX

When you scale Trino to access large distributed storage systems and expose it to many users and tools, demands on your infrastructure increase tremendously. Compute performance needs can be handled by scaling the Trino cluster itself. The queried data source can be tuned as well. Even having those optimizations all in place and tuned, however, leaves you with a gap—the connection between Trino and the data.

The lightweight data-caching framework *RubiX* (*https://github.com/qubole/rubix*) can be located between the Trino compute resources and the data sources and act as a caching layer. It supports disk and in-memory caching. Using this open source platform when querying distributed storage systems can result in significant performance improvements and cost reductions because of avoided data transfers and repeated queries on the underlying source.

RubiX is built into Trino and used by the Hive connector for storage caching. It acts as a transparent enhancement to the connector, and from the view of a Trino user, nothing really changes. All you have to do is configure the storage caching location on the workers and ensure performant storage volumes are used. Metadata about the storage as well as actual data is cached and managed by RubiX. The storage is distributed on the workers for maximum performance improvements.

Using this Hive storage caching in Trino, powered by RubiX, is an established practice to improve read performance when querying distributed object storage.

Workflows with Apache Airflow

Apache Airflow (*https://airflow.apache.org*) is a widely used system to programmatically author, schedule, and monitor workflows. It has a strong focus on data pipeline processing and is widely used in the data science community. It is implemented in Python and capable of orchestrating the executions of complex workflows written in Python, calling out to many supported systems and including the execution of shell scripts.

To integrate Trino with Airflow, you can take advantage of Trino hooks in Airflow, or run the Trino CLI from the command line. Airflow supports many data sources beyond Trino and can therefore be used outside Trino to prepare data for later consumption via Trino. You can access and work with the data using Trino to take advantage of its performance, scalability, and integration with many data sources.

The goal with Airflow and Trino is often to get the source data processed to end up with a high-quality data set that supports use in applications and machine learning models alike. Once the workflows, orchestrated by Airflow and run by Trino and potentially other integrations, have produced the desired data sets, Trino can be used to access it.

If Apache Airflow is not your tool of choice, similar functionality can be realized with dbt or Apache Flink, which have good support for Trino. You can also use other tools that support one of the client libraries such as the JDBC driver or the Trino Python client, or even resort to using the Trino CLI for running SQL scripts.

Once all your processes are running and the data is moved around and modified as desired, you can expose it to users with reports and dashboards, potentially using Apache Superset; see "Queries, Visualizations, and More with Apache Superset" on page 241.

Embedded Trino Example: Amazon Athena

Amazon Athena (*https://aws.amazon.com/athena*) is a query service that can be used to run SQL queries directly on data in files of any size stored in Amazon S3. Athena is a great example of an application that wraps Trino and uses it as a query engine to provide significant power and features. Athena is offered as a service and essentially uses Trino and the Hive connector to query S3. The Hive metastore used with the storage is another service, AWS Glue (*https://aws.amazon.com/glue*).

Figure 11-1 shows a high-level overview of the Amazon Athena architecture. Clients access Athena via the Athena/Trino REST API. Queries are run on the deployment of

Trino with Athena by interacting with the Glue Data Catalog for the metadata of the data stored in S3 and queried by Trino.

Figure 11-1. High-level overview of the Amazon Athena architecture

Athena is a *serverless architecture*, which means you do not have to manage any infrastructure such as Amazon Elastic Compute Cloud (EC2) instances or manage, install, or upgrade any database software to process the SQL statements. Athena takes care of all that for you. With no setup time, Athena instantly provides you the endpoint to submit your SQL queries. Serverless is a key design of Athena, providing high availability and fault tolerance as built-in benefits. Amazon provides the guarantees of uptime and availability of its services as well as resilience to failures or data loss.

Because Athena is serverless, it uses a different pricing model compared to when you're managing the infrastructure yourself. For example, when you run Trino on EC2, you pay an EC2 instance cost per hour regardless of how much you use Trino. With Athena, you pay only for the queries by paying for the amount of data read from S3 per query.

Amazon provides several clients to interact with and submit queries to, Athena and therefore Trino. You can use the AWS command-line interface, the REST API, the AWS Web Console, and applications using the JDBC driver, ODBC driver, or the Athena SDK.

Now, after all these benefits, it is important to understand that from a user's perspective Athena is *not a managed Trino deployment* at all. Here are a few important aspects that distinguish it from a Trino deployment:

- No use of other data sources within AWS or outside possible
- No access to the Trino Web UI for query details and other aspects
- No control of Trino itself, including version, configuration, or infrastructure

Let's look at a short example of using Athena with the iris data set: see "Iris Data Set" on page 15. After creating a database and table and importing the data into Athena, you are ready to use it.

You can run a query with Athena by using the AWS CLI with the `start-query-execution` Athena command. You need to use two arguments:

`--query-string`
>   This is the query you want to execute in Athena.

`--cli-input-json`
>   This is a JSON structure that provides additional context to Athena. In this case, we specify the database in the Glue Data Catalog where the `iris` table exists and we specify where to write the query results.

 All queries run in Athena write the results to a location in S3. This is configurable in the AWS Web Console and can be specified when using the client tools for Athena.

We are using this JSON structure, stored in *athena-input.json*, for running this query:

```
{
    "QueryExecutionContext": {
        "Database": "iris"
    },
    "ResultConfiguration": {
        "OutputLocation": "s3://trino-book-examples/results/"
    }
}
```

Let's run the Athena query with the AWS CLI:

```
$ aws athena start-query-execution \
--cli-input-json file://athena-input.json \
--query-string 'SELECT species, AVG(petal_length_cm), MAX(petal_length_cm), \
  MIN(petal_length_cm) FROM iris GROUP BY species'

{
    "QueryExecutionId": "7e2a9640-04aa-4ae4-8e88-bd6fe4d9c289"
}
```

Because Athena executes the query asynchronously, the call to `start-query-execution` returns a query execution ID. It can be used to get the status of the query execution, or the results, when it is complete. The results are stored in S3 in CSV format:

```
$ aws athena get-query-execution \
  --query-execution-id 7e2a9640-04aa-4ae4-8e88-bd6fe4d9c289

{
    "QueryExecution": {
    ...
```

```
        "ResultConfiguration": {
          "OutputLocation":
              "s3://...7e2a9640-04aa-4ae4-8e88-bd6fe4d9c289.csv"
        },
        ...
  }
  $ aws s3 cp --quiet
  s3://.../7e2a9640-04aa-4ae4-8e88-bd6fe4d9c289.csv
  /dev/stdout


  "species","_col1","_col2","_col3"
  "virginica","5.552","6.9","4.5"
  "versicolor","4.26","5.1","3.0"
  "setosa","1.464","1.9","1.0"
```

You can also use the `aws athena get-query-results` command to retrieve the results in a JSON structure format. Another choice is the open source AthenaCLI (*https://github.com/dbcli/athenacli*).

Stop and think about this. Without *any* infrastructure to manage, you can simply point a command-line interface and run SQL queries on data files stored in S3. Without Athena and Glue, you have to deploy and manage the infrastructure and software to execute SQL queries on the data. And without Trino, you have to somehow ingest and format the data into a database for SQL processing.

The combination of Athena and Glue make for a powerful tool to use. And the feature allowing you to use standard SQL against the S3 data is all powered by Trino.

This quick introduction does not provide a comprehensive look at Athena, but it gives you a glimpse at how Trino is being used in the industry and how much other offerings can differ from Trino.

Using Athena satisfies various needs and comes with specific restrictions and characteristics. For example, Athena imposes limits for larger, longer-running queries.

Since you are paying for the processed data volume rather than the infrastructure to run the software, costing is also very different. Each time you run a query, you pay for the data processed. Depending on your usage patterns, this can be cheaper or more expensive. Specifically, you can preprocess the data in S3 to use formats such as Parquet and ORC as well as compression to reduce query cost. Of course, the preprocessing comes at a price as well, so you have to try to optimize for overall cost.

Many other platforms use Trino in a similar, hidden fashion that can provide tremendous power to the user and the platform providers. If you are looking for control and flexibility, running your own Trino deployment remains a powerful option.

Convenient Commercial Distributions: Starburst Enterprise and Starburst Galaxy

Starburst (*http://starburst.io*) is the enterprise company behind the Trino open source project and a major sponsor of the project and the Trino Software Foundation. The founding team members at Starburst were early contributors to Trino at Teradata, and they started Starburst to focus on continuing the success of Trino in the enterprise. The founders of the Trino open source project from Facebook joined Starburst in 2019, and Starburst has become one of the largest contributors and committers to the Trino project.

Starburst offers commercial support for an enhanced distribution of Trino, *Starburst Enterprise*, with additional enterprise features such as more connectors, performance, and other improvements to existing connectors, a management console for the cluster and query processing on it, a built-in query editor, support for data products, and enhanced security features. Starburst Enterprise includes support for deployments anywhere. Bare-metal servers, virtual machines, and containers on Kubernetes are all supported. You can run Trino on all major cloud providers and cloud platforms, on-premises systems, and hybrid cloud infrastructure.

If you want to avoid the complexities of running Trino, Starburst offers the software-as-a-service *Starburst Galaxy*. It allows you to sign up, connect your data sources, and start querying in the built-in query editor within minutes. You can define catalogs for your data sources, and create and manage multiple Trino clusters easily. With the built-in monitoring, you can observe your clusters and analyze the query processing on the clusters. You can author SQL queries right in the user interface, save queries, and run them again in the future. The available access control allows you to easily configure read-only access or full write access and any other combination of privileges for any roles you create. Clusters can run in the major cloud providers and access numerous data sources.

Other Integration Examples

You've only scratched the surface of tools and platforms that can be used with Trino or that integrate Trino. The list of business intelligence and reporting tools known to be used with Trino is extensive, including at least these:

- Apache Superset
- DBeaver
- dbt
- Hue
- Information Builders

- JetBrains DataGrip
- Jupyter Notebook
- Looker
- Metabase
- MicroStrategy
- Microsoft Power BI
- Mode
- Querybook
- Redash
- SQuirreL SQL Client
- Tableau
- ThoughtSpot
- Toad

Data platforms, hosting platforms, and other systems using or supporting Trino include the following:

- AWS and Amazon Elastic Kubernetes Service
- Amazon EMR
- Google Kubernetes Engine
- Microsoft Azure Kubernetes Service
- Microsoft Azure HDInsight
- Qlik
- Red Hat OpenShift

Many of these users and vendors contribute to the project.

Custom Integrations

Trino is an open platform for integrating your own tools. The open source community around Trino is actively creating and improving integrations.

Simple integrations use the Trino CLI or the Trino JDBC driver. More advanced integrations use the HTTP-based protocol exposed by the Trino coordinator for executing queries and more. The JDBC driver simply wraps this protocol; other wrappers for platforms including R and Python are available and linked on the Trino website.

Many organizations take it to the next level by implementing new plug-ins for Trino. These plug-ins can add features such as connectors to other data sources, event listeners, access controls, custom types, and user-defined functions to use in query statements. The Trino documentation contains a useful developer guide that can be your first resource. And don't forget to reach out to the community for help and feedback; see "Community Chat" on page 14.

Conclusion

Isn't it amazing how widely used Trino is and how many different tools you can integrate with Trino to create some very powerful solutions? We've just scratched the surface in our tour here.

Lots of other tools are available and are used regularly, thanks to the availability of the JDBC driver, ODBC drivers, the Trino CLI, and integrations built on top of these and other extensions.

Whatever commercial or open source business intelligence reporting tool or data analytics platform you prefer to use, be sure to investigate the availability of Trino support or integration. Similarly, it is often worth understanding if Trino is used under the hood in your toolchain. This might give you a better view of potential improvements or expansions to your usage, or even a migration to first-class, direct usage of Trino.

Depending on the level of ownership of the Trino deployment, you have access to customizations, updates, and expansions as desired, or you can lean back and let your provider manage Trino for you as part of the integration. Find your own ideal fit and enjoy the benefits of Trino. And if you manage your own Trino deployment, make sure to learn more about it in Chapter 12.

Trino in Production

After learning about and installing Trino, first as a simple exploratory setup in Chapter 2 and then as a deployment in Chapter 5, you now get to dive into more details. After all, simply installing and configuring a cluster is a very different task from keeping it up and running day and night, with different users and changing data sources and entirely separate usage.

In this chapter, you therefore get to explore other aspects you need to learn about in order to be a successful operator of your Trino clusters.

Monitoring with the Trino Web UI

As discussed in "Trino Web UI" on page 38, the Trino Web UI is accessible on every Trino cluster coordinator and can be used to inspect and monitor the Trino cluster and processed queries. The detailed information provided can be used to better understand and tune the Trino system overall as well as individual queries.

> The Trino Web UI exposes information from the Trino system tables, discussed in "Trino System Tables" on page 144.

When you first navigate to the Trino Web UI address, you see the main dashboard shown in Figure 12-1. It displays Trino cluster information in the top section and a list of queries in the bottom section.

Figure 12-1. Trino Web UI main dashboard

Cluster-Level Details

Let's first discuss the Trino cluster information:

Running Queries
>The total number of queries currently running in the Trino cluster. This accounts for all users. For example, if Alice is running two queries and Bob is running five queries, the total number in this box shows seven queries.

Queued Queries
>The total number of queued queries for the Trino cluster for all users. Queued queries are waiting for the coordinator to schedule them, based on the resource group configuration.

Blocked Queries
>The number of blocked queries in the cluster. A blocked query is unable to be processed because of missing available splits or other resources. You learn more about query states in the next sections.

Active Workers
>The number of active worker nodes in the cluster. Any worker nodes added or removed, manually or by auto-scaling, are registered in the discovery service, and the displayed number is updated accordingly. Click the displayed number to access a list of workers with more details.

Runnable Drivers

The average number of runnable drivers in the cluster, as described in Chapter 4.

Reserved Memory

The total amount of reserved memory in bytes in Trino.

Rows/Sec

The total number of rows processed per second across all queries running in the cluster.

Bytes/Sec

The total number of bytes processed per second across all queries running in the cluster.

Worker Parallelism

The total amount of worker parallelism, which is the total amount of thread CPU time across all workers, across all queries running in the cluster.

Query List

The bottom section of the Trino Web UI dashboard lists the recently run queries. An example screenshot is displayed in Figure 12-2. The number of available queries in this history list depends on the Trino cluster configuration.

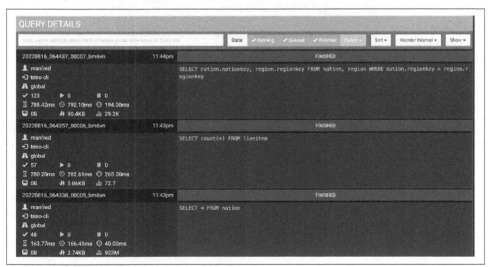

Figure 12-2. List of queries in the Trino Web UI

Above the list itself, controls are available to select the criteria that determine which queries are listed. This allows you to locate specific queries even when a cluster is very busy and runs dozens or hundreds of queries.

The input field allows you to type criteria text to use in order to search for a specific query. The criteria include the username of the query initiator, the query source, the query ID, a resource group, or even the SQL text of the query and the query state.

The *State* filter beside the text input field allows you to include or exclude queries based on the state of the query—running, queued, finished, and failed queries. Failed queries can be further detailed to include or exclude for specific failure reasons—internal, external, resource, and user errors.

Controls on the left allow you to determine the sort order of the displayed queries, the timing of the reordering when the data changed, and the maximum number of queries to show.

Each row underneath the query criteria represents a single query. The left column in the row displays information about the query. The right column displays the SQL text and the state of the query. An example of the query summary is available in Figure 12-3.

Figure 12-3. Information for a specific query in the Trino Web UI

Let's take a closer look at the query details. Each query has the same information for each query run. The text at the top left is the query ID. In this example, the value is 20220816_064437_00007_bm6vn. Looking closer, you may notice that the date and time (UTC) make up the beginning of the ID using the format YYYYMMDD_HHMMSS. The latter half is an incremental counter for the query. Counter value 00007 simply means it was the seventh query run since the coordinator started. The final piece, bm6vn, is a random identifier for the coordinator. Both this random identifier and the counter value are reset if the coordinator is restarted. The time on the top right is the local time when the query was run.

The next three values in the example—manfred, trino-cli, and global—represent the end user running the query, the source of the query, and the resource group used to run the query. In this example, the user is manfred, and we were using the trino-cli to submit the query. If you specify the --user flag when running the Trino CLI, the value changes to what you specified. The source may also be something other than trino-cli; for example, it may display trino-jdbc when an application connects to Trino with the JDBC driver. The client can also set it to any desired value with the - - source flag for the Trino CLI or JDBC connection string property.

The grid of values below is not well labeled in the Trino Web UI, but it contains some important information about the query, as explained in Table 12-1.

Table 12-1. Grid of values for a specific query

Completed Splits: The number of completed splits for the query. The example shows 123 completed splits. At the beginning of query execution, this value is 0. It increases during query execution as splits complete.	Running Splits: The number of running splits for the query. When the query is completed, this value is always 0. However, during execution, this number changes as splits run and complete.	Queued Splits: The number of queued splits for the query. When the query is completed, this value is always 0. However, during execution, this number changes as splits move between queued and run states.
Wall Time: The total wall time spent executing the query. This value continues to grow even if you're paging results.	Total Wall Time: This value is the same as the wall time except that it includes queued time as well. The wall time excludes any time for which the query is queued. This is the total time you'd observe, from when you submit the query to when you finish receiving results.	CPU Time: The total CPU time spent processing the query. This value is often larger than the wall time because parallel execution between workers and threads on workers all count separately and add up. For example, if four CPUs spend 1 second to process a query, the resulting total CPU time is 4 seconds.
Current Total Reserved Memory: The current total reserved memory used for the time of query execution. For completed queries, this value is 0.	Peak Total Memory: The peak total memory usage during the query execution. Certain operations during the query execution may require a lot of memory, and it is useful to know what the peak was.	Cumulative User Memory: The cumulative user memory used throughout the query processing. This does not mean all the memory was used at the same time. It's the cumulative amount of memory.

Many of the icons and values in the Trino Web UI have pop-up tooltips that are visible if you hover your cursor over the image. This is helpful if you are unsure of what a particular value represents.

Next you need to learn more about the different states of query processing, displayed above the query text itself. The most common states are RUNNING, FINISHED, USER CANCELLED, and USER ERROR. The states RUNNING and FINISHED are self-explanatory. USER CANCELLED means that the query was killed by the user. USER ERROR, on the other hand, signifies that the SQL query statement submitted by the user contained a syntactic or semantic error.

The BLOCKED state occurs when a query that is running becomes blocked while waiting on something such as resources or additional splits to process. Seeing a query go to and from this state is normal. However, a query can get stuck in this state for many potential reasons, and this may indicate a problem with the query or the

Trino cluster. If you find a query that appears to be stuck in this state, first check the memory use and configuration of the system. It may be that this query requires an unusually high amount of memory or is computationally expensive. Additionally, if the client is not retrieving the results or cannot read the results fast enough, this back pressure can put the query into a BLOCKED state.

The QUEUED state occurs when a query is started, or stopped from processing, and put into a waiting stage as part of the rules defined for resource groups. The query is simply waiting to be executed.

You may also see a query in the PLANNING state. This typically occurs for larger, complex queries that require a lot of planning and optimizations for running the query. If you see this often, and planning seems to take a noticeable amount of time for queries, you should investigate possible reasons, such as insufficient memory availability or processing power of the coordinator.

Query Details View

So far you have seen information about the Trino cluster overall and higher-level information about the queries. The Web UI offers even more details about each query. Simply click the name of the specific query, as shown in Figure 12-3, to access the Query Details view.

The Query Details view contains a lot of information about a specific query. Let's explore enough for you to feel comfortable using it.

> The Query Details view is often used by Trino developers and users with in-depth knowledge of Trino. This level of sophistication requires you to be very familiar with the Trino code and internals. Checking out this view may still be useful for normal users. Over time, you learn more and acquire more expertise.

The Query Details view uses several tabs for viewing more detailed information about the query. Apart from the tabs, the query ID and the state are always visible. You can see an example header of the view with the tabs in Figure 12-4.

Figure 12-4. Query Details header and tabs

Overview

The Overview page includes the information visible in the Query Details section of the query list and much more detail in numerous sections:

- Session
- Execution
- Resource Utilizations Summary
- Timeline
- Query
- Prepare Query
- Stages
- Tasks

The Stages section, shown in Figure 12-5, displays information on the query stages.

Figure 12-5. Stages section in the Overview tab of the Query Details page

This particular query was the SELECT count(*) FROM lineitem query. Because it is a simpler query, it consists of only two stages. Stage 0 is the single-task stage that runs on the coordinator and is responsible for combining the results from the tasks in stage 1 and performing the final aggregation. Stage 1 is a distributed stage that runs tasks on each of the workers. This stage is responsible for reading the data and computing the partial aggregation.

The following list explains the numerical values from the Stages section, available for each stage:

TIME—SCHEDULED
The amount of time the stage remained scheduled before all tasks for the stage were completed.

TIME—BLOCKED

The amount of time the stage was blocked while waiting for data.

TIME—CPU

The total amount of CPU time of the tasks in the stage.

MEMORY-CUMULATIVE

The cumulative memory used throughout the stage. This does not mean all the memory was used at the same time. It is the cumulative amount of memory used over the time of processing.

MEMORY—CURRENT

The current total reserved memory used for the stage. For completed queries, this value is 0.

MEMORY—BUFFERS

The current amount of memory consumed by data, waiting for processing.

MEMORY—PEAK

The peak total memory during the stage. Certain operations during the query execution may require a lot of memory, and it is useful to know what the peak was.

TASKS—PENDING

The number of pending tasks for the stage. When the query is completed, this value is always 0.

TASKS—RUNNING

The number of running tasks for the stage. When the query is completed, this value is always 0. During execution, the value changes as tasks run and complete.

TASKS—BLOCKED

The number of blocked tasks for the stage. When the query is completed, this value is always 0. However, during execution this number will change as tasks move between blocked and running states.

TASKS—TOTAL

The number of completed tasks for the query.

SCHEDULED TIME SKEW, CPU TIME SKEW, TASK SCHEDULED TIME, and TASK CPU TIME

These histogram charts show the distribution and changes of scheduled time, CPU time, task scheduled time, and task CPU time for multiple tasks across workers. This allows you to diagnose utilization of the workers during the execution of a longer-running, distributed query.

The section below the Stages section describes more details of the tasks, displayed in Figure 12-6.

Figure 12-6. Tasks information in the Query Details page

Let's examine the values in the tasks list; see Table 12-2.

Table 12-2. Description of the columns in the tasks list in Figure 12-6

Column	Description
ID	The task identifier in the format *stage-id.task-id*. For example, ID 0.0 indicates Task 0 of Stage 0, and 1.2 indicates Task 2 of Stage 1.
Host	The IP address of the worker node where the task is run.
State	The state of the task, which can be PENDING, RUNNING, or BLOCKED.
Pending Splits	The number of pending splits for the task. This value changes as the task is running and shows 0 when the task is finished.
Running Splits	The number of running splits for the task. This value changes as the task is running and shows 0 when the task is finished.
Blocked Splits	The number of blocked splits for the task. The value changes as the task is running and shows 0 when the task is finished.
Completed Splits	The number of completed splits for the task. The value changes as the task is running and equals the total number of splits run when the task is finished.
Rows	The number of rows processed in the task. This value increases as the task runs.
Rows/s	The number of rows processed per second in the task.
Bytes	The number of bytes processed in the task. This value increases as the task runs.
Bytes/s	The number of bytes processed per second in the task.
Elapsed	The total amount of elapsed wall time for the task scheduled.
CPU Time	The total amount of CPU time for the task scheduled.
Mem	Current amount of used memory.
Peak Mem	Highest peak value of memory consumption during task execution.

If you examine some of these values carefully, you'll notice how they roll up. For example, the total CPU time for all tasks in a stage equals the CPU time listed in the stage in which they belong. The total CPU time for the stages equals the amount of CPU time listed on the query CPU time.

Live Plan

The Live Plan tab allows you to view query processing performed by the Trino cluster, in real time, while it is executing. You can see an example in Figure 12-7.

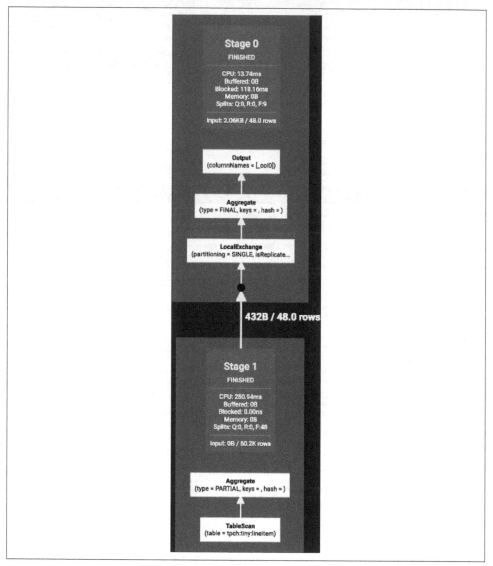

Figure 12-7. Live plan example for the count(*) query on lineitem

During query execution, the counters in the plan are updated while the query execution progresses. The values in the plan are the same as described for the Overview tab, but they are overlaid in real time on the query execution plan. Looking at this view is useful to visualize where a query is stuck or spending a lot of time, in order to diagnose or improve a performance issue.

Stage Performance

The Stage Performance view provides a detailed visualization of the stage performance after query processing is finished. An example is displayed in Figure 12-8.

Think of the view as a drill-down from the Live Plan view, where you can see the operator pipeline of the task within the stage. The values in the plan are the same as described for the Overview tab. Looking at this view is useful to see where a query is stuck or spending a lot of time, in order to diagnose or fix a performance issue. You can click each individual operator to access detailed information.

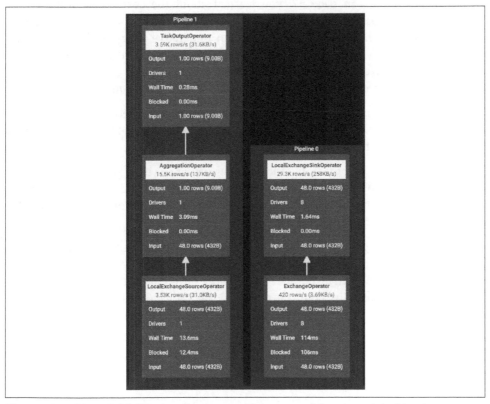

Figure 12-8. Trino Web UI view for stage performance of the `count(*)` `lineitem` *query*

Splits

The Splits view shows a timeline for the creation and processing of splits during the query execution.

JSON

The JSON tab provides all query detail information in JSON format. The information is updated based on the snapshot for which it is retrieved.

 Parts of the Web UI are helpful for copying lengthy strings to the system clipboard. Keep a look out for the clipboard icon. When you click it, the associated string is copied to the system clipboard for you to paste somewhere else.

Tuning Trino SQL Queries

In "Query Planning" on page 57, you learned about the cost-based optimizer in Trino. Recall that SQL is a declarative language in which the user writes an SQL query to specify the data they want. This is unlike an imperative program. With SQL, the user does not specify how to process the data to get the result. It is left to the query planner and optimizer to determine the sequence of steps to process the data for the desired result. The sequence of steps is referred to as the *query plan*.

In most cases, the end user submitting the SQL queries can rely on Trino to plan, optimize, and execute an SQL query efficiently to get the results fast. As an end user, you should not have to worry about the details.

However, sometimes you are not getting the performance you expect, so you need to be able to tune Trino queries. You need to identify whether a specific execution is an outlier single query that is not performing well, or whether multiple queries of similar properties are not performing well.

Let's start with tuning an individual query, assuming the rest of the queries you run are fine on the system. When examining a poorly performing query, you should first look to see if the tables that the query references have data statistics. A number of connectors, such as the Hive connector or the PostgreSQL connector, include support for gathering and maintaining table statistics. It is expected that additional connectors will start to provide data statistics.

Depending on the connector and data source configuration, column and table statistics are already available. Use the SHOW STATS command for a specific table to see what data is available:

```
trino:ontime> SHOW STATS FOR flights;
```

Use the ANALYZE command to add statistics data, if none was found.

Joins in SQL are one of the most expensive operations. You need to focus on joins when tuning the performance of your query and determine the join order by running an EXPLAIN on the query:

```
trino:ontime> EXPLAIN
              SELECT f.uniquecarrier, c.description, count(*) AS ct
              FROM postgresql.airline.carrier c,
                  datalake.ontime.flights_orc f
              WHERE c.code = f.uniquecarrier
              GROUP BY f.uniquecarrier, c.description
              ORDER BY count(*) DESC
              LIMIT 10;
```

As a general rule, you want the smaller input to a join to be on the build side. This is the input to the hash join for which a hash table is built. Because the build side requires reading in the entire input and building a hash table in memory, you want this to be the smaller of the inputs. Being able to determine whether Trino got the join order correct requires some domain knowledge of the data to further investigate. For example, if you know nothing about the data, you may have to run some experimental queries to obtain additional information.

If you have determined that the join order is nonoptimal, you can override the join reordering strategy by setting a toggle to use the syntactic order of the tables listed in the SQL query. This can be configured in the *config.properties* file as the property `optimizer.join-reordering-strategy`. However, if you want to override a single query, you often want to just see the session property `join_reordering_strategy` (see "Session Information and Configuration" on page 157). The allowed values for this property are AUTOMATIC, ELIMINATE_CROSS_JOINS and NONE. Setting the value to ELIMINATE_CROSS_JOINS or NONE performs an override of the cost-based optimizer. ELIMINATE_CROSS_JOINS is a good compromise since it reorders joins only to eliminate cross joins, which is good practice, and otherwise stays with the lexical order suggested by the query author:

```
...
FROM postgresql.airline.carrier c,
datalake.ontime.flights_orc f
...

...
FROM datalake.ontime.flights_orc f,
postgresql.airline.carrier c
...
```

Besides join optimizations, Trino includes some heuristic-based optimizations. These optimizers are not costed and do not always lead to best results. Optimizations can take advantage of Trino being a distributed query engine; aggregations are performed in parallel. This means that an aggregation can be split into multiple smaller parts that can then be distributed to multiple workers, run in parallel, and be aggregated in a final step from the partial results.

A common optimization in Trino and other SQL engines is to push partial aggregations before the join to reduce the amount of data going into the join. This can be configured with the `optimizer.push-aggregation-through-outer-join` property or the `push_aggregation_through_join` session property. Because the aggregation produces partial results, a final aggregation is still performed after the join. The benefit of using this optimization depends on the actual data, and the optimization can even result in a slower query. For example, if the join is highly selective, then it may be more performant to run the aggregation after the join completes. To experiment, you can simply turn off this optimization by setting the property to `false` for the current session.

Another common heuristic is to compute a partial aggregation before the final aggregation:

```
trino> EXPLAIN SELECT count(*) FROM tpch.sf100.orders GROUP BY orderstatus;
       Query Plan
-----------------------------------------------------------------------------
Fragment 0 [HASH]
    Output layout: [count]
    Output partitioning: SINGLE []
    Output[columnNames = [_col0]]
    │   Layout: [count:bigint]
    │   Estimates: {rows: ? (?), cpu: ?, memory: ?, network: ?}
    │   _col0 := count
    └─ Project[]
```

```
           |   Layout: [count:bigint]
           |   Estimates: {rows: ? (?), cpu: ?, memory: ?, network: ?}
           └─ Aggregate[type = FINAL, keys = [orderstatus], hash = [$hashvalue]]
                 |   Layout: [orderstatus:varchar(1), $hashvalue:bigint, count:bigint]
                 |   Estimates: {rows: ? (?), cpu: ?, memory: ?, network: ?}
                 |   count := count("count_0")
                 └─ LocalExchange[partitioning = HASH, hashColumn = [$hashvalue], ...
                       |   Layout: [orderstatus:varchar(1), count_0:bigint, ...
                       |   Estimates: {rows: ? (?), cpu: ?, memory: ?, network: ?}
                       └─ RemoteSource[sourceFragmentIds = [1]]
                               Layout: [orderstatus:varchar(1), count_0:bigint, ...
                               Estimates:

    Fragment 1 [tpch:orders:150000000]
        Output layout: [orderstatus, count_0, $hashvalue_2]
        Output partitioning: HASH [orderstatus][$hashvalue_2]
        Aggregate[type = PARTIAL, keys = [orderstatus], hash = [$hashvalue_2]]
        |   Layout: [orderstatus:varchar(1), $hashvalue_2:bigint, count_0:bigint]
        |   Estimates:
        |   count_0 := count(*)
        └─ ScanProject[table = tpch:sf100:orders]
               Layout: [orderstatus:varchar(1), $hashvalue_2:bigint]
               Estimates: {rows: ? (?), cpu: ?, memory: 0B, network: 0B}/...
               $hashvalue_2 := combine_hash(bigint '0', COALESCE("$operator ...
               orderstatus := tpch:orderstatus
                     :: [[F], [O], [P]]
    (1 row)
```

When this is a generally a good heuristic, the amount of memory to keep for the hash table can be tuned. For example, if the table has a lot of rows with few distinct values in the grouping keys, this optimization works well and reduces the amount of data early before being distributed over the network. However, if there are higher numbers of distinct values, the size of the hash tables needs to be larger in order to reduce the amount of data. By default, the memory used for the hash table is 16 MB, but this can be adjusted by setting task.max-partial-aggregation-memory in the *config.properties* file. However, with too high a count of distinct group keys, the aggregation does nothing to reduce the network transfer, and it may even slow down the query.

Memory Management

Getting the memory configuration and management for your Trino cluster right is not an easy task. Many constantly changing factors influence the memory needs:

- Number of workers
- Memory of coordinator and worker
- Number and type of data sources

- Characteristics of running queries
- Number of users

For Trino, a multiuser system using a cluster of workers, resource management is a fairly challenging problem to solve. Ultimately, you have to pick a starting point and then monitor the system and adjust to the current and upcoming needs. Let's look at some details and talk about recommendations and guidelines around memory management and monitoring in Trino.

> All memory management discussed applies to the JVM running the Trino server. The values are allocations within the JVMs on the workers, and the JVM configuration needs to consider the size of these values to allow allocation.
>
> Depending on the number of concurrent queries, the JVM needs to be adjusted to a much larger value. The next example provides some insight.

All of the preceding factors combine into what we call the *workload*. Tuning the cluster's memory relies heavily on the workload being run.

For example, most query shapes contain multiple joins, aggregations, and window functions. If the query size of the workload is small, you can set lower memory limits per query and increase the concurrency—and the other way around for larger query sizes. For context, query size is a product of query shape and amount of input data. Trino provides a way to manage memory utilization across the cluster by setting certain properties at the time of deployment in *config.properties*:

- `query.max-memory-per-node`
- `query.max-memory`
- `query.max-total-memory`

Memory management in Trino needs to allocate memory for numerous different tasks including aggregations and sorting control, as well as read, write, and shuffle on buffers, table scans, and other operations.

With these tasks in mind, you can examine the memory properties some more:

`query.max-memory-per-node`
The maximum memory a query can utilize on a specific worker. When the memory consumed by a query in allocations exceeds this limit, it is killed.

`query.max-memory`
The maximum memory a query can utilize across all workers in the cluster.

`query.max-total-memory`

    The maximum utilization of memory by a query for allocations for the entire cluster, as a result necessarily greater than `query.max-memory`.

If a query ends up exceeding these limits and as a result is killed, error codes expose the reason:

- `EXCEEDED_LOCAL_MEMORY_LIMIT` means that `query.max-memory-per-node` was exceeded.

- `EXCEEDED_GLOBAL_MEMORY_LIMIT` means that `query.max-memory` or `query.max-total-memory` was exceeded.

Let's look at a real-world example for a small cluster of one coordinator and ten workers and their characteristics:

- One coordinator
- Ten workers; typically workers are all identical system specifications
- Physical memory per worker: 50 GB
- Max JVM heap size configured in `-Xmx` in `jvm.config` to 38 GB
- `query.max-memory-per-node`: 16 GB
- `memory.heap-headroom-per-node`: 9 GB
- `query.max-memory`: 50 GB
- `query.max-total-memory`: 60 GB

Let's break down these numbers a bit more.

The total available memory on each worker is ~50 GB, and we leave ~12 GB for the operating system, agents/daemons, and components running outside the JVM on the system. These systems include monitoring and other systems that allow you to manage the machine and keep it functioning well. As a result, we determine to set the JVM max heap size to 38 GB.

When query size and shape is small, concurrency can be set higher. In the preceding example, we are assuming query size and shape to be medium to large and are also accounting for data skew. `query.max-memory` is set to 50 GB, which is at the overall cluster level. While looking at `max-memory`, we also consider initial-hash-partitions; ideally, this should be a number less than or equal to the number of workers.

If we set that to 8 with `max-memory` at 50 GB, we get 50/8, so about 6.25 GB per worker. Looking at the local limit `max-memory-per-node` set to 16 GB, we keep some headroom for data skew by allowing two times the memory consumption per node. These numbers vary significantly based on how the data is organized and what type of queries are typically run—basically, the workload for the cluster. In addition, the infrastructure used for the cluster, such as the available machine sizes and numbers, has a big impact on the selection of the ideal configuration.

A configuration can be set to help avoid a deadlock situation: `query.low-memory-killer.policy`. This can be set to `total-reservation` or `total-reservation-on-blocked-nodes`. When set to `total-reservation`, Trino kills the largest running query on the cluster to free up resources. On the other hand, `total-reservation-on-blocked-nodes` kills the query that is utilizing the most memory on the nodes that are blocked.

As you can see from the example, you just end up making some assumptions to get started. And then you adjust based on what happens with your actual workloads.

For example, running a cluster for interactive ad hoc queries from users with a visualization tool can create many small queries. An increase of users then ends up increasing the number of queries and the concurrency of them. This typically does not require a change of the memory configuration, just a scaling up of the number of workers in the cluster.

On the other hand, if that same cluster gets a new data source added that exposes massive amounts of data for complex queries that most likely blow the limits, you have to adjust memory.

This gets us to another point that is worth mentioning. Following the best practice recommendation, in a typical Trino cluster infrastructure setup, all workers are the same. All use the same virtual machine (VM) image or container size with identical hardware specifications. As a result, changing the memory on these workers typically means that the new value is either too large for the physical available memory, or too small to make good use of the overall system. Adjusting the memory therefore creates the need to replace all worker nodes in the cluster. Depending on your cluster infrastructure using, for example, virtual machines in a private cloud or containers in a Kubernetes cluster from a public cloud provider, this process can be more or less laborious and fast to implement.

This leads us to one last point worth mentioning here. Your assessment of the workloads can reveal that they are widely different: lots of queries are small, fast, ad hoc queries with little memory footprint, and others are massive, long-running processes with a bunch of analysis in there, maybe even using very different data sources. These workload differences indicate very different memory configuration, and even very different worker configuration and maybe even monitoring needs. In this scenario, you really should take the next step and separate the workloads by using different Trino clusters.

Task Concurrency

To improve performance for your Trino cluster, certain task-related properties may need to be adjusted from the default settings. In this section, we discuss two common properties you may have to tune. However, you can find several others in the Trino documentation. All these properties are set in the *config.properties* file:

Task worker threads
> The default value is set to the number of CPUs of the machine multiplied by 2. For example, a dual hex core machine uses $2 \times 6 \times 2$, so 24 worker threads. If you observe that all threads are being used and the CPU utilization in the machine is still low, you can try to improve CPU utilization and thus performance by increasing this number via the `task.max-worker-threads` setting. The recommendation is to slowly increment this number, as setting it too high can have a diminishing return or adverse effects due to increased memory usage and additional context switching.

Task operator concurrency
> Operators such as joins and aggregations are processed in parallel by partitioning the data locally and executing the operators in parallel. For example, the data is locally partitioned on the `GROUP BY` columns, and then multiple aggregation operators are performed in parallel. The default concurrency for these parallel operations is 16. This value can be adjusted by setting the `task.concurrency` property. If you are running many concurrent queries, the default value may result in reduced performance due to the overhead of context switching. For clusters that run only a smaller number of concurrent queries, a higher value can help increase parallelism and therefore performance.

Worker Scheduling

To improve performance of your Trino cluster, certain scheduling-related properties may need to be adjusted from the default settings. You can tune three common configurations:

- Splits per task
- Splits per node
- Local scheduling

Several others are explained in the Trino documentation.

Let's discuss some details about scheduling splits per task and per node next. Each worker node processes a maximum number of splits. By default, the maximum number of splits processed per worker node is 100. This value can be adjusted with the `node-scheduler.max-splits-per-node` property. You may want to adjust this if you're finding that the workers have maxed out this value and are still underutilized. Increasing the value improves performance, particularly when a lot of splits exist. In addition, you can consider increasing the `node-scheduler.max-pending-splits-per-task` property. This value should not exceed `node-scheduler.max-splits-per-node`. It ensures that work is queued up when the workers finish the tasks in process.

Network Data Exchange

Another important factor affecting the performance of your Trino cluster is the network configuration and setup within the cluster and the closeness to the data sources. Trino supports network-specific properties that can be adjusted from the defaults to adopt to your specific scenario.

In addition to improving performance, sometimes other network-related issues require tuning in order for queries to perform well. Let's discuss some of the common properties you may have to tune.

Concurrency

Trino exchange clients make requests to the upstream tasks producing data. The default number of threads used by the exchange clients is 25. This value can be adjusted by setting the property `exchange.client-threads`.

Setting a larger number of threads can improve performance for larger clusters or clusters configured for high concurrency. The reason is that when more data is produced, additional concurrency to consume the data can decrease latency. Keep in mind that these additional threads increase the amount of memory needed.

Buffer Sizes

Data sent and received during the exchange is kept in buffers on the target and source sides of the exchange. The buffer sizes for each side can be adjusted independently.

On the source side, data is written by the tasks to a buffer waiting to be requested from the downstream exchange client. The default buffer size is 32 MB. It can be adjusted by setting the `sink.max-buffer-size` property. Increasing the value may increase throughput for a larger cluster.

On the target side, data is written to a buffer before it is processed by the downstream task. The default buffer size is 32 MB. It can be adjusted by setting the property `exchange.max-buffer-size`. Setting a higher value can improve query performance by allowing retrieval of more data over the network before back pressure is applied. This is especially true for larger clusters.

Tuning Java Virtual Machine

In Chapter 2, you used the configuration file *etc/jvm.config*, which contains command-line options for the JVM. The Trino launcher uses this file when starting the JVM running Trino. Compared to the earlier mentioned configuration, a more suitable configuration for production usage uses a higher memory value:

```
-server
-Xms64G
-Xmx64G
-XX:InitialRAMPercentage=80
-XX:MaxRAMPercentage=80
-XX:G1HeapRegionSize=32M
-XX:+ExplicitGCInvokesConcurrent
-XX:+ExitOnOutOfMemoryError
-XX:+HeapDumpOnOutOfMemoryError
-XX:-OmitStackTraceInFastThrow
-XX:ReservedCodeCacheSize=512M
-XX:PerMethodRecompilationCutoff=10000
-XX:PerBytecodeRecompilationCutoff=10000
-Djdk.attach.allowAttachSelf=true
-Djdk.nio.maxCachedBufferSize=2000000
-XX:+UnlockDiagnosticVMOptions
-XX:+UseAESCTRIntrinsics
```

Typically, you need to increase the maximum memory allocation pool for the JVM with the Xmx value, in this case, upped to 64 GB. The Xms parameter sets the initial, minimal memory allocation. The general recommendation is to set both Xmx and Xms to the same value.

In the preceding configuration example, memory allocation is set to 16 GB. The actual value you use depends on the machines used by your cluster. The general recommendation is to set both the Xmx and Xms to 80% of the total memory of the system. This allows for plenty of headroom for other system processes that are running. Further details about the memory management of Trino and related configuration can be found in "Memory Management" on page 265.

For large Trino deployments, memory allocations of 200 GB and beyond are not uncommon.

While small processes such as monitoring can run on the same machine as Trino, it's highly discouraged to share the system with other resource-intensive software. For example, Apache Spark and Trino should not be run on the same set of hardware.

If you suspect Java garbage collection (GC) issues, you can set additional parameters to help you with debugging:

```
-XX:+PrintGCApplicationConcurrentTime
-XX:+PrintGCApplicationStoppedTime
-XX:+PrintGCCause
```

```
-XX:+PrintGCDateStamps
-XX:+PrintGCTimeStamps
-XX:+PrintGCDetails
-XX:+PrintReferenceGC
-XX:+PrintClassHistogramAfterFullGC
-XX:+PrintClassHistogramBeforeFullGC
-XX:PrintFLSStatistics=2
-XX:+PrintAdaptiveSizePolicy
-XX:+PrintSafepointStatistics
-XX:PrintSafepointStatisticsCount=1
```

These options can be helpful when troubleshooting a full GC pause. In combination with the advancements of JVM and the engineering of the Trino query engine, a GC pause should be a very rare event. If it does happen, it should be investigated. First steps to fix these issues are often an upgrade of the JVM version and the Trino version used, since both receive performance improvements regularly.

 JVM and garbage collection algorithms and configuration are complex topics. Documentation on GC tuning is available from Oracle and other JVM vendors. We strongly recommend adjusting these settings in small changes in test environments before attempting to roll them out to production systems. Also keep in mind that Trino currently requires Java 17. Older releases are not supported, and newer JVM versions, as well as JVM versions from different vendors, can have different behavior.

Resource Groups

Resource groups are a powerful concept in Trino used to limit resource utilization on the system. The resource group configuration consists of two main pieces: the resource group properties and the selector rules.

A resource group is a named collection of properties that define available cluster resources. You can think of a resource group as a separate section in the cluster that is isolated from other resource groups. The group is defined by CPU and memory limits, concurrency limits, queuing priorities, and priority weights for selecting queued queries to run.

The selector rules, on the other hand, allow Trino to assign an incoming query request to a specific resource group.

The default resource group manager uses a file-based configuration and needs to be configured in *etc/resource-groups.properties*:

```
resource-groups.configuration-manager=file
resource-groups.config-file=etc/resource-groups.json
```

As you can see, the actual configuration uses a JSON file. The content of the file defines the resource groups as well as the selector rules. Note that the JSON file can be any path that is accessible to Trino and that resource groups need to be configured only on the coordinator:

```
{
  "rootGroups": [],
  "selectors": [],
  "cpuQuotaPeriod": ""
}
```

cpuQuotaPeriod is optional.

Let's look at the definition of two resource groups to get started:

```
"rootGroups": [
  {
    "name": "ddl",
    "maxQueued": 100,
    "hardConcurrencyLimit": 10,
    "softMemoryLimit": "10%",
  },
  {
    "name": "ad-hoc",
    "maxQueued": 50,
    "hardConcurrencyLimit": 1,
    "softMemoryLimit": "100%",
  }
]
```

The example defines two resource groups named ddl and ad-hoc. Each group has a set maximum number of concurrent queries and total amount of distributed memory limits. For the given group, if the limits are met for concurrency or memory limits, then any new query is placed in the queue. Once the total memory usage goes down or a query completes, the resource group chooses a query from the queue to schedule to run. Each group also has a maximum number of queries to queue. If this limit is reached, any new queries are rejected and the client receives an error indicating that.

In our example, the ad hoc group is designed for all queries that are not DDL queries. This group allows only one query to run concurrently, with up to 50 queries to be queued. The group has a memory limit of up to 100%, meaning it could use all the available memory to run it.

DDL queries have their own group, with the idea that these types of queries are relatively short and lightweight and should not be starved by longer-running ad hoc SQL queries. In this group, you specify that there should be no more than 10 DDL queries running concurrently, and the total amount of distributed memory used by all queries running should be no more than 10% of the Trino clusters memory. This allows a DDL query to be executed without having to wait in the ad hoc query line.

Now that the two groups are defined, you need to define the selector rules. When a new query arrives in the coordinator, it is assigned to a particular group. Let's take a look at the example:

```
"selectors": [
    {
        "queryType": "DATA_DEFINITION",
        "group": "ddl"

    },
    {
        "group": "ad-hoc"
    }
]
```

The first selector matches any query type of DATA_DEFINITION and assigns it to the ddl resource group. The second selector matches all other queries and places those queries in the ad-hoc resource group.

The order of the selectors is important because they are processed sequentially, and the first match assigns the query to the group. And in order to match, all properties specified must match. For example, if we switch the order of the selectors, then all queries including DDL are to be assigned to the ad-hoc resource group. No queries are ever assigned to the ddl resource group.

Resource Group Definition

Let's take a closer look at the following configuration properties for resource groups:

name
: The required name of the resource group, referenced by the selector rule for assignment.

maxQueued
: The required maximum number of queries queued for the group.

hardConcurrencyLimit
: The required maximum number of concurrent queries that can be running in the group.

softMemoryLimit
: The required maximum amount of distributed memory that can be used by concurrent running queries. Once this limit is reached, new queries are queued until the memory reduces. Both absolute values (GB) and percentages (%) can be used.

softCpuLimit

The optional soft limit on the amount of CPU time that can be used within a time period as defined by the cpuQuotaPeriod property. Once this limit is reached, a penalty is applied to the running queries.

hardCpuLimit

The optional hard limit on the amount of CPU time that can be used within a time period as defined by the cpuQuotaPeriod property. Once this limit is reached, queries are rejected until the next quota period.

schedulingPolicy

The policy used to schedule new queries to select a query from the queue in the resource group and process it. Details are provided in the following section.

schedulingWeight

This optional property is to be used in conjunction with schedulingPolicy.

jmxExport

Flag to cause resource groups to be exposed via JMX. Defaults to false.

subGroups

A container for additional nested resource groups.

Scheduling Policy

The schedulingPolicy value noted in the preceding list can be configured to various values to be run in the following modes:

Fair

Setting schedulingPolicy to fair schedules queries in a first-in, first-out (FIFO) queue. If the resource group has subgroups, the subgroups with queued queries alternate.

Priority

Setting schedulingPolicy to query_priority schedules queued queries based on a managed priority queue. The priority of the query is specified by the client by using the query_priority session property (see "Session Information and Configuration" on page 157). If the resource group has subgroups, the subgroups must also specify query_priority.

Weighted

Setting schedulingPolicy to weighted_fair is used to choose the resource group subgroup to start the next query. The schedulingWeight property is used in conjunction with this: queries are chosen in proportion to the scheduling Weight of the subgroups.

Selector Rules Definition

Selector rules are required to define the group property, since it determines the resource group to which a query is assigned. It is a good practice to have the last selector in the file set to define only a group. It then acts as an explicit catchall group.

Optional properties and regular expressions can be used to refine the selector rules:

user
: Matches against a username value. Regular expressions may be used to match against multiple names.

source
: Matches against the source value. For example, this may be trino-cli or trino-jdbc. Regular expressions may be used.

queryType
: Matches against the type of query. The available options are DATA_DEFINITION, DELETE, DESCRIBE, EXPLAIN, INSERT, and SELECT.

clientTags
: Matches against the client tags specified by the client submitting the query.

To set the source or client tags from the Trino CLI, you can use the --source and --client-tags options:

```
$ trino --user mfuller --source mfuller-cli
$ trino --user mfuller --client-tags adhoc-queries
```

Conclusion

Well done! You have come a long way with Trino. In this chapter, you immersed yourself in the details of monitoring, tuning, and adjusting Trino. Of course, there is always more to learn, and typically these skills are improved with practice. Be sure to connect with other users to exchange ideas and learn from their experience and join the Trino community (see "Community Chat" on page 14).

And in Chapter 13, you get to find out what others already have achieved with Trino.

Real-World Examples

As you know from "A Brief History of Trino" on page 17, development of Trino started at Facebook. Ever since it was made open source in 2013, its use has picked up and spread widely across a large variety of industries and companies.

In this chapter, you'll see a few key numbers and characteristics that will give you a better idea about the potential for your own use of Trino. Keep in mind that all these companies started with a smaller cluster and learned on the go. Of course, many smaller and larger companies are using Trino. The data you find here should just give you a glimpse of how your Trino use can grow.

Many data platforms and other systems also embed Trino. These platforms don't even necessarily reveal that Trino is under the hood. And these platforms do not typically expose user numbers, architecture, and other characteristics.

The cited numbers and stats in this chapter are all based on publicly available information. The book repository contains links to sources such as blog posts, presentations from conferences, slide decks, and videos (see "Book Repository" on page 15). As you read this book, the data may have become outdated or inaccurate. However, growing use of Trino and the general content gives you a good understanding of what is possible with Trino and how other users successfully deploy, run, and use it.

You should also check the Trino website (*https://trino.io*), including the user testimonials and blog posts, for further information. Events like Trino meetups, Trino Summit, and the Trino Community Broadcast also regularly provide new information.

Deployment and Runtime Platforms

Where and how you run your Trino deployment is an important factor. It impacts everything from low-level technical requirements to high-level user-facing aspects. The technical aspects include the level of direct involvement necessary to run Trino, the tooling used, and the required operations know-how. From a user perspective, the platform influences aspects such as overall performance, speed of change, and adaptation to different requirements.

Last but not least, other aspects might influence your choice, such as use of a specific platform in your company and the expected costs. Let's see what common practices are out there.

Where does Trino run? Here are some points to consider:

- Clusters of bare-metal servers are becoming rather rare.
- Virtual machines are most commonly used now.
- Container use is becoming the standard and is posed to overtake VMs.

As a modern, horizontally scaling application, Trino can be found running in all the common deployment platforms:

- Private on-premises clouds such as OpenStack
- Various public cloud providers including Amazon Web Services, Google Cloud, and Microsoft Azure with their relevant VM and Kubernetes platform offering
- Mixed deployments

Here are some examples:

- Lyft runs Trino on AWS.
- Pinterest runs Trino on AWS.
- Twitter runs Trino on a mix of on-premises cloud and Google Cloud.
- Starburst Galaxy supports running clusters on AWS, Google Cloud, and Azure.

The industry trend of moving to containers and Kubernetes has made an impact on Trino deployments. An increasing number of Trino clusters run in that environment and in the related public offerings for Kubernetes use.

Cluster Sizing

The size of some Trino clusters running at some of the larger users is truly astounding, even in this age of big data everywhere. Trino has proven to handle scale in production for many years now.

So far, we've mostly talked about running a Trino cluster and have hinted at the capability to run multiple clusters.

When you look at real-world use of Trino at scale, you find that most large deployments use multiple clusters. Various approaches to using multiple clusters are available in terms of Trino configuration, data sources, and user access:

- Identical
- Different
- Mixed

Here are some advantages you can gain from identical clusters:

- Using a load balancer enables you to upgrade the cluster without visible downtime for your users.
- Coordinator failures do not take the system offline.
- Horizontal scaling for higher cluster performance can include use of multiple runtime platforms; for example, you might use an internal Kubernetes cluster at all times and an additional cluster running in a Kubernetes offering from a public cloud provider for peak usage.

Separate clusters, on the other hand, allow you to clearly separate different use cases and tune the cluster in various aspects:

- Available data sources
- Location of cluster near data sources
- Different users and access rights
- Tuning of worker and coordinator configuration for different use cases—for example, ad hoc interactive queries compared to long-running batch jobs

The following companies are known to run several Trino clusters:

- Comcast
- Facebook
- Goldman Sachs
- Lyft

- Pinterest
- Twitter

 Most other organizations mentioned in this chapter probably also use multiple clusters. We just did not find public references. The Trino-backed SaaS platform Starburst Galaxy allows users to spin clusters up and down across different cloud providers with the browser-based user interface. All users take advantage of that simplicity.

After noting the number of clusters, let's look at the number of nodes. There are some truly massive deployments and others at a scale you might end up reaching in the future:

- Facebook: more than 10,000 nodes across multiple clusters
- FINRA: more than 120 nodes
- LinkedIn: more than 500 nodes
- Lyft: more than 400 nodes, 100–150 nodes per cluster
- Netflix: more than 300 nodes
- Twitter: more than 2,000 nodes
- Wayfair: 300 nodes
- Yahoo! Japan: more than 600 nodes

Hadoop/Hive Migration Use Case

Probably still the most common use case to adopt Trino is the migration from Hive to allow compliant and performant SQL access to the data in HDFS. This includes the desire to query not just HDFS but also Amazon S3, S3-compatible systems, and many other distributed storage systems.

This first use case for Trino is often the springboard to wider adoption of Trino for other uses.

Companies using Trino to expose data in these systems include Comcast, Facebook, LinkedIn, Twitter, Netflix, and Pinterest. And here is a small selection of numbers:

- Facebook: 300 PB
- FINRA: more than 4 PB
- Lyft: more than 20 PB
- Netflix: more than 100 PB

Other Data Sources

Beyond the typical Hadoop/Hive/distributed storage use case, Trino adoption is gaining ground for many other data sources. These include use of the connectors available from the Trino project. There is also significant use of other data sources with third-party connectors from other open source projects, internal development, and commercial vendors.

Here are some examples:

- Comcast: Apache Cassandra, Microsoft SQL Server, MongoDB, Oracle, Teradata
- Facebook: MySQL
- Goldman Sachs: Elasticsearch, MongoDB
- Insight: Elasticsearch, Apache Kafka, Snowflake
- Wayfair: MemSQL, Microsoft SQL Server, Vertica

Users and Traffic

Last but not least, you can learn a bit more about the users of these Trino deployments and the number of queries they typically cause. Users include business analysts working on dashboards and ad hoc queries, developers mining log files and test results, and many others.

Here is a small selection of user counts:

- Arm Treasure Data: approximately 3,500 users
- Facebook: more than 1,000 employees daily
- FINRA: more than 200 users
- LinkedIn: approximately 1,000 users
- Lyft: approximately 1,500 users
- Pinterest: more than 1,000 monthly active users
- Wayfair: more than 200 users

Queries often range from very small, simple queries to large, complex analysis queries or even ETL-type workloads. As such, the number of queries tells only part of the story, although you nevertheless learn about the scale Trino operates:

- Arm Treasure Data: approximately 600,000 queries per day
- Facebook: more than 30,000 queries per day
- LinkedIn: more than 200,000 queries per day

- Lyft: more than 100,000 queries per day and more than 1.5 million queries per month
- Pinterest: more than 400,000 queries per month
- Slack: more than 20,000 queries per day
- Twitter: more than 20,000 queries per day
- Wayfair: up to 180,000 queries per month

Conclusion

What a huge range of scale and usage! As you can see, Trino is widely used across various industries. As a beginning user, you can feel confident that Trino scales with your demands and is ready to take on the load and the work that you expect it to process.

We encourage you to learn more about Trino from the various resources, and especially to join the Trino community and any community events.

Conclusion

Whatever your motivation for learning more about Trino, you've truly made great progress. Congratulations!

We covered everything from an overview of Trino and its use cases, to installing and running a Trino cluster. You've gained an understanding of the architecture of Trino, and how it plans and runs queries.

You learned about various connectors that allow you to hook up distributed storage systems, RDBMSs, and many other data sources. The standard SQL support of Trino then allows you to query them all and even to combine the data from different sources in one query, a federated query.

And you found out more about the next steps required to run Trino in production at scale as well as about some real-world Trino use in other organizations.

We hope you are excited to put your knowledge into practice, and we look forward to hearing from you on the community chat; remember to look up the details in "Community Chat" on page 14.

Thanks for reading, and welcome to the Trino community!

—Matt, Manfred, and Martin

Index

Symbols

A

CBO (cost-based optimizer), 66-74
  broadcast join strategy, 72
  cost concept, 66-68
  distributed join strategy, 73
  filter statistics, 70
  join cost, 68
  join enumeration, 72
  partitioned tables, statistics for, 72
  performance tuning, 264
  table statistics, 69, 74-76
cbrt() function, 186
ceiling() function, 186
CentOS, 86
Ceph, 104
certificate authentication, 224-229, 232-234
certificate authority (see CA)
certificate chain, 230
CHAR CHAR() data type, 160
chkconfig command, 86
chr() function, 188, 190
CLI (command-line interface), Trino, 19, 27-32,
    85
client libraries, 37
client-to-coordinator communication, security,
    224-229, 232-235
clipboard icon, 262
cloud installation, 88
Cloudian, 104
clusters
  coordinators and workers structure, 47-48
  creating, 79-81, 88
  encrypting communication within, 229-230
  installing Trino, 84-86
  K8s, 88, 278
  kerberized Hadoop cluster authentication,
    238
  separation for security, 239
  sizing of, 90, 279-280
  Trino Web UI to view details, 252
  Web UI cluster-level details, 252
codepoint() function, 188, 190, 191
collection data types, 161
column family (Accumulo), 124
columns
  identifying those used in query, 58
  indexing on, 127
  JMX connector, 115
  modifying a table, 155
  properties of, 151

SHOW COLUMNS statement, 142
  statistics, 69
  subquery restrictions, 178
column_mapping table property, 124
Comcast, 279
command-line interface (see CLI)
commercial distributions, 247
community chat, Trino resource, 14
complex data types
  collections as, 161
  unnesting, 194
concat() function, 188
concatenating operator (||), 42, 188
Concord, 88
concurrency, adjusting, 270
config.properties file
  about, 263
  access control, 214, 225, 235
  cluster installation, 85, 232
  deployment configuration, 79
  installing Trino, 23
  session, 158
configuration
  connectors, 94
  initial configuration file setup, 22
  JVM, 82
  logging, 80-81
  node, 81, 85
  RPM, 87
  for security, 236-237
  server, 79-81
  session, 157
  workers, 85
connecting to Trino, 35
connector.name property, 23, 24, 94
connectors, 93-118
  access control, 219-221
  Apache Cassandra, 127
  authentication, 100, 236
  black hole connector, 116
  catalogs and, 146
  configuration, 94
  data type support variations, 159
  defined, 39
  document store, 114, 130-132
  ETL, 139
  examples, 119-140
  federated queries, 133-140
  HBase with Phoenix, 119

P

pages, relationship to stages, 56
pagination of queries, 30
parallel connectors, 98
Parquet format, 103, 111
parsing
    data and time data types, 162
    queries, 58
partial aggregations, 63, 264
PARTITION BY statement, 203
_partition_id (Kafka), 129
_partition_offset (Kafka), 129
partitioned_by clause, 108
partitions
    creating, 110
    for nested arrays in ANALYZE, 75
    Hive connector, 107-109
    table statistics, 72
--password, 215
password authentication, 213-216
password property, JDBC driver, 36
password-authenticator.name property, 214
password-authenticator.properties file, 214, 216
performance
    cluster, 91
    RubiX for improvements in, 242
    Trino's design for, 5
performance tuning, 262-276
    JVM, 271-272
    memory management, 265-268
    network data exchange, 270
    query, 93, 262-265
    query tuning, 144
    resource groups, 272-276
    task concurrency, 269
    worker scheduling, 269
Phoenix, 115, 119
pi() constant, 188
Pinterest, 279
pipeline, 56
plan fragments, 54
PLANNING state, 256
plugins directory, installing Trino, 22
plugins, function in Trino, 52
PostgreSQL, 52, 94, 95-100, 133-139
power() function, 186
pre-aggregation, 63
predicate pushdown, 61, 125-127, 139
PREPARE statement, 206

prepared statements, 206
Presto, 17
Priority value, 275
privileges, access, 215, 220-221
probe side of joined table, 68
Programming Hive (O'Reilly), 102
protocols
    Kerberos authentication, 235, 238
    LDAP, 213-216
public-private key pairs, encryption, 224
publish-subscribe (pub/sub) systems, 128
push-aggregation-through-outer-join property, 264
push_aggregation_through_join property, 264
push_partial_aggregation_through_join session toggle, 64
Python, 21, 83

Q

Qlik, 67, 248
quantified subquery, 178
queries
    analysis of, 58
    Apache Superset, 241
    connector implementation's effect on, 93
    DBeaver, 32, 33
    distributed query plan, 54-57
    Elasticsearch, 130
    executing, 30, 53-57
    federated, 10, 133-140
    indexes for pushdown, 97
    optimization rules, 61-64
    pagination of, 30
    performance tuning, 262
    SQuirreL SQL Client, 33-36
    statements for catalogs, 40-43
    states of processing, 255
    subqueries, 58, 66, 177-178
    tuning, 144
    Web UI tools, 253-262
query compute resources, separation from storage, 7
Query Domain Specific Language, 114
query execution role of, 57
query plan, 53, 57-61, 66-74, 262
query pushdown, 96
query.low-memory-killer.policy, 268
query.max-memory property, 266
query.max-memory-per-node property, 266

V

value detection with IS (NOT) NULL, 186
var directory, installing Trino, 22
VARBINARY data type, 160, 190
VARCHAR/VARCHAR() data type, 160
versions
    Java requirement, 21
    Python requirement, 21
    Trino, 14, 21
    Trino CLI, 27
views, 156
visualizations of data (Superset), 241

W

WARN log level, 81
Wayfair, 280
Web UI, 251-262
    availability of, 38
    cluster-level details, 252
    query details view, 256-262
    query list, 253-256
    system table information, 144
web.pages (Kafka), 129
web.users (Kafka), 129
Weighted value, 275
wget command, 86
WHERE clause, 57, 109, 168, 179
width_bucket() function, 198
wildcard certificate, 228

window functions, 202-204
WITH clause, 112, 124, 150, 175
WITH GRANT OPTION, 220
WITH NO DATA clause, 155
word_stem() function, 188
worker parallelism, 253
workers
    about, 50
    configuring, 85
    defined, 48
    managing for memory optimization, 268
    scheduling, 269
workflow monitoring, Apache Airflow, 243
workload, memory management and, 266, 268
writing to disk, gathering statistics while, 75

X

X.509 certificate, 227
Xms parameter, 271

Y

Yahoo!, 280
YARN, 102
YEAR TO MONTH interval, 164, 196

Z

ZooKeeper, 120, 121, 123

About the Authors

Matt Fuller is a cofounder at Starburst. Prior to Starburst, Matt was a director of engineering at Teradata, where he worked to build the new Center for Hadoop division within the company. As a major part of this, Matt worked to bring Trino to the enterprise market. Matt has managed a team contributing to the open source Trino project since 2015 and led the internal Trino product roadmap. Starburst was later formed from this team at Teradata.

Before Teradata, Matt was an early engineer at Vertica, where he co-built the query optimizer. Matt is also a Very Large Databases (VLDB) published author and has US patents in the database management systems space.

Manfred Moser is a community advocate, writer, trainer, and software engineer at Starburst. Manfred has a long history of developing and advocating for open source software. He is an Apache Maven committer, wrote the Hudson book and others, and continues to be active in the open source community and his projects. He is a seasoned trainer and conference presenter, having trained well over 20,000 developers for companies including Walmart Labs, Sonatype, and Telus.

His database background includes designing databases and related applications in the RDBMS space and working as a business intelligence consultant wrangling thousands of lines of SQL by hand. He is glad he can use Trino now, and he is spreading the word about how great Trino is as cohost of the Trino Community Broadcast and beyond.

Martin Traverso is cofounder of the Trino Software Foundation and CTO at Starburst. Prior to Starburst, Martin worked as a software engineer at Facebook, where he saw the need for fast interactive SQL analytics. Martin and three other engineers worked to create what became Presto, and later Trino. Martin led the Trino development team. In spring 2013, Trino was rolled out into production, and it was made open source in fall 2013. Since then, Trino has gained wide adoption both inside and outside Facebook.

Prior to Facebook, Martin was an architect at Proofpoint and Ning, where he led development and architecture design of numerous complex enterprise and social network applications.

Colophon

The animal on the cover of *Trino: The Definitive Guide* is a southern leopard frog (*Lithobates sphenocephalus*). These true frogs are native to eastern North America. They range from New York to Florida and as far west as eastern Oklahoma, and can be found near freshwater habitats and moist vegetation in the summer months.

The southern leopard frog is known for its distinctive round spots all along its green and brown body. It has a pointed head and notably long legs, as well as prominent ridges of raised skin that extend from behind its eyes to its hips. The female southern leopard frog tends to be larger than the male. Both lack digital pads on their toes.

These nocturnal frogs primarily eat small, invertebrate insects and spiders, though larger southern leopard frogs will occasionally eat small vertebrates as well. During the day, they hide in vegetation near bodies of fresh water. They often hop in sequences of three, and jump notably high. They congregate in large colonies during breeding season, but are otherwise solitary animals. They have paired vocal sacs, which are spherical when inflated, and have a short, guttural trill, often compared to the clucks of a chicken. The call of the southern leopard frog travels farther than that of many of its related species.

The southern leopard frog is prey to birds, river otters, some fish, and many snake species, and is collected in large numbers for use as bait, scientific research, and teaching. Though their conservation status is "Least Concern" at the time of writing, many of the animals on O'Reilly covers are endangered; all of them are important to the world.

The cover illustration is by Jose Marzan, based on a black-and-white engraving from *Wood's Natural History*. The cover fonts are Gilroy Semibold and Guardian Sans. The text font is Adobe Minion Pro; the heading font is Adobe Myriad Condensed; and the code font is Dalton Maag's Ubuntu Mono.

O'REILLY®

Learn from experts.
Become one yourself.

Books | Live online courses
Instant Answers | Virtual events
Videos | Interactive learning

Get started at oreilly.com.